SCRATCH PINK AND IT BLEEDS

DOIN' IT IN PUBLIC

 PACIFIC STANDARD TIME: ART IN L.A. 1945–1980 | An initiative of the Getty with arts institutions across Southern California.

Presenting Sponsors | The Getty | **Bank of America**

OTIS Otis College of Art and Design

Doin' It in Public: Feminism and Art at the Woman's Building
is made possible by a generous grant from the Getty Foundation with additional funding provided by the Andy Warhol Foundation for the Visual Arts, Henry Luce Foundation, Department of Cultural Affairs of the City of Los Angeles, and the Barbara Lee Family Foundation.

This book is published with the assistance of the Getty Foundation as part of a two-volume set in conjunction with the exhibition **Doin' It in Public: Feminism and Art at the Woman's Building**, October 1, 2011– January 28, 2012, organized by the Ben Maltz Gallery at Otis College of Art and Design. This project is part of the Getty's initiative Pacific Standard Time: Art in L.A. 1945–1980.

Doin' It in Public: Feminism and Art at the Woman's Building
ISBN 0-930209-22-2
Copyright © 2011 Ben Maltz Gallery, Otis College of Art and Design

From Site to Vision: the Woman's Building in Contemporary Culture
ISBN 0-930209-23-0
Copyright © 2011 Ben Maltz Gallery, Otis College of Art and Design and the Woman's Building

Otis College of Art and Design
9045 Lincoln Boulevard, Los Angeles, CA 90045
www.otis.edu/benmaltzgallery; galleryinfo@otis.edu; 310. 665. 6905

Ben Maltz Gallery is grateful to all those who gave their generous permission to reproduce the publications' images. Every effort has been made to contact the owners and photographers of objects reproduced and to secure all permissions and we apologize for any inadvertent errors or omissions. Anyone having further information concerning copyright holders is asked to contact Otis College of Art and Design so this information can be included in future printings.

Editors: Meg Linton, Sue Maberry, Elizabeth Pulsinelli
Design: Susan Silton
Production assistance: Kevin Wong
Printer: CS Graphics, Singapore
Edition: 2,000

Cover: **Founders of the Woman's Building: Sheila Levrant de Bretteville (L), Arlene Raven (M), Judy Chicago (R)**, circa 1973. Photographer unknown. Woman's Building Image Archive, Otis College of Art and Design. Flyleaf: **Great Lady Rising event as part of the 5th Anniversary Celebration of the Woman's Building**, 1978. Kate Millet's sculpture being installed on the roof. Woman's Building Image Archive, Otis College of Art and Design.

DOIN' IT IN PUBLIC

FEMINISM AND ART AT THE WOMAN'S BUILDING

Ben Maltz Gallery
Otis College of Art and Design

Curators
Meg Linton and Sue Maberry

OTIS Otis College of Art and Design

TABLE OF CONTENTS

Leslie Labowitz-Starus,
A Woman's Image of Mass Media,
1978. Detail of photomural, 96" x
208". This mural is made up of
images from the performance work
of Suzanne Lacy and Leslie Labowitz-
Starus between 1977–1978.

"In Mourning and In Rage..."

Statement Read During the Performance

For all of the women here now, for all the women who will see this; we are here today in memory of the ten women who were recently slain in Los Angeles, and we are here in memory of all women who have been, and are being, battered, raped, and killed throughout this country, a result of the pervasive and ongoing attitude of violence toward women.

We are here because we want you to know that we know that these ten women are not isolated cases of random, unexplainable violence. That this violence wreaked upon them is not different, except perhaps in degree and detail, from all of the daily real-life reports which reach the news media, from those fictionalized mutilations shown by our entertainment industries, and from the countless unreported cases of brutalization of our relatives, friends, and loved ones who are women.

Today we are here to share our grief and our understanding and our rage in a public manner. That concern, which before was only expressed as isolated fear by each individual woman, we now express together, through our combined voices, and we are mourning each other loudly, mourning in rage, as we recognize our own collective strength through action. We are fighting back.

WOMEN FIGHT BACK

STREET-LEVEL SEARCH FOR KILLER

'It Sure as Hell Ain't Like Television'

HILLSIDE STRANGLER

The Victims
HERALD EXAMINER
Strangler Tips Pour In

City Hall
Eyewitness

Suzanne Lacy, "'Through the Soles:/My Struggles as a Woman Artist'/With love,/Ten years later,/Faith and Suzanne, October 16, 1980, 1980. Bronze on wood base, 10" x 13" x 7½". Courtesy Judy Chicago Papers, Schlesinger Library, Radcliffe Institute, Harvard University.

FOREWORD
DOIN' IT IN PUBLIC:
FEMINISM AND ART AT
THE WOMAN'S BUILDING

Doin' It in Public: Feminism and Art at the Woman's Building, and its companion publication, *From Site to Vision: the Woman's Building in Contemporary Culture*, offer a detailed
"herstory"[1] and account of the collaborations, performances, and courses conceived
and conducted at the Woman's Building (WB) and reflect on the non-profit organization's significant impact on the development of feminist art and literature in Los
Angeles. This two-volume set, beautifully designed by artist Susan Silton, accompa-
nies the exhibition *Doin' It in Public: Feminism and Art at the Woman's Building*, October
1, 2011–January 28, 2012, organized by Otis College of Art and Design as part of the
Getty Foundation's initiative *Pacific Standard Time: Art in L.A. 1945–1980*.

  The exhibition, publications, website, recorded oral herstories, timeline,
bibliography,[2] performances, and educational programming of *Doin' It in Public* collectively document a radical and fruitful period of art made by women at the Woman's
Building, "the first independent feminist cultural institution in the world."[3] The WB
was founded in the fall of 1973 by artist Judy Chicago, art historian Arlene Raven, and
designer Sheila Levrant de Bretteville as a public center for women's culture with art
galleries, classrooms, workshops, performance spaces, bookstore, travel agency, and
café—all dedicated to women's culture. At the time, it was described as "a special place
where women can learn, work, explore, develop their own point of view and share it
with everyone. Women of every age, race, economic group, lifestyle and sexuality are
welcome. Women are invited to express themselves freely both verbally and visually to
other women and the whole community."[4]

While the WB has been the subject of many PhD dissertations by feminist scholars and art historians; referenced and footnoted in major exhibitions like *WACK! Art and the Feminist Revolution* and *Sexual Politics: Judy Chicago's Dinner Party in Feminist Art History*; highlighted in the Sackler Center for Feminist Art's substantive feminist timeline; and the subject of essays by Lucy Lippard, Laura Meyer, Betty Brown, Faith Wilding, and others, its story has not been publicly shared, documented, or presented in depth. So, when Otis was invited by the Getty Foundation to propose a research project to be part of a regional initiative to develop an exhibition and publication focused on art made in Los Angeles between 1945 and 1980, Sue Maberry (encouraged by Suzanne Lacy) responded with the Woman's Building. Maberry, Director of the Library and Instructional Technology at Otis College, was an active member and former director of the WB, and she manages the substantial part of the WB archive that is housed at Otis. Our team at Otis pulled together an impressive group of visiting scholars and consultants who have helped research, shape, and build this project into a multifaceted exploration of the history and legacy of the WB. Our distinguished visiting scholars are Vivien Green Fryd, Alexandra Juhasz, Jennie Klein, Michelle Moravec, and Jenni Sorkin; each has contributed an insightful essay to this volume. We also worked with a dynamic group of consultants and research assistants, including Jerri Allyn, Nancy Angelo, Cheri Gaulke, Sondra Hale, Joanne Mitchell, Julia Paoli, Kayleigh Perkov, Paige Tighe, and Terry Wolverton.

WB: Brief Herstory

To understand the how and the why of the WB, one needs to start with Judy Chicago and the California Girls in Fresno.[5] In 1970, Chicago took a year-long teaching position in the art department at Fresno State College (now California State University, Fresno), where she formed the Feminist Art Project in collaboration with fifteen aspiring women artists.[6] They found and renovated a studio and worked together to answer the question prompted by Virginia Woolf's book *A Room of One's Own*: What does a woman need to become a woman artist?[7]

This collaborative educational experiment laid the foundation for what Faith Wilding, who participated in both the Fresno and WB programs, defined in her book *By Our Own Hands* as the four core activities of a feminist art education:

1. Consciousness-raising
2. Building a female context and environment
3. Female role models
4. Permission to be themselves and encouraged to make art out of their own experiences as women[8]

Consciousness-raising (C-R), an important pedagogical strategy employed at the Feminist Art Project in Fresno and the WB, is a structure for group conversation that allows each person an equal amount of time to express (or not express) her ideas/feelings about a given topic.[9] C-R created parity in the conversation and allowed the young women students to discover shared experiences that united them as women; consider topics such as power, money, sex, and work; and to find their individual voices via self-determined and focused peer-to-peer discussion. C-R was described as an essential part of the learning process by almost all of the WB alumnae we interviewed.[10]

Her experience at Fresno convinced Chicago of the importance of women creating and building their own context and work environments. In a public conversation in 2005 between Suzanne Lacy and Chicago, Lacy recalled, "I think ... [Chicago] taught us a sense of empowerment. We were all sitting around in a living room [in Fresno] ... and we were all wearing sandals. Judy looks around the room and says, 'The next assignment is to get work boots.' I was so in love with my work boots, I wore them everywhere [because] they gave me such a sense of power."[11] The process of securing and successfully renovating a building with their own hands—doing what many deemed "men's work"—gave the women in both feminist art programs a proprietary role over their physical environment and instilled a profound sense of self-sufficiency. Together, the women successfully created a physical and intellectual "safe" space in which they could encourage each other to sidestep traditionally prescribed female roles and to create work based on their own experiences as women. The women, not the misogynistic academic structure, decided what was to be meaningful and worthy subject matter for their art.

On the subject of female role models, Chicago writes in her first autobiography, *Through the Flower*, "I felt that it was important for the women to learn about the work of women of the past, identify with their lives, and use their achievements to extend their own. I personally wanted to see the work and examine it for clues that could help me in my own art. We organized a research seminar, and the women began to go to local libraries, then to libraries in Los Angeles, where they went through books, making lists of all the names of the women artists that they found. We quickly discovered that there was an enormous amount of information about women artists that had never been collated—so much, in fact, that I cried because I felt deprived of my rightful heritage."[12] Later, at the WB, mining history and claiming and honoring their foremothers was practiced in a multitude of ways through exhibitions, readings, lectures, and special workshops such as Cheri Gaulke's *Postcard Project: Celebrating Our Heroines*.[13]

In the fall of 1971, Chicago left Fresno and accepted a teaching position alongside Miriam Schapiro at the newly formed California Institute for the Arts (CalArts) in Valencia, and most of the Feminist Art Project participants followed their professor to continue their education. Together, Chicago and Schapiro led the Feminist Art Program, utilizing the four core principals of feminist art education. In January 1972, they hosted the first West Coast Women Artists Conference at CalArts and opened *Womanhouse* (January 30–February 28, 1972), a landmark collaborative installation staged in an empty house in Los Angeles.[14] The project was conceived by Paula Harper and twenty-one participants in the Feminist Art Program. It drew an enormous local audience, and the national media coverage it received introduced feminist art to the general public.

The Women Artists Conference and *Womanhouse* ignited a flurry of activity. No longer would women artists toil in isolation; they had found each other and their cause: to show, document, talk, and write about women's art. If no one was going to do it for them, they were going to do it themselves—create their own art, audience, and delivery system. The energy and work went viral via the postal service with organizations sharing information about artists, exhibitions, and programs. Armed with 35 mm slides and video-letters, such as Susan Mogul's *Feminist Studio Workshop Video Letter* (1974) (included in our exhibition), women artists, designers, and art historians traversed the country giving lectures about women's art on college campuses and in living rooms— pretty much wherever they were invited or could afford to go.[15] One pivotal result of this collective energy was the opening of Womanspace in a former laundromat at 11007 Venice Boulevard, Los Angeles. Womanspace was the first gallery in the city dedicated to exhibiting the work of contemporary women artists.[16] "[It] opened in 1973 as a women's art gallery and multifaceted center for women in the arts. As such it was comparable to the Women's Interart Center in New York, but different from it in that Womanspace was strongly interested in discovering and creating unique women's or feminist art—something most artists in New York opposed. The Southern California women's art movement at the time explored new forms of showing and working collectively, and was less interested in banding together to advance individual careers."[17]

Meanwhile, the environment at CalArts had become antagonistic toward the Feminist Art Program faculty and students. Chicago banded together with Raven, who taught art history in the art department, and de Bretteville, who ran The Women's Design Program, to leave CalArts and create an alternative art education experience exclusively for women. The Feminist Studio Workshop (FSW) was founded in the fall of 1973, and the first meetings were held in de Bretteville's living room. According to Maria Karras's 1975 artist's book about the WB, in September 1973, one of the Womanspace artists, painter Edie Gross, approached Chicago, Raven, and de Bretteville with the idea of renting a building dedicated to supporting a "community for women in the arts by creating a public space where women's art could be shown and the first feminist art school in the country, the Feminist Studio Workshop, could develop."[18] They rented the former Chouinard Art Institute building, located at 743 Grandview Avenue, near MacArthur Park in Los Angeles. A small army of women (FSW faculty and students, Womanspace members, and community volunteers) moved fast and invested a tremendous amount of sweat equity to build the space to suit their needs. The Building opened on November 28, 1973. Karras describes their vibrant community in 1975: "The Building continues to be a place of participation in the arts, collaboration of women in a variety of cultural and social activities and a place of exchange of women's services. The community in the Building has expanded and now includes the Feminist Studio Workshop; the Extension Program; the Summer Art Program; the Women's Graphic Center; the Woman's Switchboard; Womantours; Sisterhood Bookstore; seven Galleries—Grandview I & II, the Community Gallery, the Open Wall Show, the Upstairs Gallery, the Floating Gallery, the Coffeehouse/Photo Gallery; and Dr. Susan Kuhner, feminist psychologist."[19]

Chicago recounts in her autobiography how the Building's name came to be: "One day, while we were working in Womanhouse, one of the women [Nancy Youdelman] in the Feminist Program returned from a thrift-shop expedition carrying an old book. It was an out-of-print edition about something called the Woman's Building, which none of us had heard about. Opening the faded, gold-trimmed volume, we excitedly discovered that there had been a building in the 1893 Worlds' Columbian Exhibition at Chicago, designed by a woman architect [Sophia Hayden], established and run by a Board of Lady Managers, filled with work by women around the world, including a large mural by 'our' Mary Cassatt, as she was referred to by the proud women who organized the building and commissioned her mural. As we examined the book, I was struck by the quality of consciousness evidenced by the women involved in the building and by the fact that they had apparently unearthed a good deal of historical material about women artists."[20]

The 1973 women were inspired by the 1893 women's determination to make the art and craft of women visible in an international and political context for the first time. The discovery of this nearly forgotten effort to research, display, and document women's art of the nineteenth century reaffirmed for the women in 1973 the importance of recording and sharing past and present work by women artists. Like their predecessors, the women of 1973 wanted "to honor and share women's culture, to make a place in the public sector for the variety of ways women have contributed, are contributing and will contribute to our society."[21]

1893...1973...2011

As the souvenir book published to commemorate the Woman's Building in 1893 inspired the founders of the WB, *Doin' It in Public* aims to honor and share the contributions made by the artists, designers, and writers of the WB between 1973 and 1991. Our initial goal for *Doin' It in Public* was to provide a comprehensive survey of the Woman's Building. As we delved into the material housed in various public archives and searched under beds and in garages in private collections, we realized it would take literally dozens of exhibitions to truly explore the depths of all the WB activity. Over an eighteen-year period, tens of thousands of women from around the world passed through the building as students, faculty, visitors, and exhibiting or resident artists/performers/writers. At one point, there were seven functioning galleries, not including Womanspace and Double X, multiple performance spaces, artists' studios and writers' forums. *Doin' It in Public* is one attempt (of which we hope there will be many) to capture the complex and numerous histories of this dynamic space. It is this complexity and wealth of material that also drove the decision to publish, in tandem with this book, Sondra Hale and Terry Wolverton's (e)book *From Site to Vision: the Woman's Building in Contemporary Culture* (2007). The majority of the essays in *From Site to Vision* are written by women who were at the WB, while *Doin' It in Public* primarily features a new generation of scholarship.

When we first conceived of *Doin' It in Public*, we wanted to incorporate the principles of feminist art education into our process. In March 2009, we had our first week-long meeting with our visiting scholars. We gathered after hours in the Otis library and began with a mini C-R session led by Nancy Angelo—a WB/FSW alumna, member of the Feminist Art Workers, and organizational psychologist. During this time together, we conducted interviews with local WB alumnae, visited the WB video archive at the Getty Research Institute, and spent hours discussing research interests and our aspirations for the project. It was an overwhelming and exciting experience, filled with strong voices, opinions, and emotions. Over the course of a year and two more research convenings, we decided as a group to focus the exhibition and the essays in this volume on five converging themes: History, Space, Collectivity, Pedagogy, and Activism. In the exhibition, these aspects are portrayed through a broad range of media, including sculpture, photography, painting, drawing, graphic design, film, video, and historical ephemera. Within this structure, themes of identity, gender, sexuality, motherhood, race, class, spirituality, and transformation emerge.

We also decided to spotlight collaboration rather than individual production in order to showcase the work of artist collectives and projects, and to focus on key WB educational ventures, including the Feminist Studio Workshop, Women's Graphic Center, and the L. A. Women's Video Center. We took our cue from the history of feminists on the West Coast, for whom working collectively was a key mode of production and pedagogical strategy. It allowed them to experiment with non-hierarchal structures in the creation of visual art, performance, theater, and literature. Women combined forces to learn from each other as well as to maximize various skills and strengths within the group. The collaborative creative energy and output challenged the prevailing, patriarchal concept of the lone artistic genius. Women sought inclusive practices and formed artist collectives around specific subject matter and modes of production. The WB provided an encouraging environment for the following groups and projects, which are highlighted in our exhibition, to form and thrive: Ariadne: A Social Network, *Chrysalis* magazine, Feminist Art Workers, Great American Lesbian Art Show, Incest Awareness Project, Lesbian Art Project, Madre Tierra, Mother Art, Sisters Of Survival, and The Waitresses.

Sadly, the Woman's Building closed its doors in 1991, the victim of a decade of conservatism and decreased funding for the arts and alternative education under the Reagan Administration. However, the legacy of feminist education that, as Raven defined it, "raises consciousness, invites dialogue, and transforms culture," infiltrated the academy as dozens of WB alumnae began working at colleges and universities across the country.[22] When we met with Cynthia Marsh—FSW Faculty, printer, artist, designer, and now professor at Austin Peay University—to capture her oral "herstory," she remarked: "Sometimes...I'll see a name, like...Vanalyne Green's...or of somebody else that I knew at the Woman's Building, ...and I'll see them connected with another school, and I'll think wow, we are all out there...with this kind of overarching feminism, which is really to me like humanism.... [W]e have brought this humanist movement in communication and in art to the rest of the world. I think that's fabulous and I'm so thankful."[23]

I am so thankful to Sue Maberry for her stewardship of the Woman's Building archive at Otis and for her role as the instigator of *Doin It in Public*, and to the Getty Foundation and the Getty Research Institute for sponsoring this project as part of *Pacific Standard Time: Art in L.A. 1945—1980*. Organizing this endeavor has been a rollercoaster ride and it would not have been possible without our multi-generational legion of advisors, interns, dedicated colleagues, and generous patrons (who are thanked in the acknowledgments in this publication). It has been an honor to listen to and share the stories of these amazing women, and we hope to discover more from the ripples of *Doin' It in Public*. As it was then, it still holds true now: "[O]ur goal was to put feminism in the world not shelter it from the world."[24] So, whether it is named feminism or humanism, or not named at all, the legacy of the WB continues to inspire the raising of consciousness, the inviting of dialogue, and the transforming of culture.

Meg Linton
Exhibition Curator and Director of Galleries and Exhibitions
Otis College of Art and Design

Notes

1. The Oxford English Dictionary defines "herstory" thus: "In feminist use: history emphasizing the role of women or told from a woman's point of view; also, a piece of historical writing by or about women." *Oxford English Dictionary* (March 2011), http://www.oed.com:80/Entry/243412, accessed May 4, 2011. *Oxford* credits Robin Morgan with coining the term in her 1970 book, *Sisterhood is Powerful*.

2. A timeline for the Woman's Building, an exhibition checklist, and the bibliography for this volume are available at www.otis.edu. Readers are invited to submit entries to be added to the timeline.

3. Sondra Hale, "Power and Space: Feminist Culture and the Los Angeles Woman's Building, a Context," *From Site to Vision: the Woman's Building in Contemporary Culture*, Sondra Hale and Terry Wolverton, ed. (Los Angeles: Woman's Building and Otis College of Art and Design, 2011), 38–81.

4. Excerpt from a typewritten directory listing all of the tenants and services at the Woman's Building, 743 S. Grandview, Los Angeles, circa 1974. Smithsonian Archives of American Art, Woman's Building Archive 1973–1991, Box 7, Folder 8.

5. Judith Dancoff, director, *Judy Chicago & the California Girls*, 1973, videorecording. This historical documentary by and about women looks at the birth of the Women's Art Movement in Fresno, California, in 1971.

6. In addition to Judy Chicago, the fifteen women were Dori Atlantis, Susan Boud, Gail Escola, Vanalyne Green, Suzanne Lacy, Cay Lang, Karen LeCocq, Jan Lester, Chris Rush, Judy Schaefer, Henrietta Sparkman, Faith Wilding, Shawnee Wollenman, Nancy Youdelman, and Cheryl Zurilgen.

7. Laura Meyer, "A Studio of Their Own: The Legacy of the Fresno Feminist Experiment," *A Studio of Their Own: The Legacy of the Fresno Feminist Experiment*, Laura Meyer, ed. (Fresno: California State University Press, 2009), 80, exhibition catalog.

8. Faith Wilding, "Feminist Art Education," *By Our Own Hands* (Santa Monica: Double X, 1977), 10–11.

9. The following description of consciousness-raising (C-R) is excerpted from the Feminist Studio Workshop Summer Art Program orientation packet from 1979. "CONSCIOUSNESS RAISING: a process through which we raise our feelings and attitudes to a conscious level, together. // STRUCTURE: Each group consists of from four to six women. The time is divided equally between all members. Each session a particular topic is addressed. Each woman's time is her own. There should be no interruptions except for clarifications. No judgments or evaluations by others. Speak from the personal. This is each woman's time to look within herself with the support of others. The group goes around twice on a particular topic. This is the time to make the personal political— see what really is our shared experience. C-R is confidential. No woman's material should be discussed outside of C-R unless that woman brings it up. This is to ensure the safety of the group. We are most likely to reveal ourselves unto ourselves if we can trust the space. It is not recommended to eat during C-R if it is distracting. We support each other with our close attention. Sitting close together, hugs, rubs, etc. may be essential. It is important to speak from the 'I' such that our own judgments aren't dumped on others. For example, 'I am afraid of blondes' may be more appropriate than, 'Blondes are horrifying, they will kill you at the first opportunity.' It's a good idea to finish off with some sort of jollity. // ORIGINS: The format is ages old as women have supported each other. Take quilting bees. This particular format has its origins in speak bitterness groups formed by people after the Chinese Revolution." Woman's Building Archive, Millard Sheets Library, Otis College of Art and Design.

10. As part of our research for *Doin' It in Public: Feminism and Art at the Woman's Building*, Jerri Allyn, Cheri Gaulke, Sue Maberry, and I recorded one-hour interviews with thirty WB alumnae. The full interviews are in the Woman's Building Archive, Millard Sheets Library, Otis College of Art and Design. Excerpts are available online at www.otis.edu and http://www.youtube.com/otiscollege.

11. Excerpt from a video recording of a public conversation between Suzanne Lacy and Judy Chicago, March 5, 2007, Otis College of Art and Design and Skirball Cultural Center.

12. Judy Chicago, *Through the Flower: My Struggle as a Woman Artist* (Garden City: Doubleday, 1975), 86.

13. *The Postcard Project: Celebrating Our Heroines*, directed by Cheri Gaulke, artist-in-residence, the Woman's Building, 1985–88. Funding provided by the California Arts Council and the National Endowment for the Arts.

14. Judy Chicago and Miriam Schapiro, *Womanhouse* (Valencia: California Institute of the Arts, 1972), exhibition catalog; and *Womanhouse*, videorecording by Johanna Demetrakas. Conceived by Paula Harper as part of Chicago and Schapiro's Feminist Art Program, *Womanhouse* featured art and performances by professors Chicago and Schapiro along with students Beth Bachenheimer, Susan Frazier, Camille Grey, Vicki Hodgetts, Kathy Huberland, Judy Huddleston, Karen LeCoq, Janice Lester, Paula Longendyke, Ann Mills, Robin Mitchell, Sandra Orgel, Jan Oxenburg, Christine Rush, Marsha Salisbury, Robbin Schiff, Mira Schor, Robin Weltsch, Faith Wilding Shawnee Wollenmann, Nancy Youdelman, and invited fiber artists Sherry Brody, Carol Edison Mitchell, and Wanda Westcoast.

15. In addition to giving lectures about women's art, women shared information about how to become professional artists. According to a listing in *The New Woman's Survival Catalog*, "[I]n 1972, June Wayne held three consecutive seminars for women artists. Each one lasted for six 2-hour weekly sessions and covered the artist's world, budgeting, taxes and insurance, selling to collectors, and dealing with galleries." Susan Rennie and Kristen Grimstad, ed., *The New Woman's Survival Catalog: A Woman-made Book* (New York: Coward, McCann & Geoghegan, 1973), 51. Womanspace later hosted Joan of Art seminars; comparable workshops, such as Ruth Iskin's Getting Shown, Being Known, were developed for the Woman's Building.

16. "Notes on the Founders of Womanspace," *Womanspace Journal* 1 (Feb/March 1973), 21–24. The founders were Lucy Adelman, Miki Benoff, Sherry Brody, Carole Caroompas, Judy Chicago, Max Cole, Judith Fried, Gretchen Glicksman, Elyse Grinstein, Ruth Iskin, Linda Levi, Joan Logue, Mildred Monteverdi, Eugenie Osman, Beverly O'Neil, Fran Raboff, Arlene Raven, Rachel Rosenthal, Betye Saar, Miriam Schapiro, Wanda Westcoast, Faith Wilding, and Connie Zehr.

17. Wilding, 3. Founded in 1969 and opened in 1971, the Women's Interart Center is a not-for-profit cultural organization in New York City committed to the development and presentation of women artists in the performing, visual, and media arts.

18. Maria Karras, *The Woman's Building Chicago 1893/The Woman's Building Los Angeles 1973* (Los Angeles: Women's Community Press, 1975), 1, artist's book.

19. Karras, 1.

20. Chicago, *Through the Flower*, 150.

21. Sheila Levrant de Bretteville, as quoted in Karras's artist's book, *The Woman's Building Chicago 1893/The Woman's Building Los Angeles 1973*, 2.

22. Arlene Raven, interview with Lyn Blumenthal and Kate Horsfield, 1979, videorecording, Video Data Bank.

23. Cynthia Marsh, interviewed by Sue Maberry and Meg Linton, January 18, 2010, Otis College of Art and Design, Los Angeles.

24. Cheryl Swannack, interviewed by Jerri Allyn, Cheri Gaulke, Sue Maberry, and Meg Linton on February 20, 2010, Otis College of Art and Design, Los Angeles.

Feminist Art Workers, *To Love, Honor, Cherish...*, 1978. Still photograph from performance held on the
5th Anniversary of the Woman's Building when the women married the Building. Pictured L to R: Laurel Klick,
Nancy Angelo, Cheri Gaulke. (Not pictured: Vanalyne Green.) © Feminist Art Workers, Woman's Building Image
Archive, Otis College of Art and Design.

1 + 1 = 3: ART AND COLLABORATION AT THE WB

Cheri Gaulke

Alone we can do so little; together we can do so much. —Helen Keller

Prior to coming to the Woman's Building, as a young Midwestern art student I was already collaborating on making interactive video installations at my college. In 1974, my collaborator, Barbara Bouska, and I went to Scotland, where we were first exposed to performance art. We lathered suntan lotion on our bodies and lay spread-eagled in a seaside Scottish village as our mentors, Jackie Lansley and Sally Potter, wearing black ball gowns, emerged from the sea like oil-soaked birds.[1] There the notion of 1 + 1 = 3 occurred to me: when two or more collaborate, the result is greater than the sum of its parts. Upon returning to college, Bouska and I became curious oddities—performance artists working together to make art about female experience. Our newfound performance imagery included balancing on high heels, staining white clothing with red paint, and hanging spoons from our noses. Our instructors didn't know what to do with us because there were no role models; art history was the story of the male artist toiling alone in his studio. Out in California, meanwhile, women were creating feminist art education programs at Fresno State University and California Institute of the Arts. When I heard about the Feminist Studio Workshop (FSW) at the Woman's Building in downtown Los Angeles, I immediately wrote to Suzanne Lacy, the performance art faculty member. She sent a brief postcard saying, "I'm too busy to write…in the midst of organizing a conference on women's performance art…. Just come!"[2] A whole conference? A place where a bunch of women were doing what we were doing in isolation? Sign me up!

21

Cheri Gaulke and Barbara Bouska, *The Last Feat*, 1975. Still photograph of performance held at Gallery Indiscreet, Minneapolis, Minnesota. According to Gaulke, the act of balancing in high heels on ceiling studs represented a female past—isolated, painful, pointless. The artists performed this work just prior to leaving for Los Angeles to attend the Feminist Studio Workshop at the Woman's Building.

When I arrived in Los Angeles in 1975, I found a hotbed of activity. Our first job as students in the FSW was to transform an old, run-down building on North Spring Street in less than three months for the Woman's Building's grand opening.[3] We climbed scaffolds to scrape ceilings. We ached, we cursed, we sang, and we all looked the same because we were covered in a fine layer of gray dry-wall dust. Women taught us how to frame walls, sheetrock, mud and tape, sand and paint. We knew no one else was going to build us a "room of one's own."[4] In the end it was truly ours, a space for women born of our sweat, song, tears, and collective effort.

The Seventies

The Woman's Building was born at the margins of the art marketplace in a time when the art world was almost exclusively male. The New York auction and gallery scenes were highly competitive, "survival of the fittest" environments in which primordial responses of "fight or flight" ruled behavior. Women were not even invited. In 1971, the year I graduated from high school, art colleges in the United States were composed of 60 percent female students,[5] yet in the professional realm of galleries and museum exhibitions, women were barely seen, even in Los Angeles. "In 1971, for example, the Los Angeles Council of Women Artists pointed out that of 713 artists in group shows at Los Angeles County Museum only 29 had been women. Out of 53 one-person shows, only one was female."[6] Once spat out of art school into the combative world of the art marketplace, men were better equipped to fight their way to the top because they were taken seriously as artists; women retreated back into the realms of domesticity because there were no opportunities for them to show their work. It's a wonder that some women even bothered to compete when "the median income for women artists in 1970 was $3400 per year, in contrast to the $9500 figure for men."[7]

Alternative art education programs such as the FSW and the Extension Program at the Woman's Building were designed to counteract this appalling situation by giving women new tools for success. Beyond traditional art school subjects such as painting and sculpture, Woman's Building programs taught practical skills of building walls, self-promotion, and management. The tools of mutual support, constructive criticism, and intellectual investigation were also at the foundation of the curriculum. Further, there were explorations and innovations into new models for working as artists—collaboration, audience interaction and participation, use of nontraditional art media (performance, installation, video, graphic multiples), and the exploration of new settings for the work itself.

The Woman's Building became a physical place in the world and a place in our imagination where anything was possible. There was a Judy Garland-Mickey Rooney "Let's make a show" approach at the Building, and from it grew many mighty and wonderful projects. Suzanne Lacy would ask her performance students to make a list of impossible performances, encouraging them to dream big. Through this many women thought of projects for their own art, but many others teamed up with like-minded souls to realize a collective vision: Mother Art, Feminist Art Workers, The Waitresses, Sisters Of Survival, Equal Time in Equal Space, The Lesbian Art Project, Ariadne: A Social Art Network, and more. Arlene Raven, art historian and cofounder of the Woman's Building, defined the function of feminist art and it became my credo: to raise consciousness, invite dialogue, and transform culture. Although there was a playful quality in much of our work, ultimately it was more than entertainment. As collaborative groups, our work tended to focus on serious political issues, more so than our work as solo artists. We were about the business of righting wrongs, whether we saw those wrongs outside or within our walls.

The Groups

Mother Art was the first collaborative group that formed in 1973. The participants were in the founding class of the FSW at the original Woman's Building location on Grandview Street, and they came together because "As artists, feminists and mothers of young children, we were horrified at a group decision to allow dogs in the workshop studios but not children. We wanted an environment that was supportive, and we created that community. Our first act was to create space for children at the Woman's Building by building a playground in the parking lot."[8]

The Waitresses was created in 1977 when, in Lacy's performance class, Jerri Allyn and Anne Gauldin discovered their mutual and problematic experiences working in restaurants. The Waitresses addressed inequity in the work place, sexual harassment, and stereotypes of waitresses and women. They invaded restaurants and coffee shops with *Ready to Order?* (1978), a series of performances that used humor to depict the plight of the waitress as a metaphor for all women. According to Allyn, "We were ready to explode with anger at our customers. Somewhere along the line, probably in constructive crits with our fellow students, and mentoring from our professors [other kinds of collaboration], we adopted this strategy: Instead of blaming anyone, let's strive to raise their consciousnesses—humorously—about what it's like to serve, and have people treat us like their mothers or their sexy girlfriends or their lowly servants, all rolled into one."[9]

Allyn and Gauldin involved other women in The Waitresses and the performance imagery was derived from a process of sharing personal stories and collective decision-making. This was typical of the way in which the Woman's Building and Feminist Studio Workshop were run. Writer Deena Metzger taught at the Woman's Building in the seventies, and she describes how decisions were made by council—an ancient idea reinvigorated and adopted for the time: "And of course, the Woman's Building and the Feminist Studio Workshop was based in some sense on consciousness-raising and all the decisions that we made were in council. Council is a process of meeting an issue in a circle in which it is assumed that everyone has some wisdom to offer and so it is an egalitarian or a nonhierarchical form. And in that process, the other thing that was so important was that people spoke personally and you spoke from the heart and you told stories. Our own stories were essential to the wisdom and the understanding that was coming forth."[10]

> In collaborative work, one can't be stingy and only give tiny bits of oneself. If you do that, the work ends up like a thin, watery broth. To get a hearty soup that will truly nourish the audiences as well as the artists, you have to give generously—offering everything you have for the pot. —Nancy Angelo[11]

The performance art group Feminist Art Workers (FAW) embraced this collective, nurturing, and inclusive decision-making process that permeated the Woman's Building. FAW members met in an FSW feminist art education class in 1976. Candace Compton and Laurel Klick were teaching the course; Nancy Angelo and I were their students. Compton later left the group and Vanalyne Green joined. Together, we

Top: **The Waitresses, *The Great Goddess Diana*,** performance art vignette created as part of *Ready to Order?*, 1978. Still photograph of performance. Pictured: Anne Gauldin and Denise Yarfitz Pierre.

Above: **Mother Art, *Rainbow Playground*,** 1974. Electrical spools, paint, 8' x 20' x 5'. Photograph by Laura Silagi. © Mother Art.

formed a leaderless group to directly challenge the notion of hierarchy. We asked our-selves, "How is art impacted by the process of its creation in a truly egalitarian collab-oration?" Performance proved to be the best way for us to explore this thesis because in performance "we found an art form that was young, without the tradition of painting or sculpture. Without the traditions governed by men. The shoe fit, and so, like Cin-derella, we ran with it." [12]

Feminist Art Workers combined performance art and feminist education techniques (such as consciousness-raising, nonhierarchical structure, and form-following-content art instruction) into interactive experiences. We were women on a mission, traveling across the country to bring our performances, lectures, and work-shops to women in small towns and big cities. While on the road, we shared family sto-ries about food, and Angelo told her grandmother's story about the difference between Heaven and Hell. Hell was a sumptuous banquet table with platters full of delectable food. The guests had only four-foot-long forks to feed themselves and no one could get food into their mouths. Heaven was the exact same scenario, except people were using the four-foot-long forks to feed each other. This poetic image inspired FAW's signature performance *Heaven or Hell?* (1978), in which we fed each other and the audience with four-foot-long forks. We performed the work in numerous settings from women's coffee houses to activist gatherings and a National Women's Studies Association conference. [13] On a commemorative postcard, we intoned our message to feminists, artists, and political workers: "Create opportunities to feed one another in a symbolic gesture.... As you go out and affect the world, take with you our support, appreciation, and encouragement to keep nurturing and inspiring one another. For it is our abil-ity to sustain each other that will enable our political movements to endure." [14]

C-R and Collaboration

The technique of consciousness-raising (C-R) was particularly effective for social change. Based on the model of "speak bitterness" groups from the Chinese Revolution, C-R was a structured conversation. Topics in the FSW included money, power, work, and sexuality. [15] Sitting in a circle, each woman was given her own time to speak on a given topic without interruption while the other participants listened to her, or her silence. In C-R sessions, women revealed deeply private experiences and often discov-ered that other women had similar experiences. Participants came to realize that the personal is political. Within the FSW curriculum, this type of focused and intense con-versation became a place of healing and empowerment, particularly around difficult subject matter such as sexual harassment, incest, and rape. C-R was also a tool for dis-covering content and fostering collaborative experiments in performance and video art at the WB. Working as a team provided continual feedback, a never-ending source of ideas and resources, and a support system. One example of a project that was developed through a process of collaboration and C-R is Nancy Angelo's *Equal Time in*

Equal Space (*ETES*) (1979), a groundbreaking artwork that addressed the taboo subject of incest. Angelo paired camera operators (such as me) with incest survivors to create a safe space to bear witness to the survivors' recounted experiences. In its final realization as a multiple-channel video installation, *ETES*'s circle of monitors took the form of a group of women engaged in a C-R session.[16]

Collaboration was a means of production, but at its best, it was also the living, breathing embodiment of a culture transformed. In many ways it represented our utopian vision of the world, where people were truly equal and everyone's contribution was valued. However, collaboration was not always easy, successful, or sustainable. In an email exchange between members of FAW, Angelo said this about the process: "Making art collaboratively is both harder and easier than doing so by one's self. It's harder in that your vulnerability throughout the creative process is right there in the open for everyone to see. It can be quite painful to be exposed in this way. That is why I have always collaborated with people I trusted to honor that openness—and who reciprocate by revealing their inner workings as well."[17]

Having more shoulders to do the heavy lifting helped with the production of large-scale performances, but the process of collaboration had its ups and downs and its own unique challenges. Power struggles can cause a collaboration to fail. And the issue of credit is problematic. Whose idea was it anyway? Our collaborative process started with brainstorming. Ideas were thrown out, hashed around, processed, refined, and ultimately decided upon by the group. Though sometimes the origin of the idea was clear, as in Angelo's *Heaven or Hell?* story, other times it was less so. In the end it was "owned" by everyone and no one. There was no sole author, which was a source of frustration for an art world wedded to the idea of the "genius artist." FAW termed the art system's inability to deal with collective art making the "Martha and the Vandellas syndrome." The market system needed someone to be the star—the lead singer. The curators, gallerists, and journalists wanted a front person, a "Martha," to speak for the back-up singers. As critic Peter Frank recently noted, "It often takes a driven, brilliant, charismatic figure like Judy Chicago or Suzanne Lacy to galvanize a collective group, and those figures deserve the name-check, as long as the members of the collective aren't turned into mere ghostly studio assistant types...." He adds, "But that's not the only formula for group achievement."[18] Groups like FAW intentionally subverted the traditional art world organizational chart.

While the collaborative process offers significant rewards, it can also be a struggle to let go of one's ego and the artist/genius paradigm. As Angelo notes, "One of the most difficult things for me working in collaboration was having an idea, throwing it out for everyone to consider, having others make something of it and then live with some angst around 'Is this my idea? Is it hers? Is it ours?' It takes a really big person to simply let go. Sometimes I could do that. Sometimes I couldn't."[19] Peter Frank also observed that artists participating in collaborative groups understood the importance

Sisters Of Survival, *S.O.S. for Avebury*, 1983. Photograph taken during Western European tour. S.O.S. (Jerri Allyn, Nancy Angelo, Anne Gauldin, Cheri Gaulke, Sue Maberry). © Sisters Of Survival.

of "sharing power" and the necessity at times of "submerging one's individual identity" into a collaborative identity.[20] Collaboration may not be convenient, but it is a worthwhile, messy process, one that FAW member Laurel Klick describes as "a pleasurable struggle."[21]

Art as Social Change

As young feminist artists in Los Angeles, we were focused on social issues such as sexual violence, economic inequity, and recognizing the role of women in society and history. Working in new media such as video, performance, installation, and public communication—media difficult to buy and sell—we were part of an emerging art scene but not terribly concerned with the commercial marketplace. Away from the highly competitive New York art world, our seventies West Coast art forged new ground in content, form, social function, and method of production. While our New York counterparts seemed to be more involved with breaking into the traditional art market, we were creating a new paradigm in which to exist. Our concerns and measures of success were rooted in social change. Peter Frank notes, "[C]ollaboration, at least on some level, is key to making art socially relevant."[22]

Suzanne Lacy used collaboration as a tool in *Three Weeks in May* (1977), a "performance structure" in which she involved social and political agencies as partners in addressing rape in Los Angeles. She later partnered with artist Leslie Labowitz and other women in social services, government agencies, and the media to form Ariadne: A Social Art Network to focus on violence against women. Ariadne staged a media performance, *In Mourning and In Rage* (1977), to critique the media's fearmongering around coverage of a serial killer. The event resulted in rape crisis hotlines being

28

published in the front of the phone book. That was success! When the Incest Awareness Project (1979–1980) convinced the *Los Angeles Times* to change their wording from incest victim to incest survivor—that was success![23] We were concerned with changing the lives of real women through our art, our activism, and our very organizational structures. In contrast to "fight or flight," we developed new methods of survival that social scientists are now calling "tend and befriend."[24] Changing the lives of real women in the world was the content and intent of our art; exploring our relationships with each other was equally important. As FAW member Green notes, "A critical way in which FAW contributed was to do work about how women work together."[25] Images of taking care and making connections abound in our feminist art, from the many-breasted Waitress Goddess Diana to projects that networked across continents, for example, the international work of Sisters Of Survival and Suzanne Lacy's large-scale dinner party performances.[26]

The Eighties

In the early eighties, change was afoot at the Woman's Building. It was the Reagan era, a time of government censorship and withdrawal of city, state, and federal funding for the arts, education, and social services. Many alternative art spaces were closing, while business departments in universities were growing exponentially. In the seventies, other women and I had taken advantage of WB partnerships with Goddard College and Antioch University to receive graduate-level college credit for our studies in the FSW. In the eighties, women's and ethnic studies were blooming at colleges and universities, and students were returning to academia. Women were no longer flocking to alternative educational programs and numbers in the FSW were dwindling. Without a core group of students to provide funding and labor, the WB began to look for other sources of income. We began to carve up our glorious space to rent studios to artists and non-profits, and I became building manager. One of the new tenants was the Committee in Solidarity with the People of El Salvador (CISPES), and suddenly more men and different women were coming through the doors. The necessary separatist politics of the seventies (for women, lesbians and gays, people with disabilities, and people of color) resulted in a new confidence within our social movements, and we were ready for coalition building.

Reagan not only brought financial hardship for alternative organizations, his militaristic policies created a climate of fear. With increased Cold War tensions between the United States and the Soviet Union came a real threat of nuclear annihilation. A new coalition, called L.A. Artists for Survival, formed to produce Target L.A.: Anti-Nuclear Music and Arts Festival (1982). Working part-time as building manager, I became the co-director of Target L.A., with music impresario Ed Pearl, and ran it from my Woman's Building office.[27]

In 1981, Sisters Of Survival (S.O.S.) was founded by Jerri Allyn, Nancy Angelo,

Anne Gauldin, Sue Maberry, and me in direct response to Europeans protesting the threat of nuclear war on their soil. One of the last collaborative groups to emerge from the Woman's Building, S.O.S. signaled a shift in focus from "women's issues" to a global perspective. Clothing ourselves in nuns' habits in the spectrum of the rainbow, S.O.S. created a three-part conceptual project called *End of the Rainbow* (1981) to create a dialogue between people in North America and Western Europe about the nuclear threat. We employed Ariadne's media strategies and also engaged in direct political action. We embraced global issues as feminist issues, opening the door for collaborations with organizations across the country and in Europe. Seeing ourselves as citizen ambassadors, we used participatory structures to take our message directly to the people and collected 300 artworks from both continents. Our feminist doctrine to "raise consciousness, invite dialogue, and transform culture" expanded in meaning and geography.

The Woman's Building's Legacy

The lasting legacy of the Woman's Building can be seen in education, art history, and the art practices of today. The founders and teachers developed a paradigm that took form in the collaborative groups and projects that emerged. Raven gave us a theory of feminist art; Ruth Iskin connected us to our female heritage; Metzger gave us tools for sourcing content through journal writing; Sheila de Bretteville gave us printing presses and the power of public communication; Chicago taught us to be fearless and think big; and Lacy modeled strategies for merging activism and art, resulting in true social change. [28]

The Woman's Building provided an environment for working artists to experiment with new forms of education that are showing up in contemporary art pedagogy. We put into practice the ideas of interdisciplinary learning; independent, research-based projects; collaboration; constructive criticism; nonhierarchical structures; content-driven curriculum; and students making socially engaged projects within communities. Our theory-in-action style of learning now appears in educational settings across the country. [29]

Our artistic collaborations forged new territory and now collaborative art making is a recognized practice in the art world. [30] Even historic collaborations have been revealed through feminist criticism; for example, Jeanne-Claude and Coosje van Bruggen are now acknowledged as equal collaborators with their better-known husbands, Christo and Claes Oldenburg, respectively. [31]

The Woman's Building and Feminist Studio Workshop provided models of support that groups of women artists employ today. The L.A. Art Girls describe themselves as a "voluntary and non-hierarchical gathering of practices." They "provide inspiration, support, dialogue and feedback to one another and often collaborate." [32] Feminist Art Workers collaborated with non-art communities, and Sisters Of Survival

Sue Maberry and Cheri Gaulke, souvenir Polaroid portrait from the *All Girl Prom*, 1979. Organized by the Lesbian Art Project.

bypassed government to empower citizens. Today, the members of the collective Fallen Fruit "investigate ideas of neighborhood and new forms of located citizenship and community by mapping fruit trees on public property and facilitating Public Fruit Jams" in which people share fruit and make jam together.[33] The Waitresses and S.O.S. used colorful personas and interdisciplinary performance actions much like the L.A. Urban Rangers, who "come from different professions, don faux ranger outfits and take people on 'safaris' to question the line between public and private land use."[34] Ariadne and *Equal Time in Equal Space* used art for healing and intervention to change personal and public attitudes about violence against women. Similarly, A Window Between Worlds transforms the lives of women in domestic abuse shelters.[35] The worlds of art and education are much changed from the seventies, and the Woman's Building, the Feminist Studio Workshop, and the groups and projects that emerged from them should be credited.

In Conclusion

My relationship with the WB began in 1975 and continues to this day, despite the fact that the building closed its doors in 1991. For over sixteen years (possibly the longest continuous relationship anyone had with the place), I was a student, teacher, building manager, artist-in-residence, curator, publication editor, PR copywriter, and proof-reader, and I (illegally) lived in the building for a short time between homes. I even married the Woman's Building on the occasion of its fifth anniversary, in 1978, as a Feminist Art Workers' performance.[36] It is where I formed into an adult, an artist, an activist, a lesbian. It's where I met my life partner, Sue Maberry.

In 1986, I was honored with a Vesta Award from the Woman's Building for Contributions to Performance Art, but I still cleaned toilets when necessary. Today, I remain a feminist artist who often collaborates, and my complicated relationship with the Woman's Building continues. There, I learned to dive deeply into my own psyche to make art and facilitated other women to do so.[37] I am a member of the board of directors for the Building's nonprofit organization, which still legally exists. Thinking about my time with the Woman's Building, I feel excitement, exhaustion, burnout, and elation. I willingly gave my blood, sweat, and tears, and I always got back more in return. I still do.

Notes

1. I was a student at Minneapolis College of Art and Design. In the summer of 1974, I participated in Richard Demarco's Edinburgh Arts, an intensive art experience in which Sally Potter and Jackie Lansley were the performance art teachers.

2. I heard about the WB from FSW faculty members Arlene Raven and Ruth Iskin, who were doing an art historical lecture at nearby St. Catherine's College in conjunction with a Judy Chicago exhibition. In 1975 the Woman's Building hosted five conferences, including *Personal and Public Rituals: Women in Performance Art*.

3. North Spring Street was the second location of the Woman's Building. It originally opened in 1973 on Grandview Street.

4. The book *A Room of One's Own* by Virginia Woolf (London: Hogarth Press, 1929) was required reading in the Feminist Studio Workshop. Woolf's assertion that women writers (and artists) must have their own physical space in which to make work provided the philosophical underpinnings of our efforts in renovating the Woman's Building.

5. "Table 319: Degrees in visual and performing arts conferred by degree-granting institutions, by level of degree and sex of student: 1970–71 through 2007–08," National Center for Educational Statistics, United States Department of Education, http://nces.ed.gov/programs/digest/d09/tables/dt09_319.asp.

6. Rachel Spence, "How Women Artists Fought Back in the '70s," Rachel Spence, *Financial Times*, London, March 5, 2010, http://www.ft.com/cms/s/2/c181e85e-27e0-11df-9598-00144feabdc0.html#ixzz1B2fnt9EV.

7. Eleanor Dickinson, "Gender Discrimination in the Art World," paper prepared for the College Art Association, Coalition of Women, February 15, 1990, New York.

8. Email correspondence with author from members of Mother Art: Deborah Krall, Suzanne Siegel, and Laura Silagi, August 13, 2010. At various times, Mother Art members also included Velene Campbell, Jan Cook, Gloria Hajduk, Christie Kruse, and Helen Million.

9. Jerri Allyn, email correspondece with author, September 16, 2010.

10. Deena Metzger, interviewed by Jerri Allyn, February 13, 2010, at Cheri Gaulke's studio in Los Angeles. Conducted for Otis College of Art and Design.

11. Nancy Angelo, email correspondence with author, August 16, 2010.

12. Cheri Gaulke, "Acting Like Women: Performance Art of the Woman's Building," *High Performance* (Fall/Winter 1980), reprinted in *The Citizen Artist: 20 Years of Art in the Public Arena: An Anthology from High Performance Magazine 1978–1998*, Linda Frye Burnham and Steven Durland, eds. (Gardiner, NY: Critical Press, 1998).

13. The Feminist Art Workers' Midwestern tour included stops in Terre Haute, Indiana; Chicago, Illinois; and the National Women's Studies Association conference at the University of Kansas, Lawrence.

14. Feminist Art Workers, *Heaven or Hell?*, 1981. Offset postcard designed by Sue Maberry on the occasion of an evening of events called "Thanks But No Thanks."

15. The origins of "speak bitterness" are discussed by Carol Hanisch in "A Women's Liberation Tribute to William Hinton and the Women of Long Bow," a presentation at Columbia University, April 3, 1999, on a panel entitled *Understanding China's Revolution: A Celebration of the Lifework of William Hinton*.

16. *Equal Time in Equal Space* was part of the Incest Awareness Project, which also included an exhibition, readings, workshops, and a media campaign.

17. Angelo email.

18. Peter Frank, speaking on a panel called *Sisterhood City: Feminist Art in Los Angeles*, at the Los Angeles Art Show on January 21, 2011. The panel, moderated by Betty Ann Brown, included the author and Meg Linton, Director of Galleries and Exhibitions at Otis College of Art and Design, among others. Frank's comments were refined in an email to the author on January 26, 2011.

19. Angelo email.

20. Frank email.

21. Laurel Klick email correspondence with author, September 7, 2010.

22. Frank email.

23. Lacy and Labowitz were brilliant strategists for how activist artists could use electronic and print media effectively. Their models of controlling the message by staging performances to be viewed through the media had a huge impact on the work of Feminist Art Workers and Sisters Of Survival. Labowitz was working as PR director at the WB at the time of the Incest Awareness Project and was largely the architect of its media strategies.

24. "Biobehavioral Responses to Stress in Females: Tend-and-Befriend, Not Fight-or-Flight," Shelley E. Taylor, Laura Cousino Klein, Brian P. Lewis, Tara L. Gruenewald, Regan A. R. Gurung, and John A. Updegraff, *Psychological Review* 107.3 (2000): 411–29.

25. Vanalyne Green, email correspondence with author, September 6, 2010.

26. For the opening of Judy Chicago's *Dinner Party* at the San Francisco Museum of Art in 1979, Lacy organized women to host simultaneous dinner parties all over the world and called it *International Dinner Party*.

27. Target L.A.: Anti-Nuclear Music and Arts Festival took place August 6–9, 1982, with 300 artists participating and 5,000 people attending.

28. Artist Judy Chicago, graphic designer Sheila Levrant de Bretteville and art historian and critic Arlene Raven founded the Woman's Building in 1973. Chicago left after one year but the others stayed as faculty of the FSW and were joined by Iskin and Metzger, among others. Iskin and Raven also founded the Center for Feminist Art Historical Studies.

29. Examples include Otis College of Art and Design's Integrated Learning and Public Practice programs. Integrated Learning has students working across disciplines to create needed solutions for community groups. The Public Practice program was created by and is under the leadership of Suzanne Lacy.

30. Even within the unlikely setting of Hollywood films, where directing has always been considered a solo profession, we are beginning to see collaborative directing teams. Unfortunately the directors are mostly men—the Coen Brothers, the Wachowsky Brothers, etc.

31. "Recognizing Jeanne-Claude," by Kriston Capps, November 24, 2009, *The American Prospect*, an online publication, http://www.prospect.org/cs/articles?article=recognizing_jeanne_claude.

32. L.A. Art Girls website, http://www.laartgirls.com.

33. Fallen Fruit website, http://www.fallenfruit.org/.

34. L.A. Urban Rangers website, http://laurbanrangers.org/.

35. A Window Between Worlds (AWBW) website, http://www.awbw.org/awbw/home.php. AWBW is conceived as an artwork by its founder, Cathy Salser. Recently, Kim Abeles did a project in collaboration with AWBW and 800 survivors of domestic violence called *Pearls of Wisdom: End the Violence*, which culminated in a compelling exhibition and installation at the Korean Cultural Center in March 2011.

36. The performance was *To Love, Honor, Cherish...* by Feminist Art Workers (Nancy Angelo, Cheri Gaulke, Vanalyne Green, Laurel Klick), 1978.

37. After completing the Feminist Education Teacher Training Program, I began teaching at the WB. I cocreated the Summer Art Program in 1976 and taught 1 + 1 = 3: Making Performances Collaboratively. A number of FSW graduates became FSW faculty until it closed in 1981.

Anne Gauldin, Photo collage for the Woman's Building Newsletter, 1982–83. Photograph shows the women carrying the Woman's Building located at 1727 N. Spring Street, Los Angeles. © Anne Gauldin for the Woman's Building.

Sheila Levrant de Bretteville and Suzanne Lacy moving sheet rock at the Spring Street location of the Woman's Building, c. 1975. Photograph by Maria Karras. Woman's Building Image Archive, Otis College of Art and Design.

LEARNING FROM LOS ANGELES: PEDAGOGICAL PREDECESSORS AT THE WOMAN'S BUILDING

Jenni Sorkin

In 1972, Judy Chicago, Sheila de Bretteville, and Arlene Raven initiated the planning for the Woman's Building, a public center for women's culture. Comprised of an art school (Feminist Studio Workshop), a graphics and printing center (the Women's Graphic Center), art galleries, and feminist-owned businesses, the Woman's Building became Los Angeles' longest-running and most influential feminist institution.

However, at the very beginning of its existence, Chicago and de Bretteville were still on the faculty of another newly formed institution: California Institute of the Arts (CalArts), which had only opened two years prior, in September 1970. While sexism at CalArts was a clear impetus for the initiation of the Woman's Building, CalArts' male-centricism can be understood as a holdover, in effect, of its own predecessor, the Chouinard Art Institute. Chouinard, CalArts and the Woman's Building have a shared institutional history that is still largely unknown and merits serious reconsideration. Such an overlapping, unwieldy cultural history inspires a fascinating and complex amalgam of gender and pedagogical issues that spans the artistic post-war landscape in Los Angeles.

Through its cultural production, the Woman's Building became the dominant model of West Coast cultural feminism during the decade of the 1970s. Among the salient aspects of the pedagogical model at the Woman's Building was a conviction that separatism and collectivity—in a safe, inclusionary environment—were necessary criteria for women artists to achieve personal growth. Fueling the Building's formation was the ideal of consensus. In seventies-era feminism, hierarchy was widely identified as a patriarchal form of governance. Instead, equality in decision making and collaboration were seen as quintessential paradigms of community building, as was enthusiastic volunteerism, given the constant lack of financial resources. That the Woman's Building was a group exercise in creation and ownership, fostering intimate journeys toward self-awareness, was what made its members so fiercely loyal to each other and the institution itself. This included a *building up* of the building itself, both structurally and programmatically, with an important exhibition program and the piecemeal development of an art school curriculum, through trial and error.

As a setting for collective experience, the community's capacity for creativity can be differentiated distinctly from traditional notions of individual artistic practice. But women-run spaces have their own particular visual histories. The medievalist art historian Jeffrey Hamburger has explored the visual culture of female monasticism, positing the compelling argument that nuns in medieval Germany were indeed artists with a rich practice, and that their art (liturgical textiles, miniatures, drawings) had been downgraded: an overlooked, but nonetheless distinctive category of image making. Produced by cloistered inhabitants of a unique time and place, their art was at once visionary, rooted in devotional practices, and also completely insular, so as to be completely misunderstood for the greater portion of the last five hundred or so years.[1] What if we apply the gist of Hamburger's argument to the Woman's Building and think of it as a modern-day convent—a secular one, to be sure? What if we utilize similar precepts: the founding of a sister house as part of a belief-based endeavor (devotion to the feminist cause) that women had the right to partake in and produce culture in a sphere separate and distinct from men (separatism)? As an educational institution, then, what did the Woman's Building teach women, and how is the critical language of art differently defined within the context of a visionary educational community?

As I will argue, image making at the Woman's Building was also part of a visionary practice, albeit a self-actualizing one, tied to the utopian imperative of eradicating sexism and promoting creative procreation, a kind of production seemingly tied to childless women—nuns and feminist separatists alike.[2] In this context, I will define the visionary as an aspirational strain of feminism, transcendent ethically, rather than spiritually, as an affirmative practice infused with the vitality of belief in an institution (the Woman's Building) and its subsequent constructions (twice, in 1973 and 1976) as the preeminent expression of its community. But by construction, I also mean to invoke the utopian dimensions of such an endeavor.

CalArts

After all, I HATED CalArts and after one year into my two-year contract, tendered my resignation. —Judy Chicago[3]

CalArts, c. 1970. California Institute of the Arts Collection (Early Years). © California Institute of the Arts Archives

Right: **Portrait of Paul Brach**, painter and founding dean of CalArts School of Art (1969–1975), c. 1972. © California Institute of the Arts Archives.

It seems that CalArts was easy to hate during the early 1970s, as its environment was entirely inhospitable to women. The ratio of men to women students was two to one, with twenty-one as the median age of enrollment.[4] Given the youth and gender imbalance of the student populace, sexual tensions ran unsurprisingly high. There was a great deal of intrigue, for instance, around skinny-dipping in the campus pool. As well, its graduate program emphasized independent study via a "faculty mentor," rather than courses.[5] Decades prior to sexual harassment statutes, it is not hard to imagine the advantageous situation this created for male faculty, essentially encouraging their sexual impropriety. Bia Lowe, a student in the School of Design, recalls being ridiculed by the dean of design, Richard Farson, who pronounced her "uptight" for her reluctance to disrobe on a school-sanctioned trip to the natural hot springs of Esalen, located in Big Sur.[6]

CalArt's nearly all-male faculty was composed of a number of important artists renowned for their genre-bending experiments in Conceptual and performance art, such as John Baldessari, Allan Kaprow, and Wolfgang Stoerchle, whose circulation in all-male milieus must have made mentorship seem like a nearly impossible prospect for young women. Indeed, one of Stoerchle's infamous, untitled videos featured the artist extracting miniature Disney figurines from his foreskin, which, as curator Glenn Phillips recounts, was "a clear indication that the culture around CalArts in the early 1970s was a far cry from the community of fresh-faced young animators-in-training envisioned by its founder, Walt Disney."[7]

CalArts, c. 1970. California Institute of the Arts Collection (Early Years). © California Institute of the Arts Archives.

Like Chicago, de Bretteville was also "escaping" CalArts.[8] As the only woman on the faculty of the School of Design, she had established the Women's Design Program (1971–73) that ran in tandem with Chicago and Schapiro's joint Feminist Art Program.[9] At CalArts, in her first teaching position, de Bretteville had developed her pedagogical skills. *EVERYWOMAN*, for example, was a collective newspaper designed for the Fresno Feminist Art Program by de Bretteville, who had encountered the program as an invited visitor. De Bretteville replicated the feminist ethos of the program in her design, employing consciousness raising as the organizing principle: offering each participant an equal amount of space.

A number of the Feminist Studio Workshop's initial students came from these two distinct programs, including Faith Wilding from the Feminist Art Program and Vanalyne Green, Helen Alm (Roth), Bia Lowe, and Suzanne Lacy from the Women's Design Program. Lacy and Wilding came to the building as young teachers, having newly completed their MFAs at CalArts. Alm, in particular, was an instrumental figure in helping de Bretteville establish the Women's Graphic Center at the new Woman's Building, helping to find, purchase, and install the equipment necessary to run a full graphics facility.

CalArts was a place of intensive masculine bravado: *the* premiere American art school of the 1970s, the place to make a Happening alongside Kaprow, the progenitor of the genre, and one of the few art schools in the country, certainly the only school in Southern California, that taught new genres like "kinetics and environments," "post-studio art," and "video projects."[10] Which is why Paul Brach, dean of the School of Art, agreed to offer the Feminist Art Program, a separatist program, at the behest of both Chicago and his wife, Miriam Schapiro, since there were no permanent women faculty members to mentor young women.

But during the 1970s, separatism of any kind was often undifferentiated from lesbian separatism, which was a strain of particularly virulent feminism championed by figureheads such as the feminist activist Ti-Grace Atkinson and radical political collectives like The Furies. The latter lived together in a cooperative home in Washington, D.C., in the early 1970s, and produced a short-lived, self-titled journal, in which its founder, Charlotte Bunch, famously wrote, "Lesbianism is a political choice."[11] (Incidentally, The Furies also spawned one of the feminist movement's most beloved cultural producers: Rita Mae Brown, author of *Rubyfruit Jungle* [1973]).

Radical lesbian feminism also existed in Los Angeles, but distanced itself both socially and geo-politically from the Woman's Building.[12] According to the lesbian archivist and activist Yolanda Retter, the Westside lesbians (a group known amorphously as the Westside Women) also initiated their own cultural activities, such as sponsoring a Saturday night coffeehouse and staging a lesbian kiss-in at the Los Angeles County Museum of Art. Their crucial, early journal, *Lesbian Tide,* ran more or less monthly from 1971 to 1980.[13] (Incidentally, its publisher, Jeanne Cordova, wrote a book much later in life called *Kicking the Habit: An Autobiographical Novel: A Lesbian Nun Story* [1989]).

Like a convent, the Woman's Building also evokes a kind of celibacy: a separation from the perceived (sexual) violence of the heterosexual world, and a refuge into the world of lesbian love and compassion, where women nurtured and taught one another through their collective artistic practice, rooted in self-discovery and visibility. While most of the Woman's Building's core membership *was* lesbian, by and large, its constituency was not. Furthermore, if we take at its word the community's intent to be a setting for collective experience, how can we differentiate its capacity for creativity as distinct from individual artistic practice? This introduces another vexing issue regarding the consideration, then, of what constitutes student work. When does amateurism end, and the production of mature professional artwork begin? What does it mean if students do not achieve the same artistic stature as their predecessors? How do such issues, in turn, comment upon the legacy of feminist collaboration itself, since the individual aspiration, and with it, the artistic ego, was, from the beginning, something that feminist art was itself meant to redress?

This philosophy is strikingly original and fresh, fostering a kind of utopian communalism that is a world of difference from the rigorous individualism simultaneously promoted by CalArts. As its 1973/74 course catalog explained:

Annual Art Student's Ball at Chouinard Art Institute, c. 1954. Photograph from *Chouinard Art Institute Course Catalog 1954–55*. © California Institute of the Arts Archives.

Chouinard Art Institute. Photograph from Robert Perine's *Chouinard: An Art Vision Betrayed: The Story of Chouinard Institute, 1921–1972*, (Artra Publishing, 1986). © California Institute of the Arts Archives.

Young artists are inescapably responsible to and for their art, whether they enter CalArts as first-year or graduate students. We can provide the studios and workshops, the tools and the experienced artists to guide and advise. But the school cannot make art; artists make art. Students become artists the day they decide to accept the responsibility for being one. [14]

But it seems that at the Woman's Building, being an artist meant something else entirely. Rather than "accepting the responsibility for being *one* (lone artist as individual producer), being a feminist artist was about something *other* than being an artist: it was, first and foremost, about being a fully formed person, who was able to come to terms with the suffering and/or injustice she had previously experienced in her girlhood, her family, her community of origin. It meant participating in a community of like-minded women (who named their dogs Sappho) who were collectively seeking something better than what they had already experienced, and remaking themselves through the new formats offered at the Building. What could be achieved through an exclusively female vision, and how was this expression received, both within the community, and outside of it?

1921 not 1893: Chouinard as Predecessor

While the Woman's Building took its name from an historical source—the temporary exhibition and cultural space that had existed for the duration of the 1893 Columbian Exposition World's Fair in Chicago—unbeknownst to some of its participants, there was a more intimate antecedent: the Chouinard Art Institute.

Occupying a site known as the Grandview building, the Woman's Building opened November 28, 1973, in a building that had a previous illustrious history as the original site of the Chouinard Art Institute, which ran from 1921 until its closure in 1972. Founded by Nelbert Chouinard (1892–1969), a Pratt-trained artist and educator, the eponymous Chouinard Art Institute was the West Coast's first woman-run art school.[15]

Both psychically and physically, Chouinard is an important, but forgotten, forerunner to the burgeoning Woman's Building and its separatist art school, the Feminist Studio Workshop, or FSW. Chouinard itself can be interpreted as having had a single-sexed pedagogy, oriented exclusively toward men, training a generation of Los Angeles' most prized artists throughout the late 1950s and early 1960s. Chouinard had schooled a diverse population of both commercial and fine artists, including Harry Diamond, Walt Disney, Joe Goode, Robert Irwin, and Ed Ruscha. Its fashion design program, headed by Eva Roberts, had produced Bob Mackie and Rudi Gernreich. At one time or another, its distinguished faculty had included Irwin, Millard Sheets, and Emerson Woelffer.

As described by Judy Chicago in her popular autobiography, the late 1950s and early 1960s was an era of extreme sexism that ultimately created an intense need for feminist advocacy in the art world, leading Chicago to establish the Feminist Art Program at Fresno State, and later, CalArts.[16] Such insular artistic training and subsequent networks emphasize the circular relations between Chouinard, CalArts, and the Woman's Building, though these overlaps had an historical precedent as well: earlier in Chouinard's history, a group of its faculty had broken away to found Art Center in Pasadena in 1930. Similarly, after Chouinard's closure, most of its commercial design faculty was re-hired (as was Sheila de Bretteville, after 1980) at the Otis Art Institute (presently the Otis College of Art and Design), which eventually became a partial repository for the Woman's Building archives, and is the host institution for this exhibition and publication. As Chicago writes:

Entrance of the Woman's Building under construction at 743 Grand Avenue, Los Angeles, September 1973. Woman's Building Image Archive, Otis College of Art and Design.

Opposite page: **Portrait of Nelbert Chouinard, founder of Chouinard Art Institute**. California Institute of the Arts Collection (Early Years). © California Institute of the Arts Archives.

Chouinard [Art Institute] was well known but Nelbert Chouinard was NEVER mentioned—another indication of the many ways in which women's achievements were ignored by the L.A. art world (as well as the larger world)....The reputation of the school was part of the pleasure of taking it over for the Women's Building. [17]

With its Art Deco façade, the Grandview building was situated at the edge of Los Angeles' MacArthur Park, a former turn-of-the-century urban splendor, replete with lush vegetation, a spring-fed lake, and numerous pavilions and fountains. But by mid-century, the park and its surrounding neighborhood had become decidedly grittier, a middle-class neighborhood that eventually slid into poverty as the post-war era progressed. Once the site of enormous creative foment, the Grandview building itself had also fallen on hard times. During the late 1960s, in a misguided effort to save Chouinard, the school was entirely subsumed by CalArts, which in turn, became the Woman's Building's landlord.

Chouinard had always enrolled many more men than women, and the focus of its instruction was unapologetically directed toward its male students. A philanthropist only by marriage, Nelbert Chouinard returned to her hometown of Los Angeles to found an art school on a shoestring budget, or what she called "a war-widow's pension." [18] Her husband had died in 1918, at the end of the First World War. As such, her primary allegiance was toward returning veterans of both world wars. The potter Susan Peterson, who was hired to establish Chouinard's renowned ceramics program in 1952, described her own role as part of Nelbert Chouinard's desire to have something "more vocational" on hand to offer young men pursuing post-secondary education through the GI Bill. [19]

Such an insistence on preparing men for their re-entry into the professional and public spheres attests to the tenacity of pre-Second World War gender values, reinscribing women in their traditional social roles as healers, caregivers, and teachers. Nelbert herself fit this model: in both New York and Minneapolis, she had begun her teaching career in settlement houses. [20] This was a model encouraged by her teacher, the artist Arthur Wesley Dow, whose teaching was influential among the circle of American Modernists that included Georgia O'Keeffe and Max Weber. At Pratt, Dow had encouraged practical, hands-on education as a way to democratize the visual arts. [21]

For a short time, presumably in the late 1940s, Nelbert turned away women students altogether. Robert Perine, an artist, former student, and sole chronicler of Chouinard's history, offered the following story, quoting Nelbert in her own words:

One mother came in just roaring mad and she said, "I can pay my daughter's tuition just as well as anyone else. I said, "Well, you sit down and let me talk with you awhile. There are 1,000 soldiers in this

place. These eighteen-year-old boys have lived like men. I had three
or four girls in the school when they came in and they were either
married or pregnant before Christmas." I said, "I'm not going to take
care of her. If you want to come and take care of her yourself, I'll risk
her. Otherwise, no!" [22]

The rejection of women students at a woman-run art school offers a window into the
era that preceded the Woman's Building, and the kind of endurance and unconscious
demoralization that persisted in the lives of women like Nelbert Chouinard, who had
pursued a professional career as a woman artist, only to end up a little-known teacher
outside her immediate sphere of influence, which waned considerably as she aged.

Many of Chouinard's problems revolved around the common, but fatal, combination endemic to the 1950s—a lack of money, combined with declining enrollment,
owing to the expiration of GI Bill money—that hurt colleges and universities everywhere, not least of all Black Mountain College, which had closed for good in 1957.

In the early 1960s, Walt Disney emerged as the gallant anti-hero, a major
player committed to Chouinard's preservation, but with strings attached. In seeking to
pay homage to his struggling alumnus, and Nelbert Chouinard's chronically under-
funded vision, Disney sought to merge the Chouinard Art Institute with the Los Angeles Music School (also founded by a woman, Emily Valentine) onto one campus.
Called California Institute of the Arts, the entities would be allowed to retain their distinctive names and curriculums as separate colleges, but be housed as one university of
the arts.

Rather than preserve the urbanity of both institutions, a parcel of ranchland in
Valencia, belonging to Walt Disney Productions, would house the new campus.
Students and faculty were incensed by the move thirty miles deeper into the hot, rural
interior of Los Angeles County, but they had no power to stop it. As Perine describes it:

> It was the turning point in Chouinard's journey from a funky, always
> broke, dirty, little inner-city art school to a mystical, magical college
> in the sky, just a stone's throw from Symphony under the Stars. [23]

Disney generously donated the proceeds of his newest film, *Mary Poppins* (1964) in
order to fund the construction of the campus. The musical's August premiere at
Grauman's Chinese Theater was preceded by a short film that promoted the California
Institute of the Arts, as a means of attracting additional patronage. [24] However, Walt
Disney's vision was never realized due to his sudden death in 1966. His brother, Roy
Disney, abruptly changed course, entirely abolishing the Chouinard curriculum and
dismissing its remaining faculty.

We would do well to remember that *Mary Poppins* has a staunchly feminist subplot: Mrs. Winifred Banks is the dotty first-wave suffragette with a suspicious, conservative banker husband who resents his wife's political activities, which cause her to shirk her duties as a wife and mother and instead hire a nanny, the sprightly Mary Poppins, played by Julie Andrews. The aptly named Mr. Banks oozes both male and class privilege, but he is most useful here for his representation of the banking system as a sexist and classist institution. In his haughty singsong, he reminds us that during the nineteenth and most of the twentieth centuries, the field of finance and banking was an exclusively male domain.

Adverse attitudes toward women persisted into the post-war period. Despite their increased earning capacity to pay off self-incurred debt, women experienced immense bias in both credit and loan transactions, and were routinely denied the recognition of financial independence or credit status outside of marriage. Such wide-spread discrimination led to the passage of the Equal Credit Opportunity Act of 1974.[25] However, this bill had many loopholes, particularly with regard to single women in any form: divorced, widowed, or lesbian women. Such issues attracted more attention as the 1970s wore on, and the feminist movement coalesced to fight for the passage of the Equal Rights Amendment (ERA) in both 1976 and 1980.

From the onset, then, the ability to secure and raise capital impeded the growth of both Chouinard and the Woman's Building. As such, neither ever owned the Grandview building. Peterson recalled Nelbert Chouinard asking her to build kilns portable enough to dislodge with a crane in the middle of the night, lest her creditors padlock the school's front doors.[26] After Chouinard's move to Valencia, the Grandview building had fallen into a state of disrepair and neglect. When Chouinard was officially dissolved in 1972, ownership of the Grandview building transferred to CalArts, which in turn, rented it to the Woman's Building for an affordable sum of $3000 per year, in a deal brokered by de Bretteville.

Young women came from all over the country to sand, haul trash, and paint, transforming the building into a space of feminist pride and culture, culminating in a massive public opening in November of 1973 that inaugurated an unprecedented spate of feminist activity up through 1975, with myriad readings, talks, classes, workshops, and exhibitions sponsored by the Woman's Building.

It is apparent that such cherished experiences of the collective "building up" of the Building was a source of pride to the earliest FSW students, fueled by the desire for a separatist (cloistered) space. Women at the Woman's Building logged thousands of hours planning and strategizing, as well as doing the hard labor of carpentry, hanging sheetrock, rigging lights, and wiring sockets. Then, out of nowhere, CalArts sold the building in 1975, shuttering the school forever. Such a decision seems like yet another betrayal of Nelbert Chouinard, and of its ideal successors, the Woman's Building and its feminist separatist art school. In a postscript to his book, Perine speculated that, had she been alive, even Nelbert herself might have objected to the sale:

While she might not understand today's furor over women's rights, she would know what it means to be a woman with a cause. In this sense, Chouinard was always "the woman's building."[27]

The new owner, a Korean church, cancelled the Woman's Building's lease as of June 31, 1975.[28] This had dire consequences for student and faculty morale. In various interviews, de Bretteville has described the frenzied search for a new building that would offer the same amount of foot traffic and public visibility. Needless to say, the fledgling organization could never find one. But they did find a workable, if difficult, space (formerly the headquarters of Standard Oil, J. Paul Getty's company) in the industrial corridor of downtown Los Angeles, at the location that came to be known as Spring Street. In the fall of 1975, a second phase of "building up" was unwittingly repeated with a second generation of students, spearheaded by de Bretteville and the first generation of the Building's participants. Among those who had graduated to leadership and faculty roles were Suzanne Lacy and Faith Wilding, both original students of de Bretteville (Lacy) and Chicago (Lacy and Wilding) elsewhere.

Women Teachers, Feminist Pedagogy

Both beloved and demonized, Nelbert Chouinard was described as everything "from tyrant to loving mother."[29] The trio of founders at the Woman's Building also struggled with the gendered expectations and needs of students, who cast them in similarly oppressive roles, such as de Bretteville's soothing, motherly response to a prospective student:

> Regarding your statement. You will find others who come scared too so as long as you are not expecting to be unique in your attraction to feared situations, you will be at home here. It is a healthy attraction, a truly educational one as you can learn what is at the base of the fear and thus learn about yourself, making strong a part that was once hidden and weak.[30]

Nelbert, too, ministered to students who were on their own for the first time. As one Chouinard student recalled in 1931, "Every Thanksgiving she invited all the students who were away from home to her home for dinner—I always wished I could go."[31]

But like Nelbert Chouinard, Judy Chicago may also have chafed at the idea of "taking care" of her female students. Early on, this caused a rift between Chicago and de Bretteville and Raven. As de Bretteville said, in a recent interview:

> I didn't hold with the same thoughts that Judy Chicago had about women being damaged and needing to be told that and challenged in

her way. I really thought that if you came from a teaching version of unconditional love toward a student, that they were going to do what they needed to do and were far better positioned to change what they needed and wanted to change. [32]

Ultimately, Chicago had little patience for teaching, or moving beyond the pedagogical model she had already established through the short-lived Feminist Art Program. She was not going to be known as just a teacher, as another Nelbert Chouinard. Her ambition was much larger, and at its core, highly individual. Rather than remain committed to the Building, and its collaborative possibilities, she left during the first year to pursue her own art projects. But even Chicago concedes her move was ill timed, as she recently commented on her departure:

> I left because I was so driven to begin work on *The Dinner Party*, having found my way back (through the Feminist Art Programs in Fresno and at CalArts) to my own female impulses (excised while in graduate school in response to the hostility towards my imagery from male art professors); discovered the richness of women's unknown history; developed mastery in china-painting; developed the beginnings of a new, female-based iconography; found a new audience in the burgeoning women's movement. All those things came together and I felt impelled back into my studio as I needed *all* my energy. However, had I been Arlene and Sheila, I would have killed me. But they were gracious, understanding and supportive. In retrospect, I can see that my leaving made more space for others so it was probably a good thing all around but I didn't know that then. [33]

De Bretteville and Raven stayed on at the Woman's Building, using consciousness-raising (C-R) techniques as the basis for developing an intensive, two-year curriculum that acknowledged the unique vulnerabilities and social pressures faced by young women. C-R was a central ideology within second-wave feminism, employing lived experience as a barometer of widespread injustice toward women. Often described as embodying the "personal is political" credo, C-R was a group-directed, leaderless exploration in the verbalization of individual experience, using an equal power structure to foster a unique and immediate intimacy is order to examine the ways in which the private dimensions of women's lives could be used as a tool of social control and repression.

Within this framework, self-expression was of paramount importance, but the art mediums offered were atypical for an art school: at the Feminist Studio Workshop, painting and sculpture were not taught (which is not to say that there weren't practitioners in both mediums). But this alone is a radical gesture: a rejection of the mediums that only the generation before had been widely considered to be the most expressive, if not the most exclusionary, to women artists. Traditional, object-based artistic production was eschewed in favor of ephemera: video, writing, performance, and graphic design.

The Women's Graphic Center (WGC), run by de Bretteville and Alm, became one of the most important features of the Building, and its design program was, in many ways, the core of the Feminist Studio Workshop. In January of 1975, the two launched an intensive, four-month skills workshop for twenty-two women, teaching them offset lithography, silkscreen, and letterpress, and the potential for the kind of artwork each process enabled. As Alm wrote, "That program resulted in exuberant feelings about one's own creative work as well as frustration with personal and mechanical limitations to the completion of elaborate projects."[34]

The Women's Graphic Center

The WGC was built on the precepts of de Bretteville's Marxist approach, which treated design it as a public communication imbued with the efficacy of social change, rather than as a discreet art object. As she wrote in a conference paper that she presented to the American Institute of Architects in 1972:

> The process by which forms are made and the forms themselves
> embody values and standards of behavior that affect large numbers of
> people.... For me, it is this integral relationship between individual
> creativity and social responsibility that draws me to the design arts.[35]

Already fluent in the language of propaganda, de Bretteville had previously designed posters in Italy during the social unrest of the late 1960s, for Olivetti, a famed indus- trial design firm, and the Italian Communist Party. She was also a public figure in the field, writing a number of compelling articles on feminist design and its historical re- lationship to architecture and women's domestic space; many of her essays ended up in feminist publications published through the Woman's Building.[36]

FSW students learned to use a range of printing presses, beginning with the letter press, which was easy to learn but required a certain disciplined meticulousness, to set type and to think through the requisite ideas of font, size, and language. At the Grandview building, a wooden typeface called Kabel was discovered as part of the building's own past, and utilized for the Woman's Building entry signage. Offset, diazo, and rotogravure printing were introduced; the two former, almost mimeographic in quality, expanded the possibilities for the cheap and easily made copy; the latter, a fine art process, was based on intaglio, in which the image is engraved onto a copper plate, and then printed upon a reel of paper. Traditional fine art printing—such as etching and lithography—was excluded from the curriculum, on the basis that it promoted

Women's Graphic Center at the Woman's Building. 1981. Susan E. King (upper left) teaching a course. Woman's Building Image Archive, Otis College of Art and Design.

individual, rather than collective, expression. Instead, the available printing processes facilitated self-publishing of all kinds: newsletters and broadsides, as well as artists' books, poetry chapbooks, stationery, and other kinds of small-press endeavors. Additional skill proficiencies, such as photographic processes, were achieved on an as-needed basis.

Broadsides were a popular form of expression at the Woman's Building. They were often hastily written communiqués that utilized a time-based medium not unlike a poster, meant to circulate quickly among the "sisterhood." (Sisterhood was a then-widely utilized term denoting a universal network of feminist allies, initially derived from Robin Morgan's popular collection of essays, *Sisterhood Is Powerful: An Anthology of Writings from the Woman's Liberation Movement* [1970]). Broadsides were used as a rallying cry, to assert a viewpoint or address a specific issue that was time sensitive, such as announcements for rallies, workshops, teach-ins, or meetings. In a broadside titled *Growing Up* (1987), the artist Susan E. King reflected back on her own education:

> 1973: Move to California to join an experimental art program and make sculpture. Discover Artists' Books and start learning offset printing. Know nothing, print stationery on newly purchased letter-press equipment at the Women's Graphic Center. Watch two women print first-day issue for hot air balloonist commemorative stamp. Make Artists' Books. Take Bookbinding class, UCLA. Look at lots of books. Take letterpress class. Buy font of type, used job case and stick and keep it under my couch so I can set type at home. Invent nom de plume at Phillipe's Restaurant [*sic*], home of the French Dip Sandwich. Decide on way to movie with significant other that I want to make books forever. Print as much as possible. Harden myself in commercial world. Read as much as possible. Learn from elders. Find sustenance where I can. [37]

One of the footnotes under "Artists' Books" reveals some of the sources that made a distinct impression on the young bookmaker: Jumbo, Ruscha, Rebis, Poltroon. [38] Again we see circularity: a young Ed Ruscha began his student career as the editor of Chouinard's student newspaper, in the very same building that King began hers. For King, it was the "right place," as she has written elsewhere, "on the steps of the Woman's Building, listening to Helen Alm talk about artists' books. The right place was also in Sheila de Bretteville's living room, hearing her talk about commercial printing and personal voice in design." [39]

One of the key classes taught by de Bretteville was a course called Feeling to Form. More workshop than structured course, participants were asked to focus upon an object of their choice, a prized, but otherwise ordinary, possession, and speak about it.

In most cases, the object became a stand-in for the woman herself and a vehicle for initiating a discussion of form, through verbal and written exercises. De Bretteville's insistence on finding suitable forms from which women could derive content was a way of upending the traditional Modernist precepts of form *as content*, such as the Bauhaus-style graphic models that permeated American Modernism via the émigrés who brought them, such as László Moholy-Nagy at the Institute of Design in Chicago, and Serge Chermayeff at Yale University, where de Bretteville had done her graduate work. Feeling to Form, then, was a literal reversal, extracting *form from content*, rather than *content from form*.

As a result of this form-finding process, arguably the most highly realized artwork to emerge at the Building took on graphic forms, such as broadsides, posters, journals, and artists' books. As Alm described it, "I discovered women had a lot to say and wanted to say it themselves...the experience of seeing themselves in print and knowing that they did it themselves was a transforming one for each woman."[40]

Sometimes transformation became transference: even some of the best-known performance work was also the culmination of de Bretteville's graphic design pedagogy, such as Leslie Labowitz's and Suzanne Lacy's *Three Weeks in May* (1977), in which maps were used to articulate spaces of violation within Los Angeles, documenting where rape had occurred, while written press releases and posters were distributed to generate public awareness and media attention.

As King has succinctly observed, "Printing gave work power and distance."[41] But printing was also strategic: throughout the 1970s, self-publication was crucial to the success and maintenance of individual feminist communities, and came in wide ranging styles. This was in keeping with the ways in which feminist activity disseminated more broadly, nationally and internationally. I have already written elsewhere of the proliferation of an alternative lesbian press culture and its relationship to collectivity.[42] Newsletters, mimeographed manifestos, and journals were quickly printed and circulated, providing unity and critical awareness through a constantly changing body of literature, often an amalgam of politics, women's health information, poetry, and artwork.

In fact, many of the Building's performance collectives (nearly all of which had overlapping members)—the Feminist Art Workers, the Waitresses, Mother Art, the Sisters Of Survival (again, secular nuns), Ariadne, and the Lesbian Art Project—were heavily reliant upon the graphic skills they had acquired from the FSW for creating publicity and advertising for their own work through posters, mailings, press releases, and media campaigns. As sociologist Sharon Sidell-Selick wrote, "Forms of art which were considered acceptable became evident in the value placed upon internal and external organizing...the art of the Woman's Building sought action in addition to expression."[43]

Left: **Cheri Gaulke and Barbara Bouska looking at poster in the front hall,** January 1976. Welcome signage in view. Woman's Building Image Archive, Otis College of Art and Design.

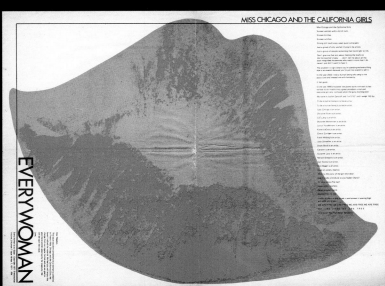

MISS CHICAGO AND THE CALIFORNIA GIRLS

EVERYWOMAN

Above: **Cover of *EVERYWOMAN*,** Volume 2, Number 7, Issue 18, May 7, 1971. This issue was produced by a woman's collective in Fresno—Miss Chicago and the California Girls—and designed by Sheila de Bretteville. Everywoman is our Sister © 1971 Everywoman. Published by Everywoman Bookstore, 1043B Washington Blvd, Venice, CA 90291.

Left: **Linda Norlen printing**, 1978. Woman's Building Image Archive, Otis College of Art and Design.

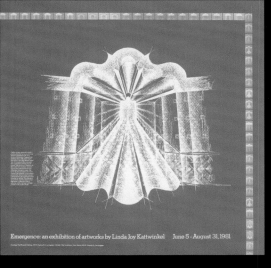

Left and below: **Linda Joy Kattwinkel,**
Emergence, 1981. Diazo print, 36" x 36".
Poster is from the *Public Announcements/*
Private Conversations Project led by Sheila
Levrant de Bretteville at the Feminist
Studio Workshop, The Woman's
Building, Los Angeles. © Linda Joy
Kattwinkel.

Emergence: an exhibition of artworks by Linda Joy Kattwinkel   June 5 - August 31, 1981

I felt a strong connection with a
public physical form, an archway,
which I identified with. In a
series of drawings, I zapped the
existing form with red to draw
attention to the part where I iden-
tify the source of the form, and
the vulnerable, private part of
myself. My process of reaction to
that attention created a central
figure who emerged from and
inhabited the space under the
arch. As she emerged, she trans-
formed the physical environment
around her: the doorway became
a long tunnel, the sculptural forms
became its ceiling. This figure is
my private creative essence: her
response to attention was to
assume visible identity and take
power in the public world.

Left: **Billy Tsien**
letterpress in t
Graphic Center
Woman's Buildi
Woman's Buildi
Archive, Otis Co
Art and Design.

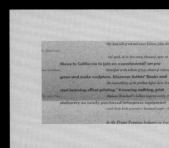

Right: **Susan E. King,**
Growing Up (in the
dying printing indus-
try), 1987. Broadside
commissioned by *Fine*
Art magazine, Paradise
Press, Venice, CA.

Feminist Art Workers, *Heaven or Hell?*, 1981. Pictured L to R: Nancy Angelo, Laurel Klick, Cheri Gaulke. Photograph by Sue Maberry. © Feminist Art Workers.

The Pedagogy of Consensus

Public Announcements/Private Conversations (1975) was another de Bretteville course that evolved into a series of site-specific art projects that took place over the course of the 1977–78 academic year, in which women installed graphic design projects in public spaces in which they were uncomfortable. The chosen space—a metaphor for the hostility and misogyny of the larger world—was a planned intrusion, as the student learned to negotiate and render a perceived "hostile" space neutral through personal efficacy. As de Bretteville described it:

> Participants in this project write, design, print, post and collect responses about and for places in the shared environment. They are asked to provide information easily accessible to as broad an audience as uses the public site, including what evokes their sense of personal connection to that place. Within this theme each woman gives graphic form to her concerns, placing this work—and thus placing herself—in public view.[44]

The lesson could be then individually tailored to meet the needs of the student. One such student, Linda Kattwinkel, who had a background in illustration, described this as the "permission for individual process [which] is one of the important ways in which this class is different from traditional academic learning and is feminist. The attention is on the individual, in support and encouragement of her finding her own personal materials and her own forms for expressing it." [45]

De Bretteville's format of direct address in a charged space, in which women entered into both self-reflexive and collective dialogues about female vulnerability, offered a highly original and compelling lesson: in feminist pedagogy, personal growth was a direct result of the search for authentic forms. Moreover, authenticity could not happen without the experience of adversity. The communal sense of self was literally "broken open," as the proto-feminist poet Muriel Rukeyser famously proclaimed, exposed in order to the pave the way for a new form of being. Hence, at the Woman's Building, *form became a transformative experience*, resultant in the perception of personal wholeness and collective unity.

This transformation, then, is twofold: first this communalism was predicated on enclosure, occurring in a sphere (the perennial "safe space") *separate* from the world at large. This is the kind of "courtyard world" that Bryan Jay Wolf writes about in his work on seventeenth-century Dutch genre painting, in which depictions of courtyard architecture acted as a permeable barrier, in effect, a threshold for sacred experiences. [46] The architecture of the Woman's Building also underscores this phenomenon: the Chouinard building had a Spanish-style courtyard that was the beloved core of the Woman's Building's social life, a central gathering point, a source, just as it had been for students at Chouinard decades before.

But the "courtyard world" extended to the interiority of the feminist studio as well. As Lacy described it:

> In those early days you could flip on a Portapak [video camera] and do whatever you wanted in the privacy of your own studio. It provided an instant access to body and other female experiences that was *safe for us* [author's italics] and gave us a way to display our bodies through performance. [47]

Lacy's notion of safety bears the mark of inclusion. Not all of us are safe, just some of us; but this zone of safety gives way to the thrilling potential for inviolable experience— collective entry into the private sphere of creation, a sphere that could *only* be achieved once the symbolic overthrow of social oppression, hierarchy, and danger had occurred, thus, the transformative experience of the studio, from a historical space of female exclusion, to a space of production informed by and infused with feminist principles.

Secondly, transformation is only completed through the collective experience of the visionary: in the case of Hamburger's medieval nuns, artistic production was the

The courtyard at the first location of the Woman's Building at 743 Grandview Avenue, Los Angeles, 1973. Woman's Building Image Archive. Otis College of Art and Design.

culmination of ritual prayer and devotion. In the case of the feminists at the Woman's Building, artistic expression was the culmination of ritual consciousness-raising, in effect, a ceremonial rite of witnessing *each other*. Being alone with your Portapak in the studio, then, was no more a solitary experience than was being a nun in her chambers.

Togetherness was constant, from emotive C-R sessions to the "feminist troubleshooting" meetings that arose around the maintenance of the building itself. Thus, isolation (which is not to be confused with misery) was not possible in such a community, which advocated for "total involvement," a term that circulated throughout the building's minutes as a way of highlighting the community's desire for daily presence not unlike nuns entering into a religious covenant with a higher power.[48] The totalizing (and perhaps unintended) effect from such an expectation (vow) of commitment amounted to a kind of secular fervor. As an anonymous staff member told Sidell-Selick in 1984,

> I have never been religious, but in a certain way I always felt like it [the Woman's Building] was a religion. You had this sort of pure, and it was pure, commitment to this cause and you had to challenge your own ingenuity and skill which was really uplifting.[49]

58

After 1976, there was even the possibility of joining the community (at the $100 level) as a "life member." [50] Of course, the Woman's Building was not the first, or the last, arts organization to have encouraged or offered lifetime memberships as a means of fundraising. But I am pointing out the language the Building used to describe its own sense of purpose, or the way in which its programming, "was alive with opportunities for you [women everywhere] to speak your own language—and be heard!" [51]

Presumably, if one's "own language," was cultivated, an act of translation would be required to disseminate such a highly specialized dialogue, reflecting the essential insularity of life at the Building—in all its facets. For instance, an eight-week course in self-portraiture called "The Photographic Speculum" (offered in Spring 1980, by Mary McNally) might very well be innocently titled, nothing more than a metaphor for interiority, but then again, it might not be. [52] To an outsider, such a heading might have been casually misconstrued as pornographic, since self-examination (gynecological and otherwise) was an intrinsic part of the feminist agenda, both at the Building, and as part of widespread (no pun intended) feminist health initiatives (such as the Boston Women's Health Collective, producers of *Our Bodies, Ourselves*). [53] Without a working knowledge of the particular dialect spoken at the Woman's Building, it would take a brave outsider to muster the courage to attend such a course.

Still, the Woman's Building proudly asserted its special brand of dominance almost as a mission statement, found, for instance, on the FSW's fall 1976 calendar:

> By working together in feminist community, we have not only creat-
> ed from present realizations of past experience, but we have had new
> and unique interactions, thus changing the content of our art. We
> have re-defined the function of art as raising consciousness, inviting
> dialogue, and transforming culture—a definition which reflects our
> awareness of the social nature of art and our commitment to the public. [54]

The politics of this self-producing, self-assured, and amorphous "we," however, became stultifying. In making sure everyone had a voice (again, the C-R structure), decision-making was notoriously inefficient and leaderless. Even the journal *Chrysalis*, housed at the Woman's Building, was mired in the bureaucracy of consensus, as their editorial decisions were (for better or worse, but probably worse) the result of a collective process. "Admittedly this is a slow process," they wrote, in describing what was involved. "But it is effective in maintaining our feminist commitment to feminist values and feminist process." [55]

This adds up to a certain kind of dystopia, which American feminism, arguably, became, particularly after the failure of the Equal Rights Amendment in 1979. [56] By the second iteration of the Building, the first generation of Chicago and de Bretteville's students: Alm, Lacy, and Wilding, as emerging artists themselves, had assumed authoritative teacher-mentor roles in the FSW, but eventually left to pursue outside projects and opportunities. This restlessness struck the remaining founders as well, since producing from within a community of students, versus a community of peers, are two very different things. Raven was the first to express dissatisfaction with the organizational model as it stood, writing to de Bretteville, in 1976:

> Somehow I feel the need to feel like a separate person instead of a cog in our group/organizational wheel, marching as I have been these last years to the sound of what I think is my duty...I love what we've built even though its maintenance is burdensome. [57]

An evolutionary process was underway, creating change, dissent, and a level of dissatisfaction roiling from within the WB's ranks. Eventually, this generation of students (those who remained, arrived, or enrolled after 1975), took over both the Building's administration and the FSW after its founders (de Bretteville and Raven) departed. From 1979 until 1981, the program's final year, a collective known as the Feminist Art Workers (Nancy Angelo, Candace Compton, Cheri Gaulke, Vanalyne Green, and Laurel Klick) took over all aspects of its pedagogy and production. [58] However, by the early 1980s, enrollment was in severe decline, as the American political climate negatively and rapidly transformed, constricting civil liberties and curtailing social services and cultural programming. In 1981, the Feminist Studio Workshop was terminated in favor of salvaging the Building itself, entirely eliminating the art school and exhibition series.

And yet, it is precisely this intensity of dedication (veneration) that elevates the Building to its mature and visionary stature, a vision that ceased to be needed in the Los Angeles community precisely because it had fulfilled its role: feminist separatism had become outmoded, while its educational model had prevailed, offering women the enormous potential for mainstream achievement and artistic recognition.

So the question remains: what did the Feminist Studio Workshop produce, if it didn't produce multiple generations of so-called important artists? To counter with a follow-up: was this really ever the point? While the dissolution of hierarchy had always been a way to counter patriarchy, the effusiveness of feminist inclusion, over time, has, for whatever reason, come down to singular ownership over collective works of art. The unfortunate squabble for acknowledgement decades later among now-middle-aged artists seems, in the end, bitterly ironic: a clear rejection of the feminist values that were espoused with such reverence during the Building's most productive years, and with it, a return to the hierarchal (and patriarchal) models of a fiercely guarded and autonomous individual artistic practice, in which individual reputation becomes inflated.

Such lessons have gone unlearned, as personal grievances also struck a later generation of feminist artists, most notably, the Guerrilla Girls, a now-iconic collective of women who, throughout the 1980s and into the early 1990s, sacrificed their individual identities as a way to advance the collective cause of gender parity. Using pseudonyms (of dead Modernist women artists such as Frida Kahlo and Kathe Kollwitz), the Guerrilla Girls appeared publicly wearing gorilla masks, using wit, humor, and theatricality in their performances and protest actions to advocate for the inclusion of women artists in New York museum exhibitions and collections. As their collective practice descended into bitter legal wrangling, two of the group's original members revealed their true identities during the course of their lawsuit, finally settling in 2005 over branding and intellectual property rights.[59]

Yet, the Woman's Building was a stubborn place, full of staunch (lesbian) feminists. Again it morphed, into a kind of community center guided by an external (outsider) board of elite (straight) women in business and finance. The most notable fallout was the alienation of core members. Mainstreaming had begun, but with little success. The Woman's Building limped through the remainder of the 1980s as its community continued to shrink, approximating the insularity of an aging artist's colony at some remove from the world, struggling, but failing to attract a younger generation of practitioners (not unlike today's besieged convents, who face dwindling numbers). In 1991, the Woman's Building closed for good, though its community remains: a diaspora of middle-aged women largely in Los Angeles, but elsewhere as well—a diffuse community, to be sure, but one that reassembles itself whenever possible, as artistic collaborators, as life-long partners, as allies and colleagues in other institutions, as small groups of friends, as big loud groups, complaining about the traffic, but good-natured enough to drive crosstown for events such as performances, book parties, and reunions. Eventually this will give way to funerals (indeed, it already has), but I refuse to see this as sad.

In 2009, I had the pleasure of attending the first Black Mountain College conference, which brought together an eclectic group of academics, curious artists, locals, and yes, former students—three, to be exact—who were still alive, well into their eighties. The conference was followed by a tour of the once-glorious campus—now a Christian summer boy's camp. To be sure, it was nostalgic and sentimental, but I am certain it was also, in some way, important. I am convinced that one day the Woman's Building will also garner a similar, if belated, recognition, taking its proper (pride of) place in post-war history. And young women will embark on a pilgrimage, and perhaps spoof former FSW student Susan Mogul's Woman's Building video tour, much as the artist herself parodied Vito Acconci videos, and a spark, somewhere, will ignite, in a way we can neither foresee nor imagine.

Notes

1. See Jeffrey Hamburger, *Nuns as Artists: The Visual Culture of a Medieval Convent* (Berkeley and London: University of California Press, 1997).

2. I am taking great liberties, departing from the literature on medieval sexualities, in which the biological imperative for artistic creation was entirely gendered male. See Fredrika H. Jacobs's excellent chapter, "(Pro) Creativity," in *Defining the Renaissance "Virtuosa": Women Artists and the Language of Art History and Criticism* (London and New York: Cambridge University Press, 1996), 27–63.

3. Judy Chicago, email to the author, July 23, 2009.

4. "Profile of the Institute's 1971–72 Student Body," *CalArts 1973/1974 Course Catalog*, 30, Sheila de Bretteville Papers, uncataloged, Hamden, Connecticut.

5. *CalArts 1973/1974 Course Catalog*, 38–39.

6. Bia Lowe to Sheila de Bretteville, 1998–99. Quoted in "The Community of Design/The Design of Community," in *From Site to Vision: the Woman's Building in Contemporary Culture*, Sondra Hale and Terry Wolverton, eds. (Los Angeles: Woman's Building and Otis College of Art and Design, 2011), 238. While not an excuse for his lewd conduct, which de Bretteville confirms later in this exchange with Lowe, in all fairness, Farson was a man of a particular time and place, a psychologist who had pioneered the 1960s encounter group, intent on "freeing" people from their repressions. Group nudity, non-sexual public touching, and screaming were among the era's accepted techniques. (For a parody of the era as it unfolded, see the film, *Bob & Carol & Ted & Alice* [1969]). Given Farson's comments to Lowe, and others, it seems clear that he failed to understand that impressionable students are not the same as consenting adults.

7. Glenn Phillips, "Introduction," *California Video* (Los Angeles: Getty Research Institute, 2008), 5.

8. Sheila de Bretteville, conversation with the author, Hamden, CT, July 13, 2009. It seems important to note that at CalArts both Chicago and de Bretteville were teaching alongside their husbands: Lloyd Hamrol (whom Chicago divorced in 1976) was on the sculpture faculty, and Peter de Bretteville also taught design. So perhaps the personal and professional overlap was also a mitigating factor in their decisions to leave, although de Bretteville had arrived in 1969, helping to plan and structure CalArts prior to its opening.

9. Miriam Schapiro continued the Feminist Art Program during its final year, 1973–74.

10. Other schools with important early video programs were the Nova Scotia College of Art and Design and the School of the Art Institute of Chicago (SAIC). In 1976, Kate Horsfield and Lyn Blumenthal founded the Video Data Bank, which is housed at SAIC. Horsfield and Blumenthal had been participants in the early life of the Woman's Building; they had been invited to conduct video workshops and, in documentarian style, had made single-channel videotape interviews of individual subjects such as Arlene Raven.

11. Charlotte Bunch, "Lesbians in Revolt," *The Furies: Lesbian/Feminist Monthly* 1:1 (January 1972), 8–9.

12. Westside Women was not Los Angeles' first. It was preceded by a spate of lesbian feminist organizing in 1971 and 1972, including: Sisters Liberation House (1972), an offshoot of the Gay Community Services Center (1971), and the Westside Women's Center, which emerged in Venice and had several iterations on Hill Street under names such as "Womonspace." See Yolanda Retter, "Lesbian (Feminist) Los Angeles, 1970–1990: An Exploratory Ethnohistory" (1995), http://www.usc.edu/libraries/archives/queerfrontiers/queer/papers/retter.html.

13. Retter.

14. *CalArts Course Catalog*, 57.

15. Robert Perine, *Chouinard, an Art Vision Betrayed: The Story of the Chouinard Art Institute, 1921–1972* (Encinitas, CA: Artra Publishing, 1985), 47.

16. See Judy Chicago, *Through the Flower: My Struggle as a Woman Artist* (New York: Doubleday, 1975).

17. Perine, 195.

18. Susan Peterson, "Ceramics in the West: The Explosion of the 1950s," in *Color and Fire: Defining Moments in Studio Ceramics, 1950–2000*, Jo Lauria, ed. (New York: Rizzoli, and Los Angeles: Los Angeles County Museum of Art, 2000), 101.

19. Ibid.

20. Perine, 47.

21. For interesting background on Dow, see Kathleen Pyne and D. Scott Atkinson, "Landscapes of the Mind: New Conceptions of Nature," in *The Third Mind: American Artists Contemplate Asia, 1860–1989*, Alexandra Munroe, ed. (New York: Guggenheim Museum, 2009), 89–99.

22. Perine, 101.

23. Ibid., 195.

24. Eddy Jo Bernal, "Mary Poppins Premiere," *Los Angeles Herald-Examiner*, August 28, 1964.

25. Martha L. Garrison, "Credit-Ability for Women," *The Family Coordinator* 25:3 (July 1976), 241.

26. Peterson, 101.

27. Perine, 101.

28. Jong Hoon Choi to Sheila de Bretteville, October 9, 1974, de Bretteville Papers.

29. Perine, 50–51.

30. Sheila de Bretteville to Melissa Hoffman, June 11, 1976, Folder: FSW Inquiries, 1976–77, de Bretteville Papers.

31. Perine, 38.

32. Sheila de Bretteville, email interview with Ginger Wolfe-Suarez, *interReview* 08 (2007) http://www.interreview.org/08/slb_interview.html.

33. Judy Chicago email correspondence with author, July 23, 2009.

34. Helen Alm, "The Women's Graphic Center," 4, Teaching Files, de Bretteville Papers.

35. Sheila de Bretteville, conference paper delivered to the American Institute of Architects, July 1973, de Bretteville Papers.

36. See in particular, Sheila de Bretteville, "The 'Parlorization' of Our Homes and Ourselves," *Chrysalis* 9 (Fall 1979), 33–45.

37. Susan E. King, *Growing Up*, 1987. Broadside written and designed by King, Paradise Press, Venice, CA. Paradise Press, Ephemera Folder, Special Collections, The Getty Research Institute, Los Angeles.

38. Jumbo was a local feminist press and Rebis a hermaphrodite character from DC Comics. Founded in 1975 by Frances Butler and Alastair Johnson, Poltroon is an avant-garde fine art press based in Berkeley that specializes in experimental writing and cover art.

39. Susan King, "Artists' Books by Women—Diaries, Notebooks, Journals, 1970–1983," in *At Home*, Arlene Raven, ed. (Long Beach: Long Beach Museum of Art, 1983), 57.

40. Helen Alm, "The Women's Graphic Center," unpublished grant application, 3, Teaching Files, de Bretteville Papers.

41. King, "Artists' Books by Women," 57.

42. See my essay, "The Feminist Nomad: The All-Women's Group Show," in *WACK! Art and the Feminist Revolution*, Lisa Mark and Connie Butler, eds. (Los Angeles: Museum of Contemporary Art, and Cambridge, MA: MIT Press, 2007), 458–72.

43. An excellent sociological study of the Woman's Building exists. See Sharon Sidell-Selick, "The Evolution of Organizational Meaning: A Case Study of Myths in Transition" (PhD Dissertation, Wright Institute Graduate School of Psychology, 1984).

44. Public Announcements/Private Conversations, course description, 1975, Woman's Building (WB) Files, de Bretteville Papers.

45. Linda Kattwinkel, "Public Announcements/Private Conversations Response," 1975, WB Files, de Bretteville Papers.

46. Bryan Jay Wolf, *Vermeer and the Invention of Seeing* (Chicago: University of Chicago Press, 2001), 60. The argument is centered specifically on the Dutch painter Pieter de Hooch, who painted many courtyard scenes as an expression of domesticity and inscribing gender ideologies.

47. *California Video*, 155.

48. "Woman's Community Inc.," board meeting minutes, July 5, 1977, de Bretteville Papers. "Feminist troubleshooting" and "total involvement" are terms that originate under the desired qualities necessary for continued involvement and participation. They also become, in this particular document, some of the desired qualities sought in a building manager, which the community wished to hire in order to alleviate the bureaucratic burden placed upon themselves in order to allocate time for artistic production.

49. Sidell-Selick, 65.

50. Woman's Building staff meeting minutes, July 13, 1977, de Bretteville Papers.

51. Feminist Studio Workshop flier/calendar, Fall 1976, unpaginated, Woman's Building Archive, Otis College of Art and Design, Los Angeles.

52. "This Spring at the Women's Graphic Center," *Spinning Off* (March 1980), 4. Woman's Building Archives at Otis.

53. For a wonderful period overview, see "Feminist Women's Health Centers: Interview with Dido Hasper," in *Women's Culture: Renaissance of the Seventies*, Gayle Kimball, ed. (Metuchen, NJ: The Scarecrow Press, Inc., 1981), 264–79.

54. Feminist Studio Workshop flier/calendar, Fall 1976, unpaginated, Woman's Building Archive at Otis.

55. Editor's note, *Chrysalis 1* (January 1977), 2.

56. The ERA was granted an extension until 1982, after it failed to pass in 1979. In 1980, Ronald Regan was elected president and the Republican Party withdrew ERA support from its national platform. Since 1982, the ERA has been introduced in each session of Congress. Passage requires ratification by 38 states. For a detailed history of the ERA, see Roberta W. Francis, "The History of the Equal Rights Amendment," www.equalrightsamendment.org.

57. Arlene Raven to Sheila de Bretteville, August 19, 1976, de Bretteville Papers.

58. As individuals, some of the artists had a longer relationship to the Woman's Building and its previous pedagogical iterations. Both Vanalyne Green and Laurel Klick had been among Judy Chicago's original students at Fresno. Nancy Angelo and Cheri Gaulke both arrived at the WB in 1975, with degrees from other institutions. Candace Compton did not remain involved in either the collective or the building's administration.

59. See Jeffrey Toobin, "The Bench: Girls Behaving Badly," *The New Yorker* (May 30, 2005), http://www.newyorker.com/archive/2005/05/30/050530ta_talk_toobin.

The Woman's Building 1893, Historical Handicrafts, March–May 1976. Installation view of the exhibition.
Woman's Building Image Archive, Otis College of Art and Design.

a monthly newsletter of women's culture published at the Woman's Building

March
50¢

Spinning Off

Art of the Woman's Building,
1893-1980

Cover of Spinning Off, March 1980. The newsletter features *Art of the Woman's Building 1893–1980: Graphics, Performance and Video*, organized by Arlene Raven with Sheila de Bretteville, Jerri Allyn, Nancy Angelo, Cheri Gaulke, and Sue Maberry for Artemisia Gallery, Chicago, March 1980. The cover image is the frontispiece from the book *Art and Handicraft in the Woman's Building* (1893). Woman's Building Image Archive, Otis College of Art and Design.

FICTIVE FAMILIES OF HISTORY MAKERS: HISTORICITY AT THE LOS ANGELES WOMAN'S BUILDING

Michelle Moravec

> Since at least the eighteenth century, feminism has used history in
> different ways at different times as a critical weapon in the strug-
> gle for women's emancipation. Feminism's History has offered dem-
> onstrations, in the form of exemplary instances from the past, of
> women's worthiness to engage in the same activities as men (wage-
> earning, education, citizenship, rulership). It has provided heroines
> to emulate and lineages for contemporary activists—membership in
> fictive families of history makers. Feminism's History has exposed as
> instruments of patriarchal power stories that explained the exclusion
> of women as a fact of nature. And it has written new histories to
> counter the "lie" of women's passivity, as well as their erasure from
> the records that constitute collective memory. —Joan Wallach Scott,
> "Feminism's History"[1]

As Joan Wallach Scott notes, the past has inspired feminists in myriad ways—justifying
women's activism, documenting heroines, providing intellectual lineages, exposing
women's exclusion from power structures, and finally, creating new histories that
include women. However, none of this useful past was available to 1970s feminists.
Indeed, as members of radical social movements, feminists seemed a group unlikely to
go foraging about in the past. The infamous injunction of the era to "never trust anyone

over thirty" attests to the tendency to avoid crossing generational divides.[2] However, among the ruins of a Whig history, fragments of a usable past gradually emerged and feminist activists began to discover the liberating power of their grandmothers' history.

Robin Morgan coined the neologism "herstory" in her influential anthology *Sisterhood is Powerful* to imply that women's versions of history would differ significantly from male narratives.[3] "Herstory" may grate on the ear now, but in its day the assertion that women had a history was a radical act. References to history dot the landscape of the early women's movement. A group of women who participated in a 1967 march against the Vietnam War called themselves the Jeannette Rankin Brigade, after the first woman elected to the House of Representatives and the only member of Congress who had the distinction of voting against both world wars. When feminists marched in New York City in 1970, they picked August 26 as the date, commemorating the fiftieth anniversary of women's suffrage. The early 1970s also saw the revival of International Women's Day, which was first celebrated in the early twentieth century by radical female labor activists.

Digging a little deeper, the thread of history is revealed as a crucial warp in the weave of the new fabric of feminism. Fundamental differences between ideologies in the women's movement in large part came down to different understandings of history. Socialist feminists well versed in Marx and Engels's analysis of the role of family in formulating capitalism emphasized the historical origins of women's oppression.[4] Radical feminists argued that women's oppression preceded class formation; instead they referenced a "pre-historical," matriarchal past.[5] Arguments over the primacy of oppressions led to a rift between radical feminists, who argued women's oppression must be seen as primary, and feminist activists who remained more tied to the Left and contended that the socialist overthrow of capitalism would also end women's oppression.[6] History, it seemed, did matter.

In this essay, I will explore the multiple uses of the past at the Woman's Building, a public center for women's culture founded in Los Angeles in 1973. The very name, which commemorates the 1893 Woman's Building at the Chicago World's Columbian Exposition, hints at the centrality of history to the endeavor. Although pavilions devoted to women had appeared at previous world's fairs, such as the Centennial Exposition of 1876 in Philadelphia, the original commission anointed by the United States Congress to organize the 1893 Columbian Exposition in Chicago included not a single woman. Despite lobbying by prominent women's activists, including Susan B. Anthony, Congress refused to appoint a woman to the commission. Instead, Congress authorized a Board of Lady Managers, which was comprised of the wives of influential men; no doubt they expected that it would be a largely ornamental and non-functional body. However, the men had not reckoned with the force that was the redoubtable Bertha Honoré Palmer, wife of the richest man in Chicago, patroness of the arts, as well as a major mover and shaker in reform circles. Despite the size and prominence of the 1893 Woman's Building, by the 1970s it had all but disappeared, both materially and historically.[7]

What is most interesting about the use of the past by feminist artists in the 1970s is that they could not allude to a glorious epoch. Women had been so systematically excluded from the art historical record that a female student could receive an entire college education in the arts without learning about a single woman artist.[8] As New York feminist artist Therese Schwartz bluntly put it, male art historians had "built women a bad art history."[9] A large part of the feminist art movement of the 1970s involved rectifying that error.

History making occurs in many ways. Most simply, history involves constructing linear narratives connecting the past to the present. However, in the process, branches get pruned in order to create a single story. Determining what gets cut and what remains involves far more complicated processes than simply putting events in chronological order. Some events, people, and things are classified as historical. That is to say, in a tautological fashion, these people, events, and things are worthy of historical attention simply by virtue of being included in the historical record. Thus taxonomy, the classifying process, is critical to history making because it determines what makes history. By reading back taxonomically, however, we can also arrive at a genealogical understanding of history making. I mean to imply both senses of the word genealogy. The more common usage refers to tracing lines of ancestry. The other, which draws on Friedrich Nietzsche and Michel Foucault, takes the emblematic element of the first sense—the tree—to explore how histories are branched as opposed to singularly unified. Reading genealogically, we find what was left behind in the creation of a seamless narrative about a complicated past that was never so irreducibly simple.

In constructing a better account of the past for themselves, members of the Woman's Building engaged a variety of strategies. These efforts initially took the shape of taxonomical interventions, by which they reclaimed some artists, artifacts, and events as art historical. In the process, new genealogies were created. At times these lineages became highly personalized. Furthermore, in reclaiming women artists of the past as ideological foremothers, the members of the Woman's Building created tangled genealogies in the secondary sense of the word, as evidenced by the way they manipulated the boundaries of time and space to craft a past to suit their present needs.

The members of the Woman's Building focused on retrieving women artists lost to art history. However, finding women artists who have been "hidden" from history only affirms the traditional art historical narrative, by merely inserting women into it. Other efforts by members of the Woman's Building served to disrupt the narrative of art history itself. For example, some women became interested in recuperating traditionally female art forms and having them aesthetically reappraised. The chronological narrative was further interrupted by the translocation of historical events, such as the 1893 Woman's Building, which challenged the story of art as a continuous narrative. Finally, members of the Woman's Building took on the fixed subject positions implied by the traditional narrative of art history—woman as muse, model, and handmaiden to male genius, but never as artist—by regenerating the figure of the artist to include women.

Mind the Gap

From its inception, history lurked in the background of the feminist art movement. In the late 1960s, Judy Chicago's reading of emerging feminist history provided inspiration for the feminist art program at California State University Fresno.[10] Later, Paula Harper, a trained art historian, joined Chicago on the faculty of California Institute of the Arts (CalArts) in Valencia.[11] Arlene Raven and Ruth Iskin replaced Harper at CalArts and founded the Center for Feminist Art Historical Studies at the Woman's Building. For female artists, finding their foremothers provided an important way of legitimizing themselves as artists. If art history exists by sorting things into two categories, those people and items worthy of aesthetic appreciation and those without such redeeming features, then a survey of art history in the early 1970s revealed women artists to basically be without a history.[12] Thus retrieving women "hidden from history" proved to be the first task of the taxonomical effort.[13] Art historian Raven remembered searching in used book stores for nineteenth-century documentation of "women artists [who] had fallen again into obscurity in the early twentieth century."[14] She describes her relief at discovering that, despite a discipline that claimed women could be at best mediocre copyists, there had been successful women artists in the past.

Yet, in the early years of the movement, art history was not merely the purview of trained academics. While searching for props to use in *Womanhouse* (1972), a project of CalArts' Feminist Art Program that involved installations about domesticity and femininity in an old house, student Nancy Youdelman found a catalog of the 1893 Woman's Building. It was one of those fortunate happenstances that make history.[15] Flabbergasted to learn that not only had women artists existed in the past, but also that they had organized to exhibit their work, Youdelman brought the book back to the Feminist Art Program, where students and teachers alike pored over its pages. After that initial, exciting discovery, the memory of the Woman's Building lingered. In the spring of 1972, student Janice Lester delivered a lecture on the Woman's Building at a feminist art conference at CalArts.[16] In January of 1973, Womanspace, a feminist cooperative gallery in Los Angeles (which later moved to the Woman's Building), celebrated its opening with, among other things, a lecture by Arlene Raven about the 1893 Woman's Building.[17] The event's description places Womanspace in the direct lineage of the original Woman's Building, describing the original "Woman's Building, [as] the first "Womanspace."[18] When Chicago, de Bretteville, and Raven decided to locate their independent art program for women—the Feminist Studio Workshop (FSW)—in a site containing other feminist organizations, Raven suggested the name the Woman's Building as "an act against the historical erasure of women's art and an acknowledgement of the heritage we were beginning to recover."[19] The inspiration members of the Woman's Building felt to their predecessors made them determined to rescue the 1893 Woman's Building from historical oblivion.

The recovery of that hidden history proved central to the mission of the Woman's Building. Initially Raven and Iskin hoped to involve FSW students in the Center for Art Historical Research. However, according to Raven, most of the students lacked the necessary research skills.[20] Nevertheless, according to Iskin, a "sense of the importance of history, that what we were doing was something that was history" pervaded the Woman's Building. Therefore, while making art and running an organization, members did their best to document their historical contributions. These efforts led the members to keep as much ephemera as possible in a now mythical closet at the Woman's Building, which eventually became the Woman's Building Collection at the Archives of American Art in the early 1990s.

Inclusion in a lofty institution like the Archives of American Art represents an achievement in rewriting the story of art. The many boxes of well-cataloged material provide scholars with a wealth of information to use as they build on the work of that first generation of art historians and critics, many of them participants in the feminist art movement, who successfully illustrated that women had been more than muses, models, or handmaidens in the service of great art. Initially, feminist art activists argued that women artists of the past simply needed retrieval and reinsertion into the art historical record. This approach reached its apotheosis in the sweeping exhibition "Women Artists: 1550–1950" (1976), curated by Linda Nochlin and Ann Sutherland Harris, which created a canonical, albeit female, version of art history.[21] In this essay, however, I am interested in the uses of the past that occurred in far less formal ways. These efforts not only attempted to rectify art historical omissions, but more importantly, provided women artists with an immediate sense of empowerment. As Harper explained, feminist art history provided "a continuous tradition within which they could see their own lives and work."[22]

In an effort to create a "continuous tradition," members of the Woman's Building mounted many exhibitions that attempted to retrieve from obscurity women artists of the past and to locate them as particular foremothers. For example, in 1975 Sheila de Bretteville arranged for an exhibition of the work of modern architect and designer Eileen Gray to travel to the Woman's Building. Gray was an Irish expatriate living in France whose life, as the *Los Angeles Times* review of the show notes, could easily pass for Hemingway's. Yet she never achieved a high degree of fame, despite her achievements.[23] "Beyond the Femininity of Eileen Gray" at the Woman's Building marked the first exhibition of her work in the United States.

The Gray exhibition took on added significance as it occurred during a landmark conference at the Woman's Building called Women in Design: The Future

Entry to the Woman's Building during the "Women in American Architecture" exhibition, April 1978. Woman's Building Image Archive, Otis College of Art and Design.

(March 1975). The architects and designers who attended the conference found Gray's example so inspiring that a few conference participants set out to find women, like Gray, who had fallen through the cracks of history. Susanna Torre, a friend of de Bretteville, eventually created "Women in American Architecture" (1978), a traveling exhibition sponsored by the Architectural League of New York for which de Bretteville designed a catalog.[24] In a sort of boomerang effect, the exhibition then traveled to the Woman's Building, the site of its original inspiration. As de Bretteville worked to "imbue it with the Woman's Building spirit,"[25] she recalled that "it brought back some of the people who had been in the Women in Design Conference…to the Building."[26] For de Bretteville, finding these women artists in the past was not about illustrating that women could be great architects. Instead, she wanted to ask larger questions about how history happens, including: "Why don't we know more about them. Why was their work not developed, why did we never hear of them? What didn't happen?"[27] In particular, de Bretteville wondered about Sophia Hayden, designer of the original Woman's Building and the first female graduate in architecture of Massachusetts Institute of Technology. Her work never developed because, after receiving the commission for the 1893 Woman's Building in a competition restricted to female applicants, she never found employment again in her field.

Blanks in the historical record not withstanding, the connections between the exhibition and the earlier conference were emphasized, as revealed by a photograph that features at center left the 1975 Women in Design conference poster and the 1978 "Women in American Architecture" exhibition poster. Tellingly, these two efforts to draw narrative lines between contemporary women designers and architects and female architects of the past were posted below a painted sign enjoining the viewer to "support our community." For a moment in 1978, an alternative timeline was created by de Bretteville based on her historical antecedents and her current community.

Early taxonomical efforts to reclassify previously excluded women such as Gray and Hayden led to deeper taxonomical interventions, such as arguing for inclusion of different art forms. A few years later, members of the Woman's Building connected formally trained women designers and architects to a still unknown artist, Grandma (Tressa) Prisbrey, who created structures out of found objects in her *Bottle Village*, located in Simi Valley, California. Suzanne Lacy initially brought Prisbrey to the Feminist Studio Workshop to speak to the students in January of 1976. Nancy Angelo, Barbara Bouska, Cheri Gaulke, and Linda Norlen, all students in the FSW, became intrigued by her.[28] They saw Prisbrey's materials, "the cast-offs of women's lives—dolls, empty bottles, broken pencils, frayed toothbrushes,"[29] as uniquely feminine and argued that her work belonged "in the tradition of quilts and crafts."[30] (The quilt became the emblematic object of feminist artists' taxonomical efforts in a hugely successful rehabilitation effort. Other women's media such as china painting and various kinds of needlework were also reclaimed as "art.") Prisbrey's *Bottle Village* had not received the same degree of recognition as other built environments made from found objects, such as Simon Rodia's Watts Towers. As Gaulke explained, "We have a very phallic culture that likes those kinds of protrusions [found at Watts Towers]. Grandma Prisbrey had never been taken seriously because she had made round structures that you had to go inside to experience the beauty, and that was all very sort of vaginal and very female."[31] The four students therefore decided to honor Prisbrey with a one woman show at the Woman's Building, which they curated, installed, and documented.

While Prisbrey would seem a somewhat anomalous peer for Gray and Hayden, all three joined a mélange of references for a 1978 issue of *Spinning Off* (a monthly newsletter of women's culture at the Woman's Building). The issue was devoted to the topic of "space" and occurred in conjunction with the "Women in American Architecture" exhibition. Images from the Prisbrey exhibition accompanied quotations that highlighted the meanings of space for women, information about the exhibition, details of lectures by Raven and Iskin about Sophia Hayden, and architect and urban historian Dolores Hayden's work on feminist architecture.[32] The inclusion of Prisbrey illustrates the way that members of the Woman's Building created chains of historical connection that progressed through a feminist lineage rather than the usual classifications of art history, which revolve around genre, style, medium, or school. The

differences between Hayden's grandiose 1893 Woman's Building, Gray's sleek in-
teriors, and Prisbrey's humble bottle village were inconsequential; what mattered was
that all these women created structures. A feminist interpretation of space connected
women ar-chitects and designers to a found object artist.

That concept of space was of crucial importance at the Woman's Building, and
was highly informed by history, albeit of the more genealogical sort. If radical feminism finds it origins in the work of Simone de Beauvoir, then certainly Virginia Woolf
stands as the grandmother of the feminist art movement. The spatial antecedent most
frequently invoked was Virginia Woolf's concept of a room of one's own. From the
beginning of the Southern California feminist art movement, the idea that women
artists needed to take themselves seriously enough to acquire space dedicated to making art was paramount. The physical spaces became progressively larger, from a studio
in Fresno, to CalArts' *Womanhouse,* and finally, the entire Woman's Building.

Judy Chicago read Woolf, as did her students at Cal State Fresno. The women
eagerly absorbed Woolf's ideas, and used them as justification for their endeavors.
Fresno student Janice Lester explains,

> The large expanse of the studio allowed us to expand our goals. We
> couldn't have thought about making ten-foot square paintings in a
> nine-foot square bedroom, and we couldn't have thought about mak-
> ing environments in a two-room apartment. More important was the
> fact that this was the first time we had a place devoted exclusively to
> making art. It forced us to make a commitment to ourselves as artists.
> Virginia Woolf said for a woman to write she must have a room of her
> own; we discovered that in order for us to make art we had to have a
> studio of our own. [33]

Miriam Schapiro, who founded the Feminist Art Program at CalArts with Chicago, saw
Woolf as "a genuine kind of myth for women who were at that time being so conscious
of the fact that they were women, and that they had a history. We needed to have role
models. Everything came together at the same time: Art and consciousness, myth and
reality." [34]

Thus one genealogical origin, based on blending myth and reality into a serv-
iceable form of history, starts with Virginia Woolf. A letter inviting women to the
Feminist Studio Workshop explicitly invoked Woolf: "Join us in the creation of the
community of learned women Virginia Woolf believed was possible. Not the daughters
of educated men, but the educated women themselves controlling their private and
professional lives according to their values, sensibility and womanity." [35] To the financial independence and privacy Woolf demanded, the pioneers of feminist art education
added a supportive female community and a new education for women artists.

Curators Nancy Angelo, Barbara Bouska, Cheri Gaulke, and Linda Norlen with the artist, Grandma Prisbrey in her installation in the Woman's Building gallery, March 1976. Photograph by Sheila Ruth. Woman's Building Image Archive, Otis College of Art and Design.

At the same time as feminist literary critics reclaimed Woolf for the canon, feminist artists placed her into their ancestry. Faith Wilding noted years later, "In *A Room of One's Own*, Virginia Woolf…suggests women create female histories by 'writing' the work of other women artists and practitioners into their own work through quotation, reference, appropriation, and fictional reconstruction."[36] Deena Metzger, who led the writing program in the FSW, approached Woolf in just such a fashion. She was drawn to "Virginia Woolf's intuitive understanding of the cyclical aspect of women's experience" even while recognizing "that if you read her books, you would not say this is women's writing."[37] Metzger found in Woolf resonances with contemporary feminism. "Suddenly I really saw it. And saw the way she wrote about the small and the domestic and what profound meaning it had and the way she was interested in relationship." In writing their own history, linking themselves aesthetically and theoretically back to Woolf, as well as to Gray, Hayden, and contemporary artists like Prisbrey, members of the Woman's Building created an alternative chronological history for themselves.

Their conceptions of history, which spiraled or curved, bent concepts of time and space.[38] This approach became particularly apparent in the extensive uses of the 1893 Woman's Building, an equally significant genealogical starting point and one

'The Woman's Building 1893, Historical Handicrafts," March–May 1976. Installation view at the Woman's Building, Woman's Building Image Archive, Otis College of Art and Design.

connected by members of the **Woman's Building** to Woolf. If Woolf demanded space for women's art, the 1893 original was **the exemplar of** that space in the past. In rediscovering a comprehensive organization so similar to what they envisioned for themselves, members of the Woman's Building found a lasting source of inspiration, but also a cautionary tale about history. The flip side of celebrating the 1893 Woman's Building was the haunting realization that the same fate could befall their organization. It could easily become another dead end of history, just as the original 1893 incarnation had disappeared, despite its elaborate national network, its leadership by powerful and influential women, and its remarkable achievements. Iskin described this phenomenon as the "doubled edge of recognition."[39] The threat of their own historical eradication was more than theoretical or based on fears derived from the past. They were aware that *Womanhouse*, perhaps the best-known exemplar of the seventies feminist art movement, had not been preserved.[40]

Iskin and Raven traveled several times to Chicago in search of the archival past of the 1893 Woman's Building. However, very little physical evidence remained. Undaunted, in 1976, Raven and Iskin curated "The Woman's Building 1893–". The exhibition consisted of reproductions of plates from the original Woman's Building catalog, and provided little more information than could have been found by perusing the 1893 catalog. However, the greatly enlarged images stretched from floor to ceiling, which gave viewers the sense of entering the original Woman's Building. Viewers were invited to imagine themselves within an approximation of the original space, which provided a means for a highly personal interpretation.

Items in a concomitant exhibition, "Historical Handicrafts," stood among the panels that documented the 1893 Building.[41] Various ephemera of the era, including "laces, costumes, watercolors, books and baskets," stood alongside an actual artifact from the 1893 Woman's Building—the first-prize winning quilt—and folk art made by a California Native American woman celebrated in the early twentieth century for her "primitive art."[42] The rather curious pairing of random Victoriana, artifacts, and Native American art was not intended to offer an exhaustive historical exploration, or even an attempt at recreation, but rather to capture the zeitgeist. Postcards of the original Woman's Building furthered a sense of the viewer being on a touristic voyage back in time. Taxonomically, the exhibition related to efforts to redefine what counted as art in order to incorporate forms dominated by women.

The exhibition also highlighted the similarities between the first and second Woman's Buildings. In discussing the art of the original Woman's Building, Raven remarked, "It is a source of pride to us that these women were able to command the kind of studio, the kind of physical strength, and the skill to be able to carve these enormous marbles."[43] While not much sculpting of monumental pieces occurred at the 1973 Woman's Building, the women who worked and studied there did, in fact, learn skills that were considered as masculine in their day as the use of the mallet and the chisel were in the time of nineteenth-century women artists. Similarly, when explaining the significance of handicrafts at the original building, Iskin pointed out that appreciation of "the so-called crafts and the so-called minor arts in the nineteenth century was very similar to the new consciousness that has been building up through the feminist movement in the twentieth century."[44]

In the minds of the 1970s feminists, the original Woman's Building was transformed into something of a proto-feminist organization. Arlene Raven claimed that the members of the 1893 Woman's Building believed "that women had a unique sensibility and point of view," which is almost exactly how she and her colleagues described their own search for a female aesthetic and efforts to contribute to women's culture. The use of the word "sensibility" would have been immediately recognizable to members of the larger feminist art movement, because the Woman's Building was allied with one side of a heated debated about the existence of a female aesthetic, which was often called a "feminine sensibility."[45]

A subsequent exhibition that used some of the same documentary panels of the 1893 Building further emphasized parallels between the Woman's Buildings. "The Art of the Woman's Building 1893–1980" appropriately appeared in 1980 at Artemisia Gallery in Chicago, the city that was the home of the original Woman's Building. The exhibition offered historical information from "The Woman's Building 1893–" alongside a retrospective of art from the first seven years of the 1973 Woman's Building.[46] As the en dash joining the two buildings in the exhibition title indicates, the curators placed the two buildings on a continuum of women's art history that traveled around the gallery walls, allowing the members of the 1973 Woman's Building to become part of the history of the 1893 Building. Similarly, in an essay about the exhibition, Raven lists in one column the names of the organizers of the 1893 Building followed by ellipses. She begins the next column with a list of the founders of the Feminist Studio Workshop, and continues with a litany of participants in the 1973 Woman's Building. Thus, she symbolically bridges the eighty years between the organizations. At least for a moment, the members of the Woman's Buildings past and present existed in one seamless timeline. This positioning created an alternative history that existed not continuously, but by leaping over the lacunae to find what remained.

In a highly imaginative artist's book made in 1975, *The Woman's Building Chicago 1893/The Woman's Building Los Angeles 1973–*, Maria Karras went even further to create a virtual community that ignored the eighty years between the two Woman's Buildings.[47] For the cover, Karras revised a well-known image from the 1893 Woman's Building catalog by inserting herself.[48] The original image contains a female figure in the foreground holding a palette and brushes, surrounded by various items representing women's art and handicrafts, such as a spinning wheel, several books, quill pen, vase, drawing table, and neo-classical statuette mounted on a pedestal. Despite the brush and palette in her hands, the artist is not engaged in the act of painting, but rather

78

looks out to the viewer.[49] In Karras's book cover collage, this artist is no longer posed in front of the original Woman's Building, which now appears as a painting. Instead she is standing outside the 1973 Woman's Building, which is in the background, along with some palm trees that highlight the California location. Karras poses as the photographer of the woman's artistic efforts, replicating the role she played frequently at the 1973 building. In this collage, past meets present and the two become part of the same community, at least pictorially.

The collaged images throughout Karras's book create an even larger imagined community that traverses the boundaries of a linear, historical narrative. Portraits of the 1893 Board of Lady Managers and busts of prominent suffragists from the 1893 exhibition catalog are interspersed among pictures of members of the 1893 Woman's Building.[50] On the steps of the 1973 Woman's Building stand visitors to the 1893 Woman's Building, taken from a picture of the west entrance of the original Woman's Building. In Karras's collages, people from the nineteenth century are invited to participate in her twentieth century Woman's Building.

Like previous uses of the 1893 Woman's Building, Karras also emphasized the parallels between the two buildings. For a young, aspiring artist like Karras, the 1973 Woman's Building provided a "space to experience ourselves in our art and our work in building and extending our community."[51] The example of the 1893 Woman's Building provided the inspiration for this community because "women knew then as we know now what aliveness there is for us in validating ourselves and making a space to turn our gifts outwards in a place we choose to create."[52] Tellingly, her book title ends with an en dash, suggesting perhaps that this 1973 Woman's Building will have an endless history.

The gaps between eras were also bridged via episodic, often intensely personal encounters with previous generations of women artists. This contact with living women artists provided another sort of lineage for emerging feminist artists, one that offered more genealogical options. Paula Lumbard's academic interest in surrealism eventually became the basis for an important personal relationship. After writing a master's thesis on the women of surrealism, Lumbard wanted to find Leonora Carrington.[53] The feminist scholar Gloria Orenstein facilitated their introduction, and Lumbard eventually spent a week and a half with Carrington in New York. Lumbard recalls the importance of her time with Carrington:

> She took me to the bookstores she went to and showed me books and bought me a book about Wicca, but she also cautioned me not to source my life out of that place. I asked why? She replied that it can be a crutch. You cannot identify so singly in that way. You have to live in the larger world.[54]

After returning to Los Angeles and the Woman's Building, Lumbard retained ties to Carrington. She curated a show centered around Carrington's work, which she exhibited alongside four artists from the Woman's Building.[55] "Artist as Magus" (1980) created "a collection of works by women who merge art, life and a female spirituality."[56] Included in the show was Lumbard's close friend Tyaga, with whom she had engaged in collaborative painting practices. At the opening, Lumbard invited her thesis supervisor, Faith Wilding, to perform *Invitation to a Burning*. Lumbard explained in an earlier article, "I use mediation and ritual...and it is from that place I receive my images; and I think it is also from that place that these women [of the surrealist movement] found their images, their symbols."[57] She also asserted, "There are parallels between the women at the Woman's Building and the visionaries of the 1930s. Each of those women sought out her own education...At the Woman's Building we are educating ourselves and each other."[58] Through the exhibition, Lumbard created a nonlinear, intricately personal narrative of women's art history based on the connections she felt to other women artists.

Different women artists filled the personal and art historical gaps for other Woman's Building members. For example, Susan King met Georgia O'Keeffe in 1970 when she was a student at the University of New Mexico. O'Keeffe was a relatively obscure artist in the 1970s; at the time she was best known for her association with the photographer Alfred Stieglitz. King, along with her friends Kristy Cruse and Cheryl Swannack, who also eventually came to the Woman's Building, spent an entire day with O'Keeffe. King became intrigued with O'Keeffe and returned with Raven for a second visit in the early 1970s. Initially, King intended to write a traditional art historical exploration of O'Keeffe, but she found formal writing unsatisfying. Instead, she began reinterpreting O'Keeffe's work from a personal point of view. She created a map of O'Keeffe's travels across the United States, and then charted the parallels with her own journey. The project lay dormant at that stage for eight years. In 1983, King received a grant from the National Endowment for the Arts and worked with the writer Eloise Klein-Healy to complete the book *Georgia*. It traces the impact of her visits with O'Keeffe in a series of prose poems that reveal how King felt emotionally inspired by O'Keeffe's lifetime of art making. As King explains in one of the prose poems, "For each year a card, tape carefully to the wall. Your life from books. My life from memory. A map with no color, only thin black borders. Both our lives drawn across the continent. And back. Your life a line. Mine still only dashes."[59]

Dashes. Again, like the en dashes in "The Art of the Woman's Building 1893–1980" and "The Woman's Building 1893–," and Raven's ellipses, we find the effort to use punctuation to unite disparate things, which here expresses King's desire "to place and read two stories on the same plane."[60] King's conundrum, how to tell two stories simultaneously, points to the complexities of using history. These tangled family trees, like King's and Lumbard's, propose alternate paths of history through the imaginative rather than the linearly reconnected. Finding specific women, filling in blanks, and imagining where necessary allowed feminists to find meaning in the past. In the hands of seventies feminists, history was transformed into examples that could justify their efforts. Through linguistic constructions that emphasized similarities, exhibitions that juxtaposed the two buildings, and photographic representations that pictorially joined the two organizations, the members of the Woman's Building incorporated the past into their own history. Ellipses and dashes—efforts to bridge the gaps in knowledge—testify to the inability to create a seamless linear narrative. Instead, like the quilt makers they so loved to reference, the members of the Woman's Building made do with what was at hand. Out of the scraps of the past, they constructed a useful historical account, but not one without complications.

Why Feminists Need(ed) History

Feminism's History is both a compilation of women's experiences and a record of the different strategic interventions employed to argue women's cause. It can, of course, stand on its own, but it is best understood as a doubly subversive critical engagement: with prevailing normative codes of gender and with the conventions and (since

> history's formation as a discipline in the late nineteenth century)
> rules of historical writing. Feminism's History has been a variable,
> mutable endeavor, a flexible strategic instrument not bound to any
> orthodoxy. The production of knowledge about the past, while cru-
> cial, has not been an end in itself, but rather (at certain moments—
> and not always in the service of an organized political movement) has
> provided the substantive terms for a critical operation that uses the
> past to disrupt the certainties of the present and so opens the way to
> imagining a different future.[61]

As Joan Wallach Scott suggests, the "doubly subversive critical engagement" of feminism's history involves challenging what counts as history, while at the same time
attempting to revise history. Members of the Woman's Building engaged in just such a
twinned effort. Through taxonomical interventions, they sought to bring women artists, aesthetic objects, and historical events into the art historical narrative. At times
these "strategic interventions" took the form of traditional art history, rewriting narratives. At other moments, members engaged in complex taxonomies that linked
seemingly disparate individuals, events, and objects through a common thread of
feminism. In the process of intervening into the historical, members of the Woman's
Building not only created their own alternative lineage of feminist artists, but also created tangled genealogies that traversed temporal boundaries. They proposed multiple
starting points, and picked from the past women artists to serve as foremothers.

   As Scott notes, feminism's engagement with history has not been simply to
"produce knowledge about the past" but rather has always been part of an activist project that uses the past to open the way to a different future. It turns out that sometimes
looking back is the only way forward. What the critic Joanna Frueh wrote in her review
of the show "The Art of the Woman's Building 1893–1980" could easily apply to the
usage of history at the Woman's Building as a whole. It "is about heritage—remembered,
invented, and because the artists of the Woman's Building think not in simplistic
chronologies but timeless patterns, prophesied."[62] Members of the Woman's Building
felt free to invent, imagine, and yes, even prophesize when it came to history. The
importance of the past lay not in the details, but in the women. In freeing themselves
from "simplistic chronologies," the members of the 1973 Woman's Building created a
"heritage" that justified their current activism. And that, in the end, was what they
really wanted from the past.[63]

   However, entering history brings consequences. What gets remembered and
how it gets remembered are important aspects of history. In their focus on the struggles
of women artists in the past and the startling parallels to their own present situation,
the members of the Woman's Building sometimes glossed over the less glorious
aspects of the 1893 original. They did not grapple directly with the disparities of race

Above: **"Georgia O'Keeffe,"
an installation about the
artist by Susan E. King,**
June 1974. Feminist Studio
Workshop's Group Show.
Woman's Building Image
Archive, Otis College of Art
and Design. Photograph by
Sheila Ruth.

Right: **Paula Lumbard and
Jane Thurmond, Signage
wall for the exhibition
"Artist as Magus,"** 1980.
© 1980/2010 Deborah
Roundtree.

ARTIST AS MAGUS

Fay Jones ☉ Leonora Carrington

Faith Wilding

Tyaga ○ Cheryl Swannack

and class at the 1893 Building. [64] They did not critique the vision of womanhood that the Victorian-era Woman's Building represented, nor did they attack the imperialist aspects of a World's Fair dedicated to Columbus's "discovery" of the Americas. [65] These omissions resulted from their desire to emphasize parallels between the two Woman's Buildings. However, parallelism denies one of the fundamental premises of historical narrative: Change unfolds over time. Parallelism also makes it difficult to draw conclusions from the past, to learn the lessons, so to speak, that our predecessors have to teach. In delving into that blend of myth and reality, in bending the timeline into a more circular form that emphasized continuities, change over time got lost.

For the remainder of this essay, I want to return to the history of the Woman's Building by reading back in that second sense of genealogy, in which histories are branched as opposed to unified. I want to briefly explore the dead ends of the Woman's Building history. I look at these not as prescriptive routes that could have been taken but in the spirit of genealogies as pruned ends. For example, in privileging the women of 1893 as their primary antecedents, members of the Woman's Building rejected other options. As Jennie Klein shows in her essay in this volume, the members of the Lesbian Art Project looked back to another sort of space for a role model—not Woolf's room of one's own, or the 1893 Building—but to the salon created in the home of expatriates Natalie Barney and Romaine Brooks.

Other, more immediate precursors to the 1973 Woman's Building existed right in Los Angeles. In many ways, the far more obvious choice of a predecessor was the Chouinard Art Institute. As Jenni Sorkin notes in her essay for this collection, this influential Los Angeles art school was founded in 1921 by a woman—Nelbert Chouinard. The first Woman's Building was located in the former site of Chouinard. In fact, the connections ran deeper. Chouinard merged with the Los Angeles Conservatory of Music to form CalArts in 1961. CalArts was the first degree-granting institution of higher learning in the United States created specifically for students of both the visual and the performing arts. CalArts opened at its present campus in Valencia, California, in No-vember 1971. [66] In an ironical, historical twist, the founders of the Feminist Studio Workshop later negotiated with CalArts to lease the space that FSW used to split from CalArts and form the Woman's Building. [67]

Origin stories have consequences for history. In choosing to trace their roots back to the 1893 Woman's Building, members of the 1973 space picked a past that celebrated what they hoped to achieve themselves—a *public* center for *women's culture*. The vision of the Woman's Building as a visible space dedicated to celebrating women's art drew heavily on the 1893 Woman's Building for aspects that could not be found in a co-educational art school like Chouinard, or a private space like Woolf's room.

Other origin stories involved women who went on to participate in the Woman's Building. In 1970, the Los Angeles Council of Women Artists (LACWA), which included de Bretteville, formed to protest the exclusion of women from an exhibition at the Los Angeles County Museum (LACMA).[68] LACWA conducted a survey of works by women in the LACMA collection, which lead to an extended dialogue with the board of trustees of the museum and ultimately resulted in the corrective exhibition, *Women Artists: 1550–1950*, which first appeared at LACMA in 1975, then traveled throughout the United States. In 1972, some of the women who participated in LACWA formed Womanspace, the first women's gallery in Los Angeles. Members of both groups became part of the Woman's Building when it opened. In fact, the first manager of the Woman's Building was not one of the three founders of the Feminist Studio Workshop, but a Womanspace member, Edie Gross, whom Judy Chicago credits with first proposing that the gallery and the new art school share a location.[69] However, the relatively short duration of each of the contemporary groups—Womanspace closed after only a year at the Woman's Building, and LACWA existed only to protest the LACMA exhibition—meant that history now records the founders of the Feminist Studio Workshop as *the* founders of the Woman's Building.

In fact, Chicago, Raven, and de Bretteville resisted the role of running the entire building, as they disdained administration. They reached back into history to formulate a way to jointly administer the Woman's Building. Despite the obvious fact that different attitudes towards gender roles, sexuality, class, and ethnicity separated the two eras, the parallels between the two buildings struck the 1970s feminists as quite literal. Art historian Iskin recalled, "I had spent many hours pouring over the minutes of the Lady Board of Managers from 1893, which [was] fascinating because some of the same problems and issues they were dealing with, we were dealing with."[70] Despite awareness of the difficulties faced by the original Board of Lady Managers, in 1974 the Los Angeles Woman's Building created their own Board of Lady Managers. However, they infused the nineteenth-century model with feminist principles such as egalitarianism and decision-making by consensus. Each tenant or group at the Woman's Building received one seat on the board. Still problems arose as competing visions of the Woman's Building vied for dominance. Meetings of the Board of Lady Managers often devolved into angry shouting matches, unfortunately mirroring the conflicts that often occurred within the original Board of Lady Managers. Within a year, the 1973 Woman's Building abandoned the Board of Lady Managers. Nevertheless, the use of the concept of the Board of Lady Managers reveals a great deal about how seventies feminists viewed the 1893 Woman's Building. They were not deterred by the difficulties they knew had existed among members of the original board. They did not feel constrained to adopt their predecessors' ideals, which were hierarchical in the extreme. They used the name because they liked the sense of connection it gave them to the past, but they felt free to create their own modern, feminist take on it, which involved far more egalitarianism that Chairwoman Bertha Honoré Palmer would have found comfortable!

In retrieving the 1893 Building from obscurity and turning it into an origin point for their own organization, members of the Woman's Building made their own choices about what to take from the past, which served more frequently as inspiration than as instruction. Sometimes the result was an uncritical celebration of women's past artistic and organizational achievements. When Raven wrote about the 1893 Woman's Building in 1980, she posited what now seems an overly optimistic celebration of the "sisterhood [that] abounded" among "queens, peasants, factory workers, matrons," and outlined a "radical spirit of sisterhood" that underlay the creation of the original Woman's Building. She claimed that a unity of women "of different nations, classes and races" came together to make the Woman's Building.[71] In reality, organized African American women sought a seat at the table with the 1893 Board of Lady Managers, but the single-minded focus on celebrating the achievements of a womanhood privileged gender over all other aspects of identity, leading Chairwoman Palmer to refuse anything more than the role of secretary to the board for black women. The issue divided the black community, with some prominent leaders like Ida B. Tarbell and Booker T. Washington organizing a boycott of the fair. During the 1970s, scholars of women's history and feminist art history began addressing these exclusionary policies.[72] However, the emphasis on sisterhood and, it must be admitted, a similar commitment to celebrating the achievements of "women's" art, allowed members of the 1973 Woman's Building to miss for a long time the racial and class-based exclusions of groups of women from the original Woman's Building.

Instead, the "double edge of recognition" that Iskin spoke of became the dominant lesson gleaned from the past: the delight in learning about the extensive efforts of feminist artists in the past, and the horror of realizing that they had been eradicated from the art historical record. Raven once remarked, "The great work of our 19th century sisters *and* the eradication of their efforts had enlarged our aspirations and sharpened our own instincts for personal and historical survival."[73] The past served not just as a template, but also as a warning. Indeed, Raven seems almost prescient, as the turning tide of feminist theory in the 1980s did increasingly consign the Woman's Building and its artists to a marginal position. Younger art historians and critics firmly relegated the Woman's Building to the "bad" camp of so-called "seventies essentialist feminists." Historians lumped them in with groups responsible for the apolitical turn taken by the women's movement.

Because of the inextricable link between the study of women's history and feminist activism, without a historical consciousness we are doomed to perpetually reinvent. Such moments of repetition have become depressingly familiar. For example, in 1989 Cynthia Navaretta, an influential 1970s feminist art activist, saw a poster about art world sexism created by members of the feminist art group the Guerrilla Girls. Navaretta recalled that the poster interested her "because it was almost identical to something we had done thirteen years before."[74] Some time in the 1980s, the members of the Woman's Building, in collaboration with Women's Caucus for the Arts, produced a flyer on blue cardstock entitled "Why are these women blue?" The flyer recounted the shockingly dismal statistics about women in the arts; its text was surrounded by the faces of famous women artists.[75] Years later, a similar technique was adopted by the Guerrilla Girls. Navaretta copied the original document and sent it off to the Guerrilla Girls with a note asking, "Had you ever seen this before? Did you know that we were active many years ago—we who are now aged and no longer go around pasting things up on walls?"[76] She received a response from a member of the Guerrilla Girls that they knew nothing of the feminist artist movement of the 1970s. I note the absence of historical memory and its consequences not to denigrate the efforts of more recent activists, but rather to point to the pitfalls of endless cycles of similar protests if we don't heed the oft-quoted advice of George Santayana, "Those who cannot remember the past are condemned to repeat it."

As a graduate student in 1993, I was hired to conduct an oral history project with members of the Woman's Building, which eventually became the topic of my dissertation. By the time I came along, members of the now defunct Woman's Building were surprised to find a young feminist interested in them and grateful that I wanted to write about the topic. Slowly, I discovered other young feminist scholars working on the feminist art movement.[77] Eventually, both Fresno and CalArts organized symposia on their campuses about the 1970s feminist art programs, which included panel discussions by participants.[78] Yet the Woman's Building still suffered from what Sondra Hale called the "book end" approach to Los Angeles feminist art, which focused on *Womanhouse* (leaving out its predecessor program at Cal State Fresno) and ending with Judy Chicago's *The Dinner Party* (leaving out, well, most of the history of the Woman's Building, which didn't open until 1973).[79] Even *WACK!,* the recent monumental show on the seventies feminist art movement, had a hard time figuring out what to do with the Woman's Building.[80]

Histories have histories. Official versions of the Woman's Building were produced over the years, for anniversaries, at the building's closing in 1991, in my oral histories, and increasingly in the memoirs of participants and in the scholarship of academics like those included in this collection. But for each woman, a highly personal, idiosyncratic history also exists, which is as it should be for a place that offered all women, regardless of talent or training, the opportunity to be what might be described as an artist, but which was really much more.

At the very end, after the Woman's Building had been closed and the remaining staff relocated to an office in the 18th Street Arts Complex of Santa Monica, the active members reached into the past once more for their final Vesta Awards ceremony in 1991. The Woman's Building began the Vesta awards, which were given annually to prominent women in various aspects of the arts, in 1981. Their inspiration once again came from history, this time reaching back into Roman mythology to Vesta, "the Roman goddess who was keeper of the flame, a woman dedicated to her work."[81] Every detail of this final Vesta awards ceremony was coordinated and executed with loving care. It was what the Woman's Building did best, paying tribute to women in a world that so frequently overlooked their contributions. Even as it exists today—in the archives, on the many academic panels comprised of alumnae, in a Facebook group, and in the many past members who continue to teach and work in the arts—the Woman's Building celebrates the ability of women to achieve their dreams, no matter what form they might take.

Notes

1. Joan Wallach Scott, "Feminism's History," *Journal of Women's History* 16.2 (2004): 10–29.

2. This slogan has been attributed to Jack Weinberg in 1965. Suzy Platt, *Respectfully Quoted: A Dictionary of Quotations* (New York: Barnes & Noble Publishing, 1993), 343.

3. Robin Morgan, ed., *Sisterhood Is Powerful: An Anthology of Writings from the Women's Liberation Movement* (New York: Random House, 1970).

4. Classic socialist feminist writings include Juliet Mitchell, *Woman's Estate* (New York: Pantheon Books, 1971); and Chicago Women's Liberation Union, Hyde Park Chapter, *Socialist Feminism: A Strategy for the Women's Movement*, 1972 (pamphlet), available at http://scriptorium.lib.duke.edu/wlm/socialist/ (accessed December 20, 2007). Heidi Hartmann's article "The Unhappy Marriage of Feminism and Socialism" inspired an entire volume devoted to discussions of socialist feminism, with contributions from many of the major socialist feminists theorists. See Lydia Sargent, ed., *Women and Revolution: A Discussion of the Unhappy Marriage of Marxism and Feminism* (Boston: South End Press, 1981). Many early statements of socialist feminism are collected in Zillah Eisenstein, ed., *Capitalist Patriarchy and the Case for Socialist Feminism* (New York: Monthly Review Press, 1979).

5. Classic radical feminist texts include Shulamith Firestone, *The Dialectic of Sex: The Case for Feminist Revolution* (New York: Bantam Books, 1970); and Kate Millett, *Sexual Politics* (Garden City: Doubleday, 1969). For an excellent treatment of the concept of matriarchy in prehistory see Cynthia Eller, *The Myth of Matriarchal Prehistory: Why an Invented Past Won't Give Women a Future* (Boston: Beacon Press, 2000).

6. The classic articulations of this position are Robin Morgan, "Goodbye to All That," *Going Too Far: The Personal Chronicles of a Feminist* (New York: Vintage Books, 1978), 121–130; and Marge Piercy, "Grand Coolie Damn," in *Sisterhood is Powerful*, 473–493. A fine analysis of the rift between socialist feminists and radical feminists is found in Alice Echols, *Daring to Be Bad: Radical Feminism in America, 1967–1975* (Minneapolis: University of Minnesota, 1991).

7. The most complete history of the 1893 Woman's Building can be found in Jeanne Madeline Weimann, *The Fair Women* (Chicago: Academy Chicago, 1981). According to Weimann, a fire destroyed most of the art from the

Woman's Building in 1895 and the building itself was demolished in 1896. The Woman's Building had not been constructed of permanent building materials. It was a façade meant to last only the six months of the exposition. That, in and of itself, makes an interesting metaphor for thinking about the perceived significance of the endeavor at the time.

8. In 1968, Joyce Kozloff and Nancy Spero began circulating accounts of art world sexism in a newsletter format called *The Rip-Off File*. These accounts were eventually compiled in Kozloff and Spero, eds., *Rip-Off File* (New York: Ad Hoc Committee of Women Artists, 1973). See also Lucy Lippard, "Sexual Politics, Art Style," *Art in America* 59 (1971): 19–20; Cindy Nemser, "Analysis: Critics and Women's Art," *Women and Art* (1971): 1–2; and Diane G. Cochrane, "Women in Art: A Progress Report," *American Artist* 36 (1972): 52–56, 71–73.

9. Therese Schwartz, "They Built Women a Bad Art History," *Feminist Art Journal* 2.3 (1973): 10–11, 22.

10. Judy Chicago, *Through the Flower: My Struggle as a Woman Artist* (New York: Doubleday, 1975), 163.

11. Paula Harper, "The First Feminist Art Program: A View from the 1980s," *Signs* 10.4 (1985): 777–781.

12. Not too surprisingly, this idea was held by many male members of the art establishment. More surprising, however, was the "greatness" debate set off when art historian Linda Nochlin published "Why Have There Been No Great Women Artists?" in *Woman in Sexist Society: Studies in Power and Powerlessness*, Vivian Gornick and Barbara K. Moran, eds. (1971; reprint, New York: New American Library, 1972), 480–510. While Nochlin's article attracted considerable attention, in reality she had simply posed more provocatively a question that earlier feminists had addressed. Virginia Woolf, for example, had pointed to societal barriers to women's quest for independence in the creative world and explored the limiting stereotypes of femininity, as did Tillie Olsen in *Silences* (New York: Delacorte Press/Seymour Lawrence, 1978).

13. Sheila Rowbotham, *Hidden from History: 300 Years of Women's Oppression and the Fight Against It* (London: Pluto Books, 1973). Here I purposefully reference Rowbotham's work, which is similar in its efforts to retrieve women for a different historical narrative, that of "western civilization." Fittingly, it was first published in 1973, the year of the Woman's Building's founding.

14. Arlene Raven, interview with Cheri Gaulke, New York, September 19, 1992, Woman's Building Oral History Project.

15. This account is drawn from Faith Wilding, *By Our Own Hands* (Culver City: Peace Press, 1977), 61; and the author's correspondence with Nancy Youdelman and Judy Chicago.

16. Program from the West Coast Women Artists' Conference held at CalArts, January 21–23, 1972. Box 3, Folder 3, California Institute of the Arts Feminist Art Materials Collection, California Institute of the Arts Library, Valencia, California.

17. Arlene Raven, "The Art of the Woman's Building: Graphics, Performance and Video," *Spinning Off* (March 1980), 1. Raven recalled this event as her first presentation of her research into the original Woman's Building.

18. "First Calendar of Events," *Womanspace* 1.1 (1973): 25.

19. Arlene Raven, *At Home* (Long Beach: Long Beach Museum of Art, 1983), 25. The idea of naming an organization for the Woman's Building was by no means unique to Los Angeles women. Many women's buildings sprang up in the early twentieth century. See for example, Karen Blair, "The Limits of Sisterhood: The Women's Building in Seattle, 1907–1921," *Frontiers* 8 (1985): 45–52. In the 1970s, a women's building also existed in San Francisco, where it still stands today.

20. Arlene Raven oral history. There were, of course, exceptions. Some of their students went on to become professional art historians. Raven recalled that Charlotte S. Rubinstein, author of two surveys about women, attended her classes at Womanspace, while Ruth Iskin taught Diane Gelon, the lead researcher on the *Dinner Party* at UCLA in the early 1970s. Paula Lumbard wrote a thesis about women in the surrealist movement, and published one of the first scholarly articles on Dorothea Tanning. (Paula Lumbard, "Dorothea Tanning: On the Threshold to a Darker Place," *Woman's Art Journal* 2.1 [1981]: 49–52.) However, most history making at the Woman's Building occurred as the members themselves made history. Sometimes that took formal shape in the articles about performance art authored by Cheri Gaulke. At other times, it consisted of self-documentation in periodicals such as *High Performance*, *Heresies*, and *Frontiers*.

21. Ann Sutherland Harris and Linda Nochlin, *Women Artists: 1550–1950*, exh. cat. (Los Angeles: Los Angeles County Museum of Art, 1976).

22. Harper, 775. Strangely, Harper writes about the program at CalArts without ever mentioning its successor, the Feminist Studio Workshop.

23. John Pastier, "Beyond the Femininity of Eileen Gray," *Los Angeles Times*, March 10, 1975, E1–2.

24. Susana Torre, ed., *Women in American Architecture: A Historic and Contemporary Perspective* (New York: Whitney Library of Design, 1977).

25. Program for West Coast Women Artists' Conference, n.p.

26. Sheila de Bretteville, interview by the author, August 8, 1992, Los Angeles, CA.

27. Jocelyn Paine, "Hidden History of a Profession," *Los Angeles Times*, April 30, 1978, H22.

28. "Grandma Prisbrey's Bottle Village Preserved," *Spinning Off* (December 1979), 2.

29. WCA program / WB calendar, n.d., circa January/ February 1977.

30. "Grandma Prisbrey's Bottle Village Preserved," 2.

31. Cheri Gaulke, interview by the author, August 6, 1992.

32. *Spinning Off* (April 1978).

33. Janice M. Lester, "Building the Studio," *Everywoman* 2.7 (1971): 13.

34. Miriam Schapiro, interview by Ruth Bowman, September 10, 1989. Archives of American Art, Smithsonian Institution, http://www.aaa.si.edu/collections/oralhistories/transcripts/schapi89.htm (accessed June 16, 2010).

35. Letter dated April 15, 1975, to prospective students of the Feminist Studio Workshop (FSW) from the staff of the FSW. Possession of the author.

36. Faith Wilding, "Don't Tell Anyone We Did It!" *Documents* 15 (1999). Available at http://faithwilding. refugia.net/ (accessed June 16, 2010).

37. Deena Metzger, interview with the author, March 24, 1994.

38. This bending reflects a similar sort of circularity noted by Alexandra Juhasz and the repetition discussed by Vivien Green Fryd in their essays for this collection.

39. Ruth Iskin, interview with the author, April 25, 1993, Los Angeles, California, Woman's Building Oral History Project.

40. The fate of *Womanhouse* is detailed in Sandra Sider, "Womanhouse: Cradle of Feminist Art," Art Spaces Archive Project, circa 2004, http://as-ap.org/sider/resources.cfm (accessed June 16, 2010).

41. Raven, *At Home*, x.

42. On this framing of the teleological narrative of primitive to modern see Laura R. Prieto, *At Home in the Studio: The Professionalization of Women Artists in America* (Cambridge: Harvard University Press, 2001), 125–135.

43. Quotations are drawn from Ruth Iskin and Arlene Raven, *1893 Historical Handicrafts Exhibition*, 1976. Videotape produced by the Woman's Building. Long Beach Museum of Art Video Archive, Getty Research Institute. Transferred by the Long Beach Museum of Art Foundation and the City of Long Beach, 2005.

44. Ibid.

45. See Miriam Schapiro and Judy Chicago, "Female Imagery," *Womanspace Journal* 1.3 (1972): 11–14. The strongest challenges to the idea of a female sensibility came from the editors of the influential *Feminist Art Journal*. They depicted the advocates of a female aesthetic as opportunists, feared that the idea created a new stereotype of women's art, and decried the essentialism at the heart of this proposed aesthetic. See Patricia Mainardi, "Feminine Sensibility: An Analysis," *Feminist Art Journal* 1.1 (1972), and 1.2 (1972): 9; and Cindy Nemser, "The Women Artists' Movement," *Feminist Art Journal* 2.4 (1973–1974): 8–10.

46. No catalog exists for the exhibit, which ran from March 28 through April 19, 1980. A double-sided sheet that was presumably distributed at the show documents the works included. The credits are listed as follow: "The Art of the Woman's Building: Graphics, Performance and Video curated by Arlen Raven, essay by Arlene Raven, printed in *Spinning Off, a monthly newsletter of women's culture at the Woman's Building.* Installation by Sheila de Bretteville, Sue Maberry, Cheri Gaulke, Cheryl Swannack, Jeri Allyn, and Arlene Raven." "Performance at the Woman's Building selected by Cheri Gaulke" and "The L.A. Women's Video Center selected by Nancy Angelo." Original document in the possession of the author.

47. Maria Karras, *The Woman's Building Chicago 1893 / The Woman's Building Los Angeles 1973–* (Los Angeles: Women's Community Press, 1975).

48. The original image, which appears to be by Madeleine Lemaire, is shrouded in confusion. It is often described as the frontispiece, but it seems clear that at least the 1893 first edition featured it as the cover. (Maud Howe Elliott, *Art and Handicraft in the Woman's Building of the World's Columbian Exposition, Chicago, 1893* [Paris, New York: Boussod, Valadon & Co., 1893]). (Viewable on the IAWA image bank, http://imagebase.lib.vt.edu/view_record_test.php?URN=IAWABK0002. Accessed June 16, 2010.) Cheaper editions that appeared subsequently do not seem to have featured it (Maud Howe Elliott, *Art and Handicraft in the Woman's Building of the World's Columbian Exposition, Chicago, 1893* [Boston and New York: Rand McNally, 1894]).

49. Dennis B. Downey, *A Season of Renewal: The Columbian Exhibition and Victorian America* (Westport: Praeger, 2000), 125. Although she is clearly an artist, she remains determinedly feminine. No artist's smock obscures her skirt and fashionable, puff-sleeved shirtwaist with deep ruffle and cascading sash. She seems in all respects to be little more than an emblematic Gibson girl, the archetype that bridged the gap between the Victorian lady and the New Woman. The Gibson girl represented no threat whatsoever to the established order, representing as she did the female ideal of beauty, not independence. While the figure may appear innocuous, members of the Woman's Building had a more radical reading of her because, as Arlene Raven pointed out, it was quite unusual to see a depiction of a woman artist at all.

50. While Karras's inclusion of suffragists may seem an unusual choice for an artist, it reflects the commitment of feminists at the Woman's Building to claim a broad feminist heritage for themselves. Raven went so far as to assert that Susan B. Anthony was "the true instigator of the 1893 Woman's Building," arguing that only her association with the controversial suffrage movement kept her from taking a more prominent position in the organizing of the Woman's Building. If suffragists were accorded only a limited organizational role, they were amply represented, albeit silently, in the Hall of Honor, which featured sculpted busts of Susan B. Anthony, Lucretia Mott, and Elizabeth Cady Stanton, who stood beside the younger generation represented by Lucy Stone and Harriet Beecher Stowe. Suffragists were most visible in the World's Congress of Representative Women that occurred from May 15 through 21, 1893, which drew many famous American suffragists such as Susan B. Anthony, Jane Addams, Elizabeth Cady Stanton, and Lucy Stone. This led Raven to conclude that the Woman's Building "became an important political gathering space for women." By showing that explicitly political women, and you could not get much more radical than suffrage in the late nineteenth-century, were involved in an endeavor like the 1893 Woman's Building, the 1970s feminists laid claim to that same radical tradition. (Raven, "The Art of the Woman's Building," 1.)

51. Karras, *The Woman's Building*, n.p.

52. Ibid.

53. Paula Lumbard, "Visionaries of the Wicca: The Women of Surrealism," Master's thesis, Goddard College, 1980.

54. Paula Lumbard, interview with the author, March 6, 2009, Los Angeles California.

55. In the late 1970s, Carrington's work was rarely exhibited in the United States, although she continued to be shown in her native England and her adoptive home of Mexico.

56. Paula Lumbard, "The Artist as Magus," *Spinning Off* (March 1980), 13.

57. Paula Lumbard in conjunction with Geraldine Hanon, "Vision and the Artist," *Spinning Off* 2.16 (1979): 1.

58. Ibid.

59. Susan E. King, *Georgia: A Series of Prose Poems on Georgia O'Keeffe* (Los Angeles: Paradise Press, 1985), n.p.

60. Ibid.

61. Scott, 18.

62. Joanna Frueh, "The Women's Room," *Chicago Reader* (n.d.), 40. This undated press clipping from the Woman's Building Archives is a review of the exhibition at Artemisia Gallery. (It is presumably circa March 1980, concurrent with the exhibition. But I have been unable to date it precisely because this alternative newspaper is not indexed, cataloged or microfilmed prior to 1988.)

63. I do not in any way mean to impugn the scholarship of any art historian associated with the Woman's Building. Raven herself admitted that she had taken the path towards art criticism that led away from tradition-ally academic art history. Lise Vogel outlined the difficulties faced by feminist art critics and the extent to which they are forced to work outside academia. Vogel, a truly remarkable scholar, became so disenchanted with the field of art history after completing a doctorate in art history at Harvard that she returned to graduate school to earn a second doctorate in sociology from Brandeis. See Lise Vogel, "Fine Arts and Feminism: The Awakening Consciousness," *Feminist Studies* 2.1 (1974): 3–37. Raven was a well respected art critic who published three highly influential critical anthologies. See Arlene Raven, *Crossing Over: Feminism and Art of Social Concern* (Ann Arbor: UMI Research Press, 1988); Arlene Raven, *Art in the Pubic Interest* (Ann Arbor: UMI Research Press, 1989); and Joanna Frueh, Cassandra L. Langer, and Arlene Raven, eds., *New Feminist Criticism: Art, Identity, Action* (New York: Harper Collins Publishers, 1994). A sort of follow up to the kind of research as excavation that Raven and Iskin practiced in the 1970s can be found in Charlene G. Garfinkle, "Lucia Fairchild Fuller's 'Lost' Woman's Building Mural," *American Art* 7.1 (1993): 2–7; and Carolyn Kinder Carr and Sally Webster, "Mary Cassatt and Mary Fairchild MacMonnies: The Search for Their 1893 Murals," *American Art* 8.1 (1994): 52–69.

64. Early treatments of racism at the 1893 Woman's Building include Ann Massa, "Black Women in the 'White City,'" *Journal of American Studies* 8.3 (1974): 319–37; and Erlene Stetson, "A Note on the Woman's Building and Black Exclusion," *Heresies* 8 (1979): 45–47. A more complicated consideration can be found in Gail Bederman, *Manliness and Civilization: A Cultural History of Gender and Race in the United States, 1880–1917* (Chicago: University of Chicago Press, 1995). Finally, Christopher Robert Reed documents participation in the World's Fair in "All the World Is Here!" *The Black Presence at White City* (Bloomington: Indiana University Press, 2000).

65. The dominant interpretation of imperialism at the 1893 World's Fair is Robert Rydell's *All the World's a Fair: Visions of Empire at American International Expositions, 1876–1916* (Chicago: University of Chicago Press, 1984) and the work he did for the Smithsonian exhibition in Robert Rydell and Carolyn Kinder Carr, eds., *Revisiting the White City: American Art at the 1893 World's Fair* (Washington, D.C.: Smithsonian Institution, 1993). Erik Larson offers a riveting account of gender at the World's Fair in *Devil in the White City: Murder, Magic, and Madness at the Fair That Changed America* (New York: Crown, 2003).

66. http://calarts.edu/aboutcalarts/history

67. Raven, *At Home*, 29.

68. This history of the early feminist art movement in Los Angeles is drawn from Wilding, *By Our Own Hands*.

69. Chicago, *Through the Flower*, 201.

70. Ruth Iskin, interview with the author, April 25, 1993.

71. Raven, "The Art of the Woman's Building," 1.

72. Two of the earliest such pieces appeared in the influential feminist art journal *Heresies*. See Terree Grabenhorst-Randall, "The Woman's Building," *Heresies* 4 (1978): 44–46; and the response to her by Stetson, "A Note on the Woman's Building and Black Exclusion." See also Joelynn Snyder-Ott, "Woman's Place in the Home (That She Built)," *Feminist Art Journal* 3 (1974): 7–8; and Frances K. Pohl, "Historical Reality or Utopian Ideal?" *International Journal of Women's Studies* 5 (1982). An excellent review of recent literature on the 1893 Woman's Building can be found in T.J. Boisseau, "White Queens at the Chicago World's Fair, 1893: New Womanhood in the Service of Class, Race, and Nation," *Gender & History* 12.1 (2000): 33–81. Along with Sondra Hale, I have written about the complex issue of race at the 1973 Woman's Building in "'At

Home' at the Woman's Building, But Who Gets a Room of Her Own?: Women of Color and Community," in *From Site to Vision: the Woman's Building in Contemporary Culture*, Sondra Hale and Terry Wolverton, eds. (Los Angeles: Woman's Building and Otis college of Art and Design, 2011.)

73. Raven, "Art of the Woman's Building," 1.

74. "'Visual Arts' Leader Cynthia Navaretta, Rapporteur: Leslee Corpier," in *The Stubborn Green Bud: Women's Culture at Century's Close*, Kathryn F. Clarenbach and Edward L. Kamarck, eds. (Metuchen, N.J., London: The Scarecrow Press, 1987), 99.

75. Cheri Gaulke recalls the flyer being made for "the Women Artists Visibility Event (WAVE) produced by the Southern California Women's Caucus for the Arts, co-directed by Cheri Gaulke and Carol Newman." Author's correspondence with Sue Maberry, February 8, 2010.

76. "'Visual Arts' Leader Cynthia Navaretta, Rapporteur: Leslee Corpier," 99.

77. At the time I was aware of Denise Bauer, Jennie Klein, and Margo Hobbs Thompson.

78. In 1998, CalArts hosted "F-word" to explore the Feminist Art Program. In 2007, a student-organized event entitled "Exquisite Acts & Everyday Rebellions" again reflected on the feminist past at CalArts. In 2009, at California State University Fresno, Laura Meyer organized the exhibition "A Studio of Their Own: The Legacy of the Fresno Feminist Art Experiment."

79. Sondra Hale, "Power and Space: Feminist Culture and the Los Angeles Woman's Building, a Context," in *From Site to Vision*, 68.

80. In March of 2008, the Bronx Museum exhibition *Making It Together* corrected some of these omissions by including the work of important collaborative art groups from the Woman's Building, such as Mother Art, the Feminist Art Workers, the Waitresses, and Sisters Of Survival (www.bronxmuseum.org/content/080102_Making_It_Together.pdf).

81. Terry Wolverton, *Insurgent Muse* (San Francisco: City Lights Books, 2002), 180.

First day group meeting, second year of Feminist Studio Workshop. 1974. Woman's Building Image Archive, Otis College of Art and Design.

At Home

by Arlene Raven

A PROCESS ARCHIVE: THE GRAND CIRCULARITY OF WOMAN'S BUILDING VIDEO

Alexandra Juhasz

Usually we go around the room in almost any learning situation to find out who is here; to get a sense of everyone's name. This time we are doing it with video so you get a picture of yourself back to yourself. This is how education works here. You do work to see yourself outside yourself. I'm here because I think that's a fabulous process.
—Sheila Levrant de Bretteville sharing with the circle in *First Day Feminist Studio Workshop* (videotape by Nancy Angelo, 1980)[1]

Video was omnipresent, preserving the voices of women who had dropped everything to be part of the Feminist Studio Workshop. Among these were lesbian students seeking role models, black women writers, and incest survivors who shared their experiences long before such speaking became acceptable. —Nancy Buchanan, "Women Video Artists and Self-Articulation"[2]

Doing It with Video: Now & Then

"This time we're doing it with video," proclaims Sheila Levrant de Bretteville. What did that mean in 1980, and what might it mean in 2010, while revisiting the Woman's Building's awesome archive of one medium's "omnipresence"? At the Woman's Building, video played a central role in a unique feminist art education organized around the

97

risks of female representation and its associated pleasures of self-realization. According to Amelia Jones, "In the early '70s it was assumed that if you put yourself out there and expressed hitherto forbidden feelings (at the time it was inadmissible to talk about things like menstruation or rape) that was itself a political act."[3] At the Building this political act was *videotaped*. For example, in her article here, Vivien Fryd covers the complex ways in which video was used to initiate conversation and memory, record testimony, and in so doing create possibilities for the witnessing necessary for healing, as understood through the radical rape and incest work spearheaded at the Building. For these reasons, video was simultaneously a favored method, medium, and record:

> "I'm Joy. I'm from Kansas. I came here because I heard about it, and there's nothing like it where I'm from. No feminist support community and I'm anxious for that." "I'm Lyricon Jazzwomin McCaleb. This is my 2nd year. I'm nervous. I quit smoking. I hate microphones and now I have a camera to go with it. I think I'll die. I'm a visual artist. I came here because I was a grape turning into a raisin." (*First Day Feminist Studio Workshop*)

Countless Woman's Building videos, capturing untold bits of self-expression like those from *First Day Feminist Studio Workshop*, were made and saved by innumerable (often anonymous) women, who were mutually developing and enjoying a uniquely feminist theory and practice of video fundamentally informed by a form of consciousness-raising that was itself conversant with contemporary art. Over its two hours, *First Day Feminist Studio Workshop* delivers fifty or so testimonies that share an earnest and joyous, if tough, linking of feminism, art, community, self-empowerment, and video. Using video as process and register to make public the private and female within a safe community often culminated in feminist analysis. Michelle Moravec explains: "This process represented the ideal outcome of consciousness-raising, which was meant to help individual women understand that the sexism they experienced was not individual but systematic in patriarchal society."[4] Within feminist art education, feminist analysis could enable another outcome: a critical feminist art practice. At the building, video would initiate a process, enhance it, record it, and ultimately deliver a "picture of yourself back to yourself," which could allow for a new type of seeing of the self, and thus a feminist art intervention. This picture of a radical self was preserved for later generations: a picture of themselves put forward for ourselves. For it was the video that lasted even as—or precisely because—their processes were mostly shelved, taken up and modified by other avant-gardes, lost to the waning of community, or evaporated in the very living of them.

Throughout feminist art education at the building, process was valued and documented. All of these documents of processes were meant to be made public (often through video), and saved for history (as video), even as they also, most critically, mark something internal and ephemeral. Thus, the archive of the omnipresent video of the Los Angeles Woman's Building performs the perplexing, inspiring, and incongruous work of holding still moving documents of and for feminist learning and transformation. Finally pinned down in the patriarchal digs of the Getty Research Institute (GRI), the Building's haphazard records of radical process and feminist change enjoy a contradictory state of preservation.

The GRI archive contains one hundred and eighty-one eclectic videos that register personal alteration, communal growth, aesthetic development, and multiple methods for and records of expanding voice and vision. In the hushed special collections reading room, contemporary feminists can appraise unruly documents that, by "doing it on video," enabled essential transformations for earlier generations of women. What might initially appear to be a cluster of random personal insights expressed on any one tape found amongst this slapdash archive in fact serves to demonstrate a consistent and self-aware project. The video archive of the Woman's Building forms a complex link between video and feminist process and preservation.

Because they manifest this uniquely feminist theory and practice of an *archive of process*, the collected tapes display what continues as a highly relevant project of women's visibility: a theory and practice for being seen and remembered. At first glance, the current catalog of Woman's Building videos is defined primarily by the heterogeneity and disorganization of its entries. Thankfully, I received invaluable assistance from Woman's Building video artist Jerri Allyn, who graciously aided me in navigating what otherwise would have been a truly opaque assortment of tapes. The collection includes, for example, sloppy recordings of art shows and poetry readings (the camera as often facing the floor as the speaker's face), unidentified footage shot for art tapes never made, hours of the now-familiar circle of women introducing themselves to each other, fully realized art videos (some well-known, most forgotten), cable access television programs made by artists at the building from 1987–89, and random tapes donated to the building by indiscriminate feminist parties from across the country. This hodgepodge also comes in a wide range of original recording formats, includes work from 1973–91, and is identified in the catalog only by the esoteric titling found on the tapes' original labels, often without dates or authors. In any case, most of the tapes are not yet transferred into a viewable format. The humble feminist researcher can only guess what hidden riches might be found in the yet-to-be-transferred *Scenes never to be seen beyond the scene (videorecording): hidden eye takes a long look at the FSW, 1975–1976* (1976).[5]

But I did get to see *First Day Feminist Studio Workshop*, twice, and it serves as a primer for the first of three categories of video found in the Building's unique archive of process. In our many conversations about the archive, Allyn and I have named this most common category of video *documentary footage*. In her quote above, Buchanan describes this use of video as "preserving the voices." The many tapes of documentary footage in the archive capture, in unedited form, the activities, exercises, and methods of the unique feminist art education invented and refined at the building from 1973–1991. The archive also holds the video production that resulted from the Building's ubiquitous taking and saving of footage of the difficult private processes of building a public feminist personhood and community. Two forms of "product" (rather than process) tapes are also preserved in the collection; these forms are edited and completed videos, made as an outcome of the processes that were so central at the building: *documentary videos* and *video art*. Woman's Building documentary videos intentionally structure lived time and space with an eye towards feminist analysis and education; art videos do the same while also engaging in a feminist conversation with historical and contemporary aesthetic traditions. In all three categories, every one of the collected tapes performs and documents transformative processes, which are often focused on multiple, perhaps competing, practices—including seeing, speaking, and being seen—and the related project of making these practices public and preserving them.

Thus in its totality the collection reveals a distinctive, highly relevant, and uniquely feminist archival project that is primarily devoted to the *now* of video-aided process—of seeing "yourself outside yourself"—while also being committed to the potentially incompatible goal of entering history through an anticipated (but perhaps under-thought) dialogue with feminists of the future. These are both systems for feminist history built on the circle—of a narcissism where the artist looks at her self across generations and back again, which is an idea explored by Michelle Moravec in this volume. In her essay, Moravec uses as an example Susan King's "conundrum": "how to tell two stories simultaneously" of the Woman's Building's past and present. Video proved an excellent medium with which to work through this challenge of how to express a shared, complex, and sometimes contradictory theory of a mutual and multiple space, time, and self. Doing it with video, women at the building engaged in collective, circular practices developed to acknowledge simultaneous points of view. Today, their videos create a different simultaneity: representing the building, its women, and their loss(es), as well as the multiple and conflicting views of the feminists of the seventies and their progeny. From today's vantage of yesterday's videos, not only are the women of the seventies lost to history (once they were young, now they are not, as will be the case for us as well), but also many of their values and practices no longer seem relevant (lost perhaps to post-identity politics and post-structuralism).

In her essay in this volume, Jennie Klein identifies these "certain qualities—reciprocity, mutuality, equality" as "lesbian." With this I agree, and I note as well that while some of these qualities seem lost, others have been revisited or reinterpreted. Similarly, in their critical contributions to feminist art/archival studies, Ann Cvetkovich and Diana Taylor observe related contradictions that arise from studying archives of ephemera. Cvetkovich explores affect and trauma; Taylor investigates the repertoire of performance.[6] I contribute to this branch of feminist archival/art studies by "doing it with video," just as my forebears did so conscientiously before me. While Cvetkovich and Taylor also rely on video for traces of what would have otherwise been lost to history, I study the Woman's Building's self-conscious move to video, in the face of loss, as my central concern. In his introduction to the photo exhibition *Archive Fever: Uses of the Document in Contemporary Art,* Okwui Enwezor remarks, "The camera is literally an archiving machine, every photograph, every film is *a priori* an archival object."[7] Acknowledging video's unique relation to archives, my claim will be that the Woman's Building engaged this *a priori* power in a uniquely feminist fashion.

The (Waning) Power of Process (Across Space and Time)

The contradictions of documenting process on video via feminist art education expands the reach of video, the archive, and process. I return to *First Day Feminist Studio Workshop* because, as does every tape in the collection, it exhibits the incongruous pulls experienced, documented, and preserved in an archive of process. The tape captures two workshop exercises experienced and relayed over two unedited hours (save for a rough, in-camera edit between exercises and during which it seems the group watched yet another videotape). The processes of videotaping and being videotaped are explicit; answers are performed for the camera and the room, the public and the personal, the future and the now. The first exercise is the one described by de Bretteville above—a building requisite—the personal introduction, around the circle, of all participants and teachers, to the group and the camera:

> "I'm Terry Wolverton. I'm here because I want to be a better writer and I want to work with women in an artist's community." "I'm Cheri Gaulke, core faculty in the workshop. I came five years ago. The reasons I came then are the reasons I'm here now. I want to do my work in a community and get feedback and have my work grow from the experiences of feedback from other women." "This is so nerve wracking. My name is Diana. I don't know why I am here. This is my second year. I never cried so much as last year. I don't know why I am here. I've asked myself a million times, why am I coming back? Because I want more. I want more from myself and I want more for other women." "I'm Deirdre Beckett. I'm here to do this sort of thing we're doing right now. I find it very difficult. I find it very difficult talking in a group. But I came here after going to art school. I got confused about whether I was being produced by the institution or I was the producer. The question of my being a person or not was unclear to me."

Annette Hunt documenting with video on the first work day of the Feminist Studio Workshop, October 22, 1975. Woman's Building Image Archive, Otis College of Art and Design.

The tension, fear, and excitement in the room are palpable in the women's comments, faces, and gestures. It's also greatly exacerbated by the camera. The subjects are saying out loud things they've never said before (as a personal and political act), taping it for their own later view (to see themselves outside themselves), and also for posterity (to see themselves by ourselves). They tell us how hard it is to speak to each other, to the camera, and to us.

As a feminist professor and artist myself, I've been in many such rooms, enjoying our matrilineal inheritance of videotaping exercises around a circle. I know the power of this process. However, I must attest that it came as somewhat of a surprise to find that *watching* such a process at the Getty, rather than engaging in it myself in my own room with my students, proved to be another matter entirely. I'll be frank. *First Day Feminist Studio Workshop* is basically unremarkable, tedious, and somewhat impenetrable when watched thirty years later in the hushed special collections reading room of the GRI. While its reel-to-reel, black-and-white, seventies feel, as well as the haircuts, are initially entertaining, watching hours of other women's unprocessed process is, well, boring. However, when I watch the tapes with Jerri Allyn, that's a different matter altogether. Allyn recognizes everyone, and narrates aloud many levels of information that would be utterly inscrutable without her: who the mostly unnamed women are, who is probably behind the camera, what's become of them all, and what was *really* going on in the room at the time—all the exciting, unspoken drama and tension. It's delightful to engage with the tapes through her animated nostalgia; it's like watching home movies. (Home movies are also prime examples of the category documentary footage, although home videos are not made with a view towards a larger, theorized process that will involve their later use by researchers.)

In *First Day Feminist Studio Workshop*, de Bretteville eloquently addresses this gap between the seen and felt (or lived) aspects of process, between its now and its later, its public and private, its participant-users and its projected-but-ill-defined-future-audience. She identifies a well-known trouble with realist documentary footage (one often satisfied by making fiction or art video): it only records the surfaces or facts of things. For this essay, I will focus on this particular problem and how the Woman's Building developed unique theories and practices that used video as both record and resource for the now, while also committing it towards a somewhat less coherent project of the future. For this reason, the video footage and video documentary output found in the collection—not the video art—will take up my primary consideration. Furthermore, while the feminist video art of the Woman's Building has already received some critical and curatorial attention, the work that comprises the majority of the archive has not.[8] Thus, video's documentary, rather than aesthetic, problems and potential will be of greatest concern to me. (It was thus for women at the Building who, as Jenni Sorkin establishes in this volume, were not primarily committed to the making of great—or sometimes any—works of art.)

The documentary concerns related to preserving feminist process with video were central to women at the building, which is eloquently elaborated by de Bretteville during the second recorded exercise of *First Day Feminist Studio Workshop*. In this case, women were asked to explain the metaphorical and/or physical importance of the Woman's Building. De Bretteville remarks:

> This place embodies our energy. If I measure it under feminist ener-
> gy, there's a strange gap between reality and what we made happen.
> In rational, logical, linear thinking it stands as proof for that which is
> not measurable, that which is based on our wanting it, our needing it.
> We are vulnerable to a kind of naïveté. We've accomplished a lot, and
> we can accomplish more, as long as there are enough of us. I am
> scared that there won't be enough women to carry us into the future.
> If there aren't women, there won't be a building.

De Bretteville expresses that the Woman's Building is nothing more than their own irrational, illogical (and undocumentable) wants, needs, and energies—the lived process of those who are there, now, creating (and documenting) it. Note, as ever, the power of the now, and its tug against an implicit theory of future (as well as the condemnation of the linear). De Bretteville remarks that this place will stop being the Woman's Building when women stop doing and wanting in the way that they are. They did stop, and the building is no longer, just as she anticipated. All that is left is its collection of videos.

Documentary videos can only capture the visible and audible aspects of that feminist energy, not the unquantifiable, interpersonal, and private stuff: the feeling, wanting, and needing. (Again, that is the project of video art.) Alone with the videos these many years later, I find that even when the women speaking are as eloquent as de Bretteville (and most are not, I must admit), I am *not* riveted by their process. I can see and hear them attesting to their wanting and needing, but I can't *feel* it. My mind wanders, I start scanning the tapes at 4X speed, hoping not to miss a crucial moment amidst the mundane revelations, hoping the other researchers (careful, attentive art historians) don't catch my sloppy methods. I realize: Wow, come to think of it, this video actually isn't for me, the feminist future, even as it could have been preserved for no one else but me. It clearly worked as part of *their* process, in its time, in its now. It even seems to continue to work today for the women like Allyn who made it; it retains value in their ongoing feminist process. But what is the meaning and purpose of process video for others once it is archived?

It seems that the contradictions inherent in gathering and saving evidence of *feminist process*—something that is most critical in the doing and living of it, in its present, and within its community—are paled by those raised by the ensuing process of

sitting in a subdued research room, years later, watching long, eclectic, often unau-
thored and untitled bits of evidence of someone else's daring development. Saving
process is weird enough, but watching someone else's saved process feels downright
crazy. While I may be revealing myself as a bitchy archivist (daughter), or I might be
hinting that this is an unpleasant (mother's) archive, it is the complex meanings raised
by this collection's many paradoxes that I will attempt to illuminate for the rest of this
essay. Centrally, I am interested in the powerful and productive ambivalence that the
archive produces in relation to its own feminist theories of time, place, self, community, generation, and consequence. I intend to highlight, upfront, the many irreconcil-
able theories and practices at the heart of these feminist videos and their preservation
between past, present, and future; archiver and archivist; mother and daughter; public
and private; and importance (or quality) and insignificance.

A/No Document for the Daughters of Posterity

Across this essay, I engage in a curious mapping of the contradictions found in a *process
archive*, using the videos found therein to help answer what might be, in more familiar
archival settings, some relatively straightforward questions: Why were these tapes
made and for whom? Why and how were they archived? What does the archive, and the
fact of its archiving, tell us about video and feminist art education at the Woman's
Building? Some of what is learned is to be expected. For instance, it is now accepted
wisdom that feminists in the seventies, like others breaking past the confines of high
Modernism, used this new technology against art objects and in celebration of the
quotidian. "Woman's art and video were largely responsible for transforming the pre-
dominantly male monoliths of minimalism into the cluttered, chatty, often messy
objects of post-minimalism and post-modernism," explains Ann-Sargent Wooster in
her introduction to *The First Generation: Women and Video, 1970–75*.[9] Chris Hill builds
on this history in *Video Art and Alternative Media in the United States 1969–1980*. "The
valorization of 'process' and 'an almost religious return to experience' was shared by
both political and cultural radicals of the late '60s, even though their agendas and
strategies varied considerably."[10]

While notable for their eclecticism of purpose, style, and method, the fifty
or so tapes from the Woman's Building archive currently available deliver what any
student of video would expect from work of the seventies (and eighties): a host of predictably low production values used to record the social and cultural world of a community of diverse female artists, where a distinct value is placed on process over product.
"Low production values characterized the emergent feminist video art of this era,"
explains Christine Tamblyn, who then enumerates "long, unedited takes, minimal
camera angles or movement, and a reliance on synch sound."[11] The work in the collection establishes how the act of shooting, and thereby owning and preserving women's
voices, bodies, and experiences, proved as paramount for these feminist artists as

it did for others inventing the field in the seventies. Deidre Boyle elaborates in *Illuminating Video*:

> Video's unique ability to capitalize on the moment with instant play-back and real time monitoring of events also suited the era's emphasis on 'process, not product.' Process art, earth art, conceptual art, and performance all shared a de-emphasis on the final work and an emphasis on how it came to be. The absence of electronic editing equipment—which discourages shaping a tape into a finished "product"—further encouraged the development of a 'process' video aesthetic.[12]

Across the decades, the focus of early feminist video stays consistently on women's voices, bodies, and daily experiences; self-growth, healing, and self-definition; and advancing feminist community and art. "Without the burdens of tradition linked with other media, women video artists were freer to concentrate on process, often using video to explore the body and the self," writes JoAnn Hanley in her introduction to *The First Generation: Women and Video, 1970–75*.[13] The significance of self-expression to seventies feminism is everywhere evident: most videos focus upon women talking about themselves, their experiences, and the power of feminist representation. Predictably, a feminist methodology including reflexivity and collaboration, an action orientation and activist stance, and an affective focus on the everyday is demonstrated across the work.[14] These shared forms, contents, and methods arise from and often refer to the central place of consciousness-raising and collectivism within the building and the feminist art education developed there. "Feminist art forms stressed performance and group reception and foregrounded the values of collaboration, participation, empowerment, consciousness-raising, and the belief in art's ability to create change," write Mary Jo Aagerstoun and Elissa Auther in "Considering Feminist Activist Art."[15]

In regard to both form and content, the videos appear exactly as we might expect, and precisely as they've been described by previous feminist scholarship. Take, for example, the tape *la la la workshop* (1976)[16] listed thus in the Getty's catalog: "[produced by?] the Woman's Building, 1976. Video documentation of the second day of the la la la workshop held at the Woman's Building, June 5-6, 1976, 10 mins." The video opens and closes to black and is without identifying titles of any sort. The first image is a close-up of a woman who begins to tell a joke "about a wide-mouthed frog" that "you need to both see and hear to really enjoy." But "you" don't get the punch line because an in-camera edit cuts to the body of the tape, which is comprised of two real-time, brief segments. In each, a different group of three women sit in a semi-circle on plastic chairs facing the camera and a camerawoman with whom they are openly interacting. They pass a microphone between them and answer interview questions posed by one

Video workshop with Jerri Allyn, 1979. Woman's Building Image Archive, Otis College of Art and Design.

member of the visible group. The first begins, "This is Sheila Ruth at la la la speaking with Linda and Marilou. I'd like to ask you two lesbians several questions." The questions relate to how they told their mom, dad, best friend, and boyfriend that they were lesbians. They are about to tape lesbians saying out loud what's rarely been made public before. It's no small thing, as Buchanan describes above. They are sharing "their experiences long before such speaking became acceptable."

Each woman answers in her own way—charming, funny, but also fast because the off-screen voice keeps reminding them that they only have two and a half minutes. Ruth does not even get to finish her answer, as the tape is abruptly cut (at the ominous time limit, we assume) by another rough, in-camera edit. A new group of women pops into place, beginning their segment with the statement, "Our group is so creative." They have decided that for their part of what now seems an exercise, they will answer the question "What is la la la?" The answers are multiple, uncertain, and passionate, including "Being with a lot of women. It's all a celebration," and "Lesbians Are Living and Loving Amazons." Then we begin to hear what was so powerful about la la la, which seems to have included lectures and workshops. One woman explains: "I would love access to Ruth Iskin's slide show. I wish that had been videotaped. I'd like to see a book of the photo exhibition to be available for future reference, for future study. My interest has been sparked in things I will continue on my own. My fantasy is that this sort of thing is happening for a lot of women. What is happening at the Woman's Building is almost synonymous with what's happening this weekend…" But we've run out of time to finish her thoughts. From off-screen: "We're winding up. Good-bye."

I describe the tape in detail so that you might begin to understand the complicated process of viewing and making sense of this and most of the other works in the collection. Toward what goal, and for whom was this tape made? Why was it archived? Why do I watch it today? Whatever would they like me to make of it, here and now? At first, answers seem hard to come by (in that unappreciative daughter sort of way). This is no document for the daughters of posterity. The direct-to-camera address seems to be an acknowledgement of the videographer in the room rather than an outside, or even future viewer, who would certainly need more context, background, and a more coherent structure to be able to engage meaningfully with these vaguely structured fragments of video. *la la la workshop* is not the coherent chronicle of two days of events that would be of any real use to the future (like the video the woman in the tape said she wanted "for future reference"). Apparently, the video is instead one component of one exercise from one workshop from la la la, where six women were asked to use video to interview each other about the event, quickly. The video is not future-oriented, but rather process-oriented. It is for and of the now. While Jennie Klein (in this anthology) writes about la la la as one of several gestures produced by the Woman's Building towards an imagined lesbian future—"THE FUTURE IS FEMALE" she quotes Raven as writing in 1979—the primary value of the tape of this utopian action is in the act of its taping; it gave these lesbians coming into art and voice a structured activity around public speaking and its record. "The Woman's Building in L.A. taught liberation as a broad-based action imbedded in real time, not as an abstraction," explains Marlena Doktorczyk-Donohue in her essay about one of the building's performance collectives, The Waitresses.[17] Videotaping served to formalize and give shape, as well as make public and permanent, this small and private action experienced within one sparsely attended workshop, which was itself part of a larger set of events and activities that we will never see again because they were not adequately recorded with video.

And yet, there *is* more. There is *abstraction* and a future, too! Yes, this video, like all the others in the archive, was originally for process. But it was also carefully saved, meaning that someone (or many) deemed it of value for an intangible future. Moreover, it is highly self-reflexive and self-aware (and therefore abstract). Discussions about its own making, structure, and the value of video run consistently across what initially appears as ten haphazard minutes of videotaping an exercise. There's more to this video than its one-time use value. For *la la la workshop* is a video documentary, structured in three (albeit weird) acts, each consistently relaying several linked and coherent themes and practices. At once entirely about and for its own moment and community, feminist method and theory are at play in the consideration and construction of the multiplicity of time, space, and self that extends this one tape beyond video's cherished function as a playback machine that easily records and represents process. The woman quoted above ends the tape by imagining herself, or a feminist like her, wanting to re-visit and re-use all the ephemera produced at the Woman's Building, particularly the stuff experienced during la la la (slide shows, art exhibits, workshops). She expresses a radical, lesbian, future-oriented video fancy: that others in her present, as well as the future, will be as lucky as is she—recorded on tape, and accessible again and again, "for future reference, for future study."

She and this exercise *were* videotaped, archived, and made available for future reference by me, a feminist media scholar who is the middle-aged daughter of a seventies feminist, Suzanne Juhasz, who was a first-generation women's studies professor, and one-time visitor to the Woman's Building for a program on feminist poetry about which she was an early expert.[18] And for you, curious reader, diligent student of feminist art history, video, or documentary studies. We are that woman of the future, referencing and studying, and yet sadly, problematically, so little like *her*, what with her ungainly seventies fashion and heart-wrenching enthusiasm for the endless exercises and events of la la la. At the same time, I prove not to be the woman she imagined me to be, longing for access to the minutiae of her generation's self-education. I gain little from watching the tape, because—let's face it—that was her process, not mine. So, in the face of my coldhearted disinterest and unforgivable lack of gratitude, and in the name of their narcissistic projection of a future populated not by *all* women (as Klein suggests was their stated utopian desire) but only by more of themselves, I'd like to attest that what remains compelling is the fact of the feminist video archive itself. This seriously messy collection, housed for years in dusty boxes on the shelves of the venerable Long Beach Museum of Art's Video Annex, goes truly public, and ends up accomplishing the impossibly stimulating work of unsettling the staid structures between contemporary feminist scholars and (the histories of) their activist artist foremothers.

Feminist Archives Are(n't) Made for their Archivists

la la la workshop is only the first example of the heartbreaking failures and unimaginable successes of this archive of feminist process. So rightfully caught up in the moment were they that they somehow didn't realize that the feminist process that they created and documented would itself create new feminist processes, and that feminism would change, not simply carry on in their likeness. So moved were they by their own present that they planned for a future littered with the documents that they needed *then*. Women at the building diligently shot and preserved the archive that *they* wished to study, as if they would give birth to another generation that would study the tapes just as their foremothers had already studied themselves. But some archives aren't made for their archivists. For an article about the Woman's Building published for the Getty's exhibition *California Video*, which included several tapes from the Woman's Building collection, Meg Cranston worked closely with Allyn. Cranston writes that she asked Allyn: "What constitutes the Woman's Building video collection?"

> "It's everything!" Jerri Allyn said, and then her hubris made her laugh. She explained, "It sounds strange now, but then...everything was important. That was part of the feminist ethos. Everything was political and everything was important. So that's what got put into the collection—everything." [19]

Yep...everything. As Ilya Kabakov ponders in "The Man Who Never Threw Anything Away," "But if you don't do these sortings, these purges, and you allow the flow of paper to engulf you, considering it impossible to separate the important from the unimportant—wouldn't that be insanity?" [20] I will attest to how exhausting and confusing the post-facto sorting of an undifferentiated archive can be. I see that the women at the building had an articulated, feminist rationale behind their incessant archiving. Something critical and revolutionary defined their archival impulse; they believed in their archive's consequence, as well as the worth of every woman who made video there, and the value of every tape she ever made. But to whom was it important, and how?

In relation to the toxic misogyny of the period (and henceforth), the radical feminist art education at the building taught its students several related, political ideals, including that their work and their voices were important in their own right, and to history. In this volume, Moravec quotes Ruth Iskin: "There was a sense of the importance of history, that what we were doing was something that was history." You and I are now that history, sorting the meaning of their significance. Cranston continues:

> In the halls and archives of the Woman's Building, women—as artists and subjects, as students and instructors, as employees and volunteers—are taking action in the belief that all work is important, and that creative construction can produce social change. This conviction is the basis of the feminism that constructed the Woman's Building and the video collection is a testament to that view. [21]

Women at the building knew that if their important work was going to enter and stay in history, then they would need to "get shown and be known" (one course offered through the Woman's Building Continuing Education Program was called Getting Shown, Being Known), by and for themselves, because no one would do it for them. Well, that is, no one except for me (and you), here. For there's the rub in all this: the taping and the saving of the tapes actually *worked*. The seventies feminist theories and politics of voice and preservation were right on. The women at the building understood that video would enable them to enter the archive, thus insuring their own power; they did, and it *was*. Writes Jacques Derrida: "There is no political power without control of the archive, if not of memory. Effective democratization can always be measured by this essential criterion: the participation in and the access to the archive, its constitution, and its interpretation." [22] They made the work and it has been archived, and not simply because the women from the building saw value in it, and in themselves (the ultimate feminist act) but also because the Getty did as well (the ultimate patriarchal fact). The unique feminist art education at the building—which produced these tapes, as well as some other objects archived elsewhere, and a slew of ephemera only available to memory—played a part in real cultural shifts that ultimately allowed for feminist art, method, and education to move into dominant institutions like the Getty and other major museums, universities, and libraries. Of course, feminist work is sometimes still considered marginal, but mostly it's not. Major shows of feminist art have been recently staged across the country, and the Woman's Building Video Archive and other feminist archives have been readily accepted by some of our foremost cultural institutions.

This raises a related question as to the associated matter of (my) tone. Given their preeminently housed archive, and its related visibility and power, why do the women from the building, and feminists from the seventies more generally, continue to feel unseen and undervalued? Are they in or out of history? And who is the best judge? While conducting research for this article, I made use of a significant and consistent body of scholarship that clearly defines the form and content of seventies feminist video and art education, as well as the role that the Woman's Building played in its history and development. Now, there may not be as much written on this topic as, say, the work of Pablo Picasso or John Baldessari, but that is definitive of feminist production and scholarship and comes as no surprise. Thus, in the end, what seems more noteworthy are the interrelations between the previous generation's insatiable anxieties about invisibility in the face of their own consistent visibility project (via video) and my own, somewhat contradictorily resistant response as I make this and other small gestures towards ensuring their ongoing visibility. Hal Foster explains: "Perhaps the paranoid dimension of archival art is the other side if its utopian ambition—its desire to turn belatedness into becomingness, to recoup failed visions of art, literature, philosophy and everyday life into possible scenarios of alternative kinds of social relations, to transform the no-place of the archive in to the no-place of utopia." [23]

But whose paranoia is this: the archiver's or the archivist's? Gayatri Spivak uses the terminology of "transference" to describe the complex relations between these subjects of past and present, "in the modified psychoanalytic sense of a repetition-displacement of the past into the present as it necessarily beats on the future." [24] For, given that these participants in the Woman's Building are very much alive and playing central roles in the reevaluation of this archive, the repetitive relations between generations of feminists displacing past into present, as modified and supported by this archive, seems impossible to avoid. Michel Foucault writes, "The analysis of the archive, then, involves a privileged region: at once close to us, and different from our present existence, it is the border of time that surrounds our presence, which overhangs it, and which indicates its otherness: it is that which, outside ourselves, delimits us." [25] And yet, nothing is so simple between generations of women. While the feminist mother is not outside ourselves as simply as the forefather is to his son, the point of the video process was to see "ourselves outside ourselves," remember? Jennie Klein sheds some light on my complicated amalgam of transference, resistance, and receptivity in the face of this work. She writes that it is the "aura of distance that is misleading" when confronting these tapes. [26] When I do research in this archive, do I see my mother (and her sisters) or myself (and my sisters), and to whom am I obligated? Is it me seeing them seeing themselves? Is it their process or mine? Their archive or ours? Whose importance does it signify? These tensions between author and archivist, feminist past and feminist future, are duly noted, but I will leave them unresolved to haunt their archive and my writing about it. As a media studies scholar, I find it easier to note and then run away from the intransigent psychodrama at the heart of the feminist archive. Turning from feminist discourse and relations, I will conclude, instead, by engaging with a less loaded but equally important battle for provenance. For the remainder of this piece, I will demonstrate how the archive of Woman's Building video forces us to re-think the accepted wisdom about histories of documentary and video.

Accepted narratives of various art histories all move past seventies feminist art to end with a celebration of movements and ideas that are considered to have been built from and improved upon it—critical theory, deconstructive form, and postmodern method. However, as I believe I've shown, the feminist practice at the Woman's Building was thoroughly theorized and politicized. Art histories need to be reevaluated in light of what this archive demonstrates.

I will attempt to conclude my thoughts on the contradictions of the process archive by explaining how the diverse but coherent body of video work from the Woman's Building demands a rethinking of the tautological hierarchies developed by art and feminist history, as well as those of documentary studies. Video at the Woman's Building might be contradictory, but it is neither preliminary, nor "pre" anything else that might be dismissively called upon to compare this collection to the better, brighter videos of today.

Multiple Views: Things Are(n't) This or That

I have forcefully objected to oppositional labels like "first wave" and "second wave," for these only rehearse male-conceived dualistic Cartesian symbolic systems wherein things are with "this" or "that." This type of fractured/territorialist thinking runs counter to what was and is a holistic feminist social program. —Marlene Doktorczyk-Donohue [27]

So far we have regarded all films made from natural material as coming within this category [documentary]….They all represent different qualities of observation, different intentions in observation, and, of course, very different powers and ambitions at the stage of organizing material. I propose, therefore, after a brief word on the lower categories, to use the documentary description exclusively of the higher. —John Grierson [28]

John Grierson, considered the father of documentary film, looked scornfully on the "lower categories" of the form as being so base that they did not even deserve the name. In so doing, he programmatically rehearsed a type of the "male-conceived dualistic Cartesian symbolic systems" to which Doktorczyk-Donohue objects. The kinds of films Grierson disdains include those videos most commonly found in the Woman's Building archive: "different qualities of observation" of events, activities, and the processes of women's lives and feminist education. Take, for example, the first three videos listed in the archive's alphabetically organized holdings: *1893 Historical Handicrafts exhibition, 1976*; *Adrienne Rich and Mary Daly, 1979—readings*; and *Alcoholism Center for Women (Summary: Videos probably contain documentation of an event organized by the Alcoholism Center for Women)*.[29] Grierson calls such records "snip-snaps of some utterly unimportant ceremony."[30] Note the importance of the word *importance* again, and, as ever, my question: Important to whom? This aside, what Grierson is attempting to define in the 1940s, as he invents our contemporary documentary form as well as its academic studies, is how using the camera to record "natural material," the stuff of daily life, does not become a *documentary* until it is edited and organized into an argument, and made into art.

However, for the women of the building, this record keeping—these documents of daily practice, this process—*was* their art. "Video moves well beyond the function of the artistic," explains Deidre Boyle, "to encompass every discursive function of documentary media: recording, preserving, persuading, and analyzing events—public and private, local and global."[31] As I've been establishing throughout, this archive is quite special in that it holds evidence of a complex and unique feminist practice where "art" and the "discursive functions of documentary media" are produced *in tandem,* or even perhaps as the very same thing, as one messy but still coherent project, where neither tautology nor priority is given to the "this" or the "that," the "lower" or "higher." All the work is the work; all the process is the process; and thus, everything is in the archive. For the women at the building, documentary footage and art video were two equivalent and supporting parts of their multifaceted video archive process. "At the Feminist Art Program artists would create performances out of psychodynamic situations (ones drawn from consciousness-raising sessions) which would finally find their way into the visual imagery," explains Amelia Jones in an interview about women's art in California. "I also have a problem with the dichotomy made between conceptual work and feminist work whereby the former is thought of as obviously theorized and the latter as intuitive, naïve, and overly sincere."[32]

As a renowned scholar of early cinema, Tom Gunning repudiates yet another accepted academic hierarchy. Gunning nuances the dichotomy between the preliminary forms, which Grierson names "actualities," and the ones that come later, which Grierson more righteously called "documentaries." "Confronting a gaping abyss that separates the earlier and later modes of nonfiction filmmaking," Gunning notes that the actualities of documentary's "prehistory" have gone under-studied because they are understood to be merely "descriptive," "uninterpreted," "too raw, too close to reality, and bereft of artistic or conceptual shaping."[33] They are characterized by single shots, as editing was yet to be matured, and little attention was given to narrative clarity and logic. As you've probably noticed, I've been discussing just this sort of work, found in the Woman's Building archive seventy years later.

In his work on early documentary, Gunning makes an unexpected and helpful move that provides media scholars of other periods a critical vocabulary for understanding "primitive" work. Rather than discarding the earliest forms, as most are wont to do for their embarrassing lacks and "snip-snaps," Gunning chooses to carefully enumerate their distinct stylistic subtleties. "This *Urform* of early nonfiction film I propose to call the 'view,'" he writes. "I mean to highlight the way early actuality films were structured around presenting something visually, capturing and preserving a look or vantage point."[34] He then delineates the two common forms of the "view:" the tour that presents space, and "films dedicated to activities and processes" that are more temporal in nature.[35] While Gunning's description eerily foretells the video practices found in the archive under consideration, the feminist underpinnings of Woman's Building video profoundly distinguish, and complicate, the form and function of their videos' "actualities."

For the remainder of the paper, I will continue to demonstrate how video in the Woman's Building, whether "high" or "low," "actuality" or "documentary," differentiates itself from other process work—and documentary—in that the varied but related productions all embody a consistent theory built from the coherent, self-aware project of feminist art education developed at the Building. Facing the camera, eyes obscured by purple glasses, Judy Chicago proclaims in *Judy Chicago in 1976* (Sheila Ruth, 1980): "Feminism is a new world view, a whole philosophical system that challenges the value system of Western civilization."[36]

I am particularly interested in how feminist challenges to theories of time and space, expressed through their practices of mutuality and circularity, are illuminated in every video in this collection. Masterfully manifested in the archive as a totality, they defy commonsense understandings of the ordering of artistic development already being questioned by feminist scholars. The contradictions of a process archive create a coherent artistic theory and practice, "a new value system," structured by feminist multiplicity and collectivity. In this part of the essay, I will look closely at several videos to demonstrate how the collective, the circle, and the archive form a distinct and lucid feminist practice rooted in process, voice, and memory. *From Reverence to Rape to Respect, Leslie Labowitz and Suzanne Lacy* (Leslie Labowitz and Suzanne Lacy, 1978)[37] documents one hour of group process towards a public artwork that will be staged later by a diverse group of feminist activists who have been cobbled together by Lacy and Labowitz in Las Vegas. The visitors from the building are keen on educating this group about the unique role of collective criticism in feminist art education: "We need criticism to move from isolation to support community. Criticism is a central aspect of support. Does that make sense to you?" A woman in the circle responds: "I disagree. I'm beginning to believe criticism is not a factor of the social function." Lacy reacts, "We're not talking about art critics, we're talking about how criticism works within a group. Can we think of a framework for the group, when we criticize or give feedback without splitting up? So we can talk to each other and communicate?...Raven says it's an essential part of any feminist community. But you need trust, and willingness to be open and vulnerable and to be able to learn." The women sit in the predictable circle of consciousness-raising. What is more, the entire tape is not only shot in black-and-white long-takes, but the circle sits within what is called an iris-shot—an early cinematographic technique that takes the form of a circle; part of the screen is blacked so that only a round portion of the image can be seen by the viewer. It's an idiosyncratic view to be sure: based on the circle, which represents the collective, which produces a new kind of knowledge based in trust and criticism. This feminist epistemology under-pins the work in the building's video archive, and is manifested, again and again, in the content and form of its eclectic holdings.

One of the categories of documentary film that Gunning discusses is the *tour* film. He describes it thus: "The view of the tourist is recorded here, placing natural or cultural sites on display, but also miming the act of visual appropriation, the natural and cultural consumed *sights.*"[38] Interestingly, the women at the building shot a large number of such tours: several of the building itself, and many more of the shows they put on there. However, if we think of *all* the video from the Woman's Building as tours (putting cultural sites on display) of "everything important," what is striking about the collection is that the "view" in these tours differs from more traditional forms in that it is circular, mutual, collective, and interactive. In *Arlene Raven* (Kate Horsfield/Lyn Blumenthal, 1979), one of the Building's founders explains how Sapphic education "takes into account mutuality."[39] I am suggesting that this video might be understood as a guided tour not of a place but of Raven's *analysis.* The video is shot in their signature style, including black-and-white long-takes and often extreme close-ups. Similarly, in the "tour" *Adrienne Rich, 1976* (1976), the celebrated poet remarks upon the new and "intense reciprocity between individuals" that distinguishes her experience at the Woman's Building.[40] These careful articulations of theories of collectivism fill the archive, and color our understanding of it. Writes Moravec, "The Woman's Building explored the multiplicative aspect of collaboration. What Cheri Gaulke once described as 'one plus one equals three.'"[41]

This mutual view is also enacted in what was perhaps the most bizarre video that I viewed from the collection, *1893 Historical Handicrafts Exhibition* (The Woman's Building, 1976), which documents an exhibition of historical objects related to the original, 1893 Woman's Building at the Chicago World's Columbian Exposition. This literal tour of the exhibition follows the curators—de Bretteville and Ruth Iskin—for thirty or so minutes as they move clockwise around the room. Sharing the microphone, de Bretteville and Iskin stop before each panel and discuss minute historical details and background, as well as their exacting curatorial thinking, about everything, yes everything, in the exhibition. They know a lot about this history and they address all of the many works on the wall. Says Iskin: "We're going to go through each board and go through the different aspects of the exhibition." Why I call this bizarre is that the view-er cannot see what is on the wall, given that the entire video is shot in real time in a medium long shot. The *women* are our focus, and in particular their shared words and analysis. This tour is actually a staid, if circular and shared, lecture. It is also, somewhat eerily, the imagined video that the woman from *la la la workshop* tried to conjure: "I would love access to Ruth Iskin's slide show. I wish that had been videotaped.... To be available for future reference, for future study."

However, this video is unlike a more traditional tour film or the document of the slide show that we might really have wanted to watch (where we could see the slides). It is also distinct from much of the process work, with its emphasis on the now of the making and using of the tape, that I have discussed so far. *1893 Historical Hand-icrafts Exhibition* displays a much more complicated relation to time as well as to place than what one might initially expect. The video records two women in the present "touring" illegible pictures from an art show about the past, while standing in the Woman's Building of the present, and lecturing in direct-address to putative students in the future. Chicago gives words to this feminist theory of time in her discussion of *The Dinner Party* (1974–79) in *Judy Chicago in 1976*: "We create a wedge in the culture. If we can bring in women's history, we can bring in women's future." Hence, the mutuality enacted in Woman's Building tour videos is across multiple registers: in terms of point of view of the "tourist" or guide, and also in relation to temporality—all at once the past, present, and future of Woman's Buildings. Here we find evidence of what Moravec, in this anthology, understands as the building's "circular conception of history, not one that rested on linear progress, but one that spiraled or curved at times, and bent concepts of time and space...particularly apparent in the extensive uses of the 1893 Woman's Building."

This is evidenced with more success by *Constructive Feminism: Reconstruction of the Woman's Building 1975* (Directed by Sheila Ruth; Produced by Sheila Ruth, Diana Johnson and Annette Hunt, 1976),[42] which also makes explicit a complex register of spatiality. One woman guides this tour, which begins outside the building. Speaking to the camera with a microphone in hand, she takes up the familiar stance of a live TV correspondent. "The Woman's Building is a public center for women's culture," she begins. Here, the video cuts to a close-up of the front of the building, tour guide missing. (Why didn't they do this in the previous tour?!) She continues in voiceover:

> When we speak of the Woman's Building we are not just talking about the physical building. But the physical space has been part of our process: taking responsibility for the creation of the kind of environment we need to produce our work and the space we need to make our work public. We have created not only a room, but a building of our own. Please join me inside.

And so, the mutual and multiple spatiality, temporality, and visuality of the tour begin: seeing oneself outside oneself, seeing themselves by ourselves. Later in the tape, in one of many interviews with her, de Bretteville explains this theory of collective vision:

> The experience that you always have at the Woman's Building is that while you are seeing one thing, you can, out of the periphery of your vision, see something else going on and in that way it never feels like one thing is happening at a time. There are many points of view existing concurrently.

Just so. While we see a video image of the entry desk, we hear the voice of de Bretteville describing the decisions made, practical and philosophical, about the function and meaning of the Building's face to the public. "I am now speaking with Sheila de Bretteville," explains our tour guide after the fact. We cut to a two-shot, and hear the cut (some period-specific formal snafu that occurs in most seventies videos). Our guide then diligently escorts us to each room and area of the building, from bottom to top. At each stop we meet a different woman who narrates the work done on that space, as well as the feminist principles embodied in the design choices. Says one:

> A part of feminist education is not only to create one's art but also the wall in which the piece will hang. This is about ownership. Owning the space: the gallery and classroom. They own that space and it belongs to them. The other reason for physical work [is] to halt the separation, people's problem of separating out different kinds of work. We want to work and play. It gives us another way of being together, building our community and working together.

We cut to images, from some earlier time, of women collectively painting a ceiling and singing together.

The video juggles, with little temporal logic or coherence, photographs and moving documents of past processes of construction, the present of the interview, and the anticipated future of its viewing. A fully realized "video documentary," this tape, more than most that we've seen (but also like the previous tour) is clearly for viewers (of the future) outside the often closed world of the building. The same can be said for *FSW Videoletter* (Susan Mogul, 1975), which is similarly structured but much funnier, in Mogul's signature style.[43] This video tour was made to be sent to women's groups in Chicago, New York, and Washington. Two guides, Pam McDonald and Mogul, go from room to room, interviewing teachers, visitors, students, and yet again circling the walls and halls of the building. With their loving, laughing testaments to the architectural and metaphorical space and time of feminist art education, all of these many tour tapes preserve and educate with a complexity of vision unimagined in the early (preliminary, actuality) film tours that they might at first seem to resemble.

The Grand Circularity of an Archive of Process

Woman's Building video begs us to reconsider the possibilities of archiving process. Gunning describes the second, more temporal form of early documentary as "a view of a process." He explains that these are records of "the production of a consumer good through a complex industrial process, the creation of an object through traditional craft, or the detailing of a local custom or festival...the most fully developed narrative pattern is the transformation of raw materials into consumable goods."[44] Again, while the archive under consideration is rife with such videos, it is their specifically feminist analysis of process that serves to truly differentiate feminist video from the predictable plots (and products) of their patriarchal predecessors. Here I will focus again on the prevalence of the circle in consciousness-raising and the videos it inspired as a direct contest to the linearity of industrial production celebrated in the early films of modernity (and elsewhere across patriarchal production).

As has become quite clear, passing the camera around a circle is a recurring format and trope in the Woman's Building archive. "Feminists often employed egalitarian structures. At the most basic level, this effort translated into the venerable feminist institution of the circle, around which each woman speaks in turn, having equal opportunity to voice her views," explains Moravec.[45] *Feminist Studio Workshop—student self-portraits* (FSW Students, 1979) has a similar structure, although it is more figurative.[46] All twenty-four participants introduce themselves, then produce a short, rudimentary, autobiographical video with the help of their classmates. "Julie James. I am seed. I am heart. I am healing. I am power. I am smooth. I am alive. I am dark red. I am pulsing. I am magic. I am clearing. I am self." "Laurine DeRocco. I was five years old, heard my baby brother's cry and knew there was no more time for me." And so on. The video ends with the group joining together in a moving class portrait culminating with a chant, "Feminist Studio Workshop, 1979–80," and a loud "YEAH!" A quick fade to black bumps us against an unanticipated snippet of yet another circle. We suddenly see the last five minutes of a consciousness-raising meeting of a group of deaf women. (Perhaps the other tape was taped over this one.) The women speak together about the role of affection in their lives (we hear through an interpreter while they sign), and end their meeting (and the tape) with a group (circle) hug. This process leads to no product (other than its video documentation), but rather to affection, collectivity, and self-expression. But I'm starting to bore myself. That's their theory, and it is represented in everything they made.

Finally, the kind of process Gunning finds in early documentary is perhaps most closely modeled in *Kate Millet 1977* (Claudia Queen and Cyd Slayton, 1977), where the documentarians show the production (from inception to installation) of a set of naked "fat lady" sculptures that Millet made as a commission while she was an artist in residence at the building.[47] While the video imagery is primarily of Millet and a team of unnamed assistants, who produce the sculptures from wire mesh and papier-mâché, and of the exhibition opening, the views of the process are multiple. In her voiceover Millet discusses how these powerful figures came to be made. She explains, "What was really great was working with other people." The unidentified voices of her assistants from the building say in chorus: "I learned a lot of skills, and took chances and took responsibility. I gained my voice." "I learned a lot from Kate. We didn't work for her. We worked with her. We didn't do it for nothing. We did it because we wanted to, and getting to know Kate Millett." Where patriarchy, and its documentary, see linear, singular, goal-oriented processes resulting in commodifiable products, Woman's Building video produces and preserves a multiple, messy vision of the development of collective experience and growth en route. As de Bretteville says in *Constructive Feminism: Reconstruction of the Woman's Building 1975*, "There are many points of view existing concurrently."

By "doing it with video" in their time and in their building, de Bretteville and many others augmented their feminist epistemology to allow for a permanent record of their theory of process. This process turns out to be a transformative practice of feminist history-making: a varied, collective point of view that reverberates across the present and into the future. By doing it with video today as I watch their compelling archive of process, I am humbled by the complexity and originality of their vision even as I realize that it takes the hard work of their daughters' voices and (re)visions—which are rife with ambivalence, judgment, admiration, boredom, and anger—to produce coherence out of contradiction. This, of course, is the work of any archivist—making stuff into stories. In *Dust: The Archive and Cultural History*, Carolyn Steedman writes in familiar terms about how the archival work of history is less about the objects we find than the *process* of making use of them:

> We have to be less concerned with History as *Stuff* (we must put to one side the content of any particular piece of historical writing, and the historical information it imparts) than as *process*, as ideation, imagining and remembering.... It is indexed, and catalogued, and some of it is not indexed and catalogued, and some of it is lost. But as stuff, it just sits there until it is read, and used, and narrativized.[48]

By visiting her theory of dust—the ephemeral traces that remain in the archive, easily lost but ever calling us to reach, touch, breath, intake, and inhabit the things made and saved for us—I can best make my feminist conclusion. The archive has taught me to name for myself the empowering legacy of a feminist epistemology and preservation of process that describes and is described by the circle. Moravec discusses in this volume how women at the building used history: "At least for a moment, the members of the Woman's Buildings past and present existed in one seamless timeline." Their video archive multiplies this impulse and weaves women of the present into their process. In her study's conclusion, Steedman writes, "Dust—the Philosophy of Dust—speaks of the opposite of waste and dispersal; of a grand circularity, of nothing ever, ever going away."[49] This grand circularity, evidenced in the Woman's Building's feminist video archive, is what I salute in all I have said and seen.

Notes

1. Long Beach Museum of Art Video Archive, Getty Research Institute. Transferred by the Long Beach Museum of Art Foundation and the City of Long Beach, 2005.

2. Nancy Buchanan, "What Do We Want? The Subject Behind the Camera: Women Video Artists and Self Articulation," in *Art/Women/California 1950–2000: Parallels and Intersections*, Diana Fuller and Daniela Salvioni, eds. (Berkeley: University of California Press, 2002), 324.

3. Amelia Jones interviewed by Fuller and Salvioni, "Burning Down the House: Feminist Art in California (an interview with Amelia Jones)," in *Art/Women/California*, 167.

4. Michelle Moravec, "In the Name of Love: Feminist Art, the Women's Movement and History," in *The Waitresses Unpeeled: Performance Art and Life*, Jerri Allyn and Anne Gauldin, eds. (Los Angeles: Spectrum Digital, 2008), 67.

5. Long Beach Museum of Art Video Archive, Getty Research Institute.

6. Ann Cvetkovich, *An Archive of Feelings: Trauma, Sexuality and Lesbian Public Cultures* (Durham: Duke University Press, 2003); and Diana Taylor, *The Archive and the Repertoire: Performing Cultural Memory in the Americas* (Durham: Duke University Press, 2003).

7. Okwui Enwezor, *Archive Fever—Uses of the Document in Contemporary Art* (New York: ICP, 2008), 12.

8. The works of feminist art, cinema history, and theory that comprise these footnotes are ample testament to the substantial and rigorous body of writing dedicated to both early feminist video and its place at the Woman's Building.

9. Ann-Sargent Wooster and JoAnn Hanley, *The First Generation: Women and Video, 1970–75* (New York: Independent Curators, Inc., 1993): 21–22.

10. Chris Hill, *Video Art and Alternative Media in the United States 1969–1980* (Chicago: Video Data Bank, SAIC, 1996), 2.

11. Christine Tamblyn, "Significant Others: Social Documentary as Personal Portraiture in Women's Video of the 1980s," in *Illuminating Video*, Doug Hall and Sally Jo Fifer, eds. (New York: Aperture, 1991): 406.

12. Deirdre Boyle, "A Brief History of American Documentary Video," *Illuminating Video*, 52.

13. JoAnne Hanley, *The First Generation: Women and Video, 1970–75* (New York: Independent Curators, 1993), 10.

14. Sharlene Nagy Hesse-Biber, Christina K. Gilmartin, and Robin Lydenberg, eds., *Feminist Approaches to Theory and Methodology* (New York: Oxford, 1999).

15. Mary Jo Aagerstoun and Elissa Auther, "Considering Feminist Activist Art," *NWSA Journal* 19.1 (2007): viii.

16. Long Beach Museum of Art Video Archive, Getty Research Institute.

17. Marlena Doktorczyk-Donohue, "The Waitresses in Context," *The Waitresses Unpeeled*, 13.

18. Suzanne Juhasz, *Naked and Fiery Forms* (New York: Octagon Books, 1977).

19. Meg Cranston, "Everything's Important: A Consideration of Feminist Video in the Woman's Building Collection," *California Video: Artists and Histories*, Glenn Phillips, ed. (Los Angeles: Getty Research Institute, 2008), 269.

20. Ilya Kabakov, "The Man Who Never Threw Anything Away, c. 1977," in *The Archive: Documents of Contemporary Art*, Charles Merewether, ed. (Cambridge: MIT Press, 2006), 33.

21. Cranston, 273.

22. Jacques Derrida, *Archive Fever: A Freudian Impression*, 4, quoted in Charles Merewether, "Introduction: Art and the Archive," *The Archive*, 13.

23. Hal Foster, "An Archival Impulse," in Merewether, *The Archive*, 146.

24. Gayatri Spivak, "The Rani of Sirmur: An Essay in Reading the Archives," in *The Archive*, 166.

25. Michel Foucault, "The Historical a priori and the Archive," in *The Archive*, 30.

26. Jennie Klein, "Bad Girls Video," *Afterimage* (1995): 2.

27. Doktorczyk-Donohue; 17.

28. John Grierson, "First Principles of Documentary," in *Grierson on Documentary*, Grierson and Forsyth Hardy, eds. (Berkeley: University of California Press, 1966), 145.

29. All three videos from the Long Beach Museum of Art Video Archive, Getty Research Institute.

30. Grierson, 145.

31. Boyle, 52.

32. Jones, 170.

33. Tom Gunning, "Before Documentary: Early Nonfiction Films and the 'View' Aesthetic," in *Uncharted Territory: Essays on Early Nonfiction Film*, Daan Hertogs and Nico de Klerk, eds. (Amsterdam: Stichting Nederlands Filmmuseum, 1997), 8, 24.

34. Ibid., 14.

35. Ibid., 14–15.

36. Long Beach Museum of Art Video Archive, Getty Research Institute.

37. Ibid.

38. Gunning, 15.

39. Long Beach Museum of Art Video Archive, Getty Research Institute.

40. Ibid.

41. Cheri Gaulke interview with Jerri Allyn, August 12, 1992, Las Cruces, New Mexico; Woman's Building Oral History Project, 44; quoted in Moravec, 7.

42. Long Beach Museum of Art Video Archive, Getty Research Institute.

43. Ibid.

44. Gunning, 17.

45. Moravec, 65.

46. Long Beach Museum of Art Video Archive, Getty Research Institute.

47. Ibid.

48. Carolyn Steedman, *Dust: The Archive and Cultural History* (New Brunswick: Rutgers University Press, 2002), 67–68. Original italics.

49. Ibid., 166.

The cast of *An Oral Herstory of Lesbianism,* **directed by Terry Wolverton**, 1979 as part of the Lesbian Art Project. Pictured L to R: Jerri Allyn, Brook Hallock, Nancy Angelo, Cheri Gaulke, Terry Wolverton, Catherine Stifter, Leslie Belt, Chutney Lu Gunderson, and Louise Moore. Not Pictured: Sue Maberry, Arlene Raven, Cheryl Swannack, and Christine Wong. Woman's Building Image Archive, Otis College of Art and Design. © Bia Lowe.

AN ORAL HERSTORY OF LESBIANISM

Storytelling, Theater and Magic for Women Only

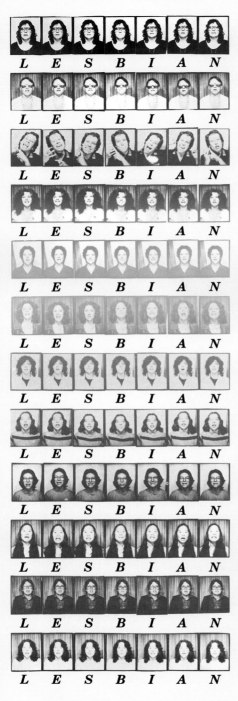

L E S B I A N
L E S B I A N
L E S B I A N
L E S B I A N
L E S B I A N
L E S B I A N
L E S B I A N
L E S B I A N
L E S B I A N
L E S B I A N
L E S B I A N
L E S B I A N

May   2, 3, 4   9, 10, 11   16, 17, 18   23, 24, 25

8:30 p.m.   (No one seated after the performance begins)

Tickets $5   Reservations Advised   Call 221-6161

The Woman's Building   1727 North Spring Street in Los Angeles

a Lesbian Art Project production   directed by Terry Wolverton

THE GHOST OF DESIRE: THE LESBIAN ART PROJECT AND THE WOMAN'S BUILDING

Jennie Klein

> Why is it so difficult to see the lesbian—even when she is there, quite
> plainly, in front of us? In part because she has been "ghosted"—or
> made to seem invisible—by culture itself. It would be putting it mildly
> to say that the lesbian represents a threat to patriarchal protocol:
> Western civilization has for centuries been haunted by a fear of
> "women without men"—of women indifferent or resistant to male
> desire. Precisely because she challenges the moral, sexual, and psy-
> chic authority of men so thoroughly, the "Amazon" has always pro-
> voked anxiety and hatred. —Terry Castle [1]

Reading Castle's book today, one cannot help but be struck at how very different things
are for lesbians now, especially in major metropolitan areas. In Los Angeles, a number
of women live openly as lesbians. And these women have not been ghosted. They have
their own television show (*The L Word*), movies (*But I'm a Cheerleader, High Art*), bars,
restaurants, and bookstores. Los Angeles has always been a mecca for creative bohemi-
ans, and there is no dearth of lesbian-identified artists with national and international
reputations, including Catherine Opie, Judie Bamber, Millie Wilson, Kaucyila Brooke,
and Angela Ellsworth. Haunting this fairly recent visibility of lesbian-identified
artists, however, are the ghosts of the first lesbian art movement in Los Angeles, a
movement that was based at the Woman's Building. In the summer of 1975, the

Woman's Building moved from the former Chouinard Art Institute on Grandview Avenue to Spring Street, in a rather barren warehouse district. As Laura Meyer has speculated, the geographical isolation of the building probably contributed to the psychic isolation of the community of women who used the Woman's Building or took classes at the Feminist Studio Workshop (the art school housed in the Woman's Building).[2] Women, particularly women who identified as lesbians, found a community of like-minded women who craved a separate sphere that was free of the mind games and inequities of patriarchal culture. During the mid to late seventies, the Woman's Building was the locus of a efflorescence of lesbian culture that included collectives, conferences, workshops, lectures, classes, exhibitions, and consciousness-raising sessions, all of which were concerned with the articulations of lesbians and the promotion of lesbian art.

The epicenter of the lesbian art movement was the Lesbian Art Project (LAP). Arlene Raven and Terry Wolverton founded the LAP in 1977, after Wolverton attended a workshop titled "Lesbian Art Worksharing" given by Raven at the Woman's Building, in which artists came together and presented their work to one another. A group of approximately six women, who called themselves the Natalie Barney Collective (NBC), committed to working on the LAP. The project's mandate included the goals of creating a lesbian pedagogical practice, promoting lesbian art and artists, and writing a lesbian history of art. The NBC disbanded after less than a year. In spite of this, Wolverton and Raven continued to run the LAP. They were astonishingly productive: integrating the LAP with the curriculum of the Feminist Studio Workshop at the Woman's Building, proposing a radical but only partially realized pedagogical model of lesbian education, creating a database of lesbian artists, and organizing two major performance events at the Woman's Building based on science fiction and lesbian identities: *FEMINA: An IntraSpace Voyage* and *An Oral Herstory of Lesbianism*. The LAP disbanded after *Oral*, with Wolverton and Raven going their separate ways without completing the book they had planned. Wolverton went on to help Tyaga, another artist associated with the Woman's Building, organize and curate "GALAS: The Great American Lesbian Art Show."[3] Raven meanwhile continued to promote feminist and lesbian art through her curatorial and pedagogical practices.

Articles and advertisements about the LAP, *FEMINA*, and *Oral* appeared in most of the major feminist and performance magazines at that time, including *Spinning Off*, *Frontiers*, *Heresies*, *High Performance*, and *The Lesbian Tide*.[4] Wolverton devoted two chapters of her autobiography, *Insurgent Muse* (2002), to the LAP, *FEMINA*, and *Oral*. Images from *Oral* have been included in important feminist exhibitions such as "Sexual Politics" (1996) and "WACK! Art and the Feminist Revolution" (2007–08). Despite the renascence of interest in seventies feminist art in the past two decades, very little has been written about this important moment in lesbian feminist art production by anyone other than Wolverton.

Promotional photographs and button from *An Oral Herstory of Lesbianism*, directed by Terry Wolverton, 1979, as part of the Lesbian Art Project. Woman's Building Image Archive, Otis College of Art and Design.

An Oral Herstory of Lesbianism was not a standalone performance. Rather, it was part of a larger project—the LAP—that tried to build a cohesive community of artists who were feminists and lesbians. In this essay, I am particularly interested in how the LAP "iterated" lesbianism in a post-Stonewall, pre-AIDS, and pre-queer theory landscape. How did Wolverton and Raven embody the terms lesbian, artist, woman, and feminist? How did they negotiate the territory between normative and non-normative? Can the failure of the LAP, which disbanded before the third year, be reconciled with the stated goals of its founding members? Does that failure invalidate the work that came before?

The questions asked in this paper have been motivated by the work of Judith Butler, who argued in *Gender Trouble* (1990) and *Bodies That Matter* (1993) that gender—and gender identity—is "performative," insofar as it consolidates the subject through reiteration. The performativity of gender is not voluntary, or even consciously acknowledged. Rather, it is what Butler has termed a "ritualized production" that "enables a subject and constitutes the temporal conditions for the subject."[5] Butler is therefore interested in how certain bodies are materialized (rendered matter) through a ritualized and repetitive iteration of language. She is also interested in how certain bodies come to matter (to society, to others) whereas other bodies do not. Questions about what makes us human—and what constitutes the human—continued to preoccupy Butler in her book *Undoing Gender* (2004). "What might it mean," Butler asks, "to learn to live in the anxiety of that challenge, to feel the surety of one's epistemological and ontological anchor go, but to be willing, in the name of the human, to allow the human to become something other than what it is traditionally assumed to be?"[6] The women involved in the LAP were willing to take this risk.

When Wolverton and Raven met at Raven's home to hash out lesbian artistic identity, aesthetics, and culture, they were breaking new ground. The idea of a lesbian identity as distinct from a gay male identity was a new and powerful concept. Following a model proposed by writers such as Adrienne Rich, Kate Millet, and Mary Daly, all of whom had presented or exhibited at the Woman's Building, women who desired other women cast off their medical identity as sexual invert for a political identity, arguing that lesbians were better feminists than their heterosexual sisters. The LAP engaged in a performative relationship with both lesbian feminism (as they understood it in the late seventies) and heterosexual norms in the art world and the feminist art community

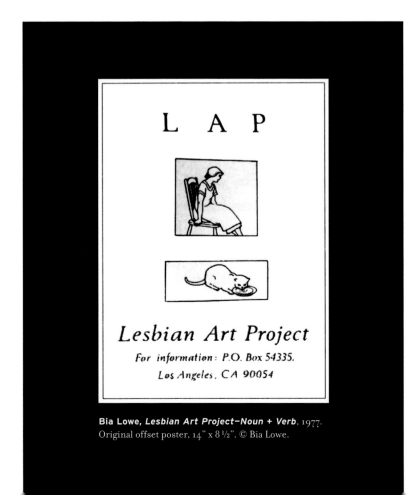

Bia Lowe, *Lesbian Art Project–Noun + Verb*, 1977.
Original offset poster, 14" x 8½". © Bia Lowe.

to which they belonged in order to assert their identities as lesbians, feminists, and, most of all, artists. In *Undoing Gender*, Butler advocated developing a critical distance from societal norms, "an ability to suspend or defer the need for them, even as there is a desire for norms that might let one live."[7] The members of the LAP critically distanced themselves from the norms of both lesbian feminism and heterosexuality through actions that simultaneously embraced and disavowed these norms. They had respect, tempered by a healthy suspicion, for pre-Stonewall lesbian stereotypes of butch and femme. They went so far as to parody and honor these norms as the NBC; and they arranged for photographer E.K. Waller to record this moment. Many of the skits in *Oral* parodied the more dogmatic tenets of lesbian feminism, such as no leather, no meat, no cigarettes, and no men—not even as friends. As an antidote to the continuing homophobia of representatives of the Christian Right, as personified by Anita Bryant, they embraced feminist spirituality. Wolverton and Raven devoted an inordinate amount of time (and ink) to analyzing their relationship with one another, and thinking about what it meant to be a lesbian, a woman, a feminist, a human, and a witch—or a goddess. In short, they tried to make lesbian feminists "normal," or even better than normal.

By the mid eighties, most if not all of this lesbian activity at the Woman's Building had ceased. The Woman's Building lesbians were still around, still making art, and in some cases working as administrators at the Building. But they were no longer an active presence in the way that they had been in the late seventies, when *Spinning Off*, the newsletter of the Woman's Building, advertised frequent lesbian events.[8] They had become, in the words of Terry Castle, "something ghostly, an impalpability, a misting over, an evaporation."[9] The lesbian presence in the Los Angeles art world would not make itself known again until 1990, the year that Pam Gregg mounted the exhibition "All But the Obvious: A Program of Lesbian Art" at Los Angeles Contemporary Exhibitions (LACE) in an industrial section of downtown. Gregg's postmodern, pro-sex, and sadomasochistic version of lesbian art, which included the work of Opie, Wilson, Brooke, Monica Majoli, and Della Grace, was very different from the work that had been presented at the Woman's Building a scant twelve years earlier. The work in "All But the Obvious" dealt explicitly with sexual identity and pleasure, as a result of the burgeoning discipline of queer theory as well as the sex-positive response on the part of the Gay Lesbian Bisexual Transgender (GLBT) community to the AIDS crisis.[10] The year 1990 signaled a new visibility for lesbian artists and visual art that was informed by lesbian concerns and issues. At the same time, this new, "in your face" lesbianism supplanted, rather than built upon, the work that had been made at the Woman's Building. No objects made by lesbian artists associated with the Woman's Building were included in the show, although Cheri Gaulke and Phranc were invited to curate a performance series for two weekends entitled "Muff 'n Stuff," which included Girls in the Nose from Texas.[11] Wolverton was commissioned to write a review of the exhibition for *High Performance*.[12] In her autobiography, Wolverton recalled her

Above: **The Natalie Barney Collective butches up, Lesbian Art Project**, 1977. Pictured L to R: Terry Wolverton, Nancy Fried, Arlene Raven, Sharon Immergluck, Maya Sterling. © E.K. Waller Photography.

Opposite: **Femme version of the Natalie Barney Collective, Lesbian Art Project**, 1977. Pictured L to R, seated: Nancy Fried, Arlene Raven; L to R, standing: Maya Sterling, Sharon Immergluck, Terry Wolverton. © E.K. Waller Photography.

disappointment when Gregg admitted to having no knowledge of either the LAP or the "Great American Lesbian Art Show," and expressed only mild interest when Wolverton approached her to talk about it. Several months later, Wolverton was asked to write an article for *The Advocate* on the new generation of lesbian artists. "During my interviews I asked them what they know of lesbian art in the seventies. I am stunned that almost none of them has any idea of their predecessors.... I felt profound discouragement at my findings—it seems all of our work has been so entirely erased."[13]

I. Lesbian Feminism and Essentialism

At the time that Wolverton approached Gregg, a new generation of feminist and queer theorists, many of them informed by postmodern theories of identity construction, were having a profound impact on the way in which lesbian identity and representation was conceptualized. I was in graduate school at the University of Southern California in 1990, and I can attest that the members of this new generation, including me, were eager to distance ourselves from a group of women that we perceived as being hopelessly mired in unproductive, separatist politics and essentialist notions about the nature of female identity. The LAP was founded during the waning years of the Lesbian Feminist Movement. At the time, it appeared as though 1970s lesbian feminism and 1990s queer theory (which included, but was not limited to, lesbian identity) had nothing in common. History has not been kind to lesbian feminists, dismissing them as a monolithic group that advocated separatism—a Lesbian Nation—and political correctness. In actuality, this characterization of lesbian feminism as an overly rigid lifestyle blueprint is not entirely fair. As Annamarie Jagose has suggested, lesbian feminism "actually describes a range of sometimes contradictory political and theoretical positions.... Some of queer's most trenchant demonstrations of how gender functions in licensing heterosexuality as normative originate in early lesbian feminist theorizing."[14]

Twenty years later, it is easier for many scholars to accept that seventies lesbian feminism was not as dogmatic as it was believed to be in the early nineties, and that it actually had much in common with postmodern feminism. In 2001, Linda Garber argued: "The pejorative tag *essentialist* has stuck to lesbian feminism despite the decades-old preoccupation of lesbian poets and critics with definitions and constructions of lesbian identity, and despite more recent postmodern understandings of the strategic deployment of provisional essentialisms. Within GLBT studies the essentialism/constructionism debate has been claimed by 'queer theory,' which tends to characterize 1970s lesbian feminism as unreflectively essentialist, when it is addressed at all. In fact, early lesbian-feminist writers were not only participants in the social construction of lesbian identity, they were actively engaged in a version of the essentialism/construction debate itself."[15] In 2008, Deirdre Heddon, who identified herself as lesbian in the introductory pages of her book on autobiographical performance, takes Garber's assertion as given. "Recognising that all identities are discursive constructions and therefore historically and culturally located does not make the various experiences that adhere to any 'identity' less real or felt. This is as true today as it was in the 1970s."[16]

The Lesbian Feminist Movement, which was born from the radical leftist politics of the 1960s, radical feminism, and the gay rights movement, was very different from queer theory and the GLBT movement, which was primarily motivated by postmodern theory and the AIDS crisis.[17] The Lesbian Feminist Movement kicked off in 1970 when the Lavender Menace preempted the scheduled proceedings of the Second Congress to Unite Women in order to raise the issue of lesbianism.[18] The Lavender Menace, which was subsequently renamed Radicalesbians, circulated an important paper entitled "The Woman Identified Woman," which conceptualized lesbianism as the most efficacious form of feminism. The positions taken in "The Woman Identified Woman" were echoed by Adrienne Rich, whose enormously influential essay "Compulsory Heterosexuality and Lesbian Existence," argued for a "lesbian continuum" between all women, even those who continued to identify as heterosexual, since the lesbian experience, like motherhood, was a profoundly female experience.[19] Rich argued against grouping lesbianism with other "sexually stigmatized existences" because it precluded an understanding of how lesbians were oppressed first as women. To be a lesbian was a way to embody and enact one's feminist politics. Fueled by New Left politics and radical feminism, seventies lesbians became "lesbian-feminists," women who often made a deliberate political choice to embrace lesbianism.

Raven, who hosted the first lesbian worksharing event, was enormously influenced by lesbian feminist theory. She was particularly indebted to the views espoused by Rich, who was a frequent contributor to *Chrysalis: A Magazine of Women's Culture.* The editorial board of *Chrysalis*, a feminist publication produced at the Woman's Building, included Raven and her then-partner Ruth Iskin. Raven decided to host the lesbian worksharing evening in order to establish a lesbian presence in the Feminist Studio Workshop (FSW). At a second worksharing in April, which took place at her home, Raven announced that she was beginning a research project on the history and meaning of lesbianism.[20] The six women—Kathleen Berg, Nancy Fried, Sharon Immergluck, Maya Sterling, Wolverton, and Raven—who formed the LAP, in 1977, ommitted themselves to putting in at least a year's worth of work on the project. They called themselves the Natalie Barney Collective after the openly lesbian, expatriate, American writer who hosted a salon in Paris in the twenties. The influence of lesbian feminist ideas on the formation of the LAP and the NBC were readily apparent. Complete egalitarianism was the rule rather than the exception. Everyone shared in the "shitwork." Drug use was tolerated. Most importantly, nobody, not even Raven, who was a faculty member while the others were students, was to take precedence over anyone else. Commitment to the LAP meant weekly meetings and paying tuition at the Feminist Studio Workshop.[21] The collective sought to develop a lesbian cultural community, engage in research and analysis, and address a larger audience. In a collective statement issued shortly after the founding of the LAP, they proposed their mission: "To promote strong and positive images of lesbian women by exploring the artistic and cultural contributions we make to civilization." In order to realize these goals, the collective met weekly to engage in consciousness-raising sessions, and they sponsored a gay/straight dialogue with FSW students, worksharing groups—which were open to all lesbians whether or not they were registered at the FSW—and salons in which writers such as Alice Bloch and Joanne Parrent shared their work. Raven, in her role as educator at the FSW, began to push the lesbian perspective in all of the classes that she taught.

II. A Lesbian Aesthetic

Is there such a thing as a lesbian aesthetic? A similar question was asked recently by Pam Meecham and Julie Sheldon, who wrote in 2005 that "as with other groupings within art made on the basis of the personal or political relations of the artist, the designation queer art begs the question: What is queer art? Is it anything painted by a man or woman who happens to be gay or lesbian or is queer art something more specific than that, in the sense of being the representation (or suggestion) of same-sex relations?"[22] The members of the LAP were equally concerned with understanding what it meant to label a work of art "lesbian." At the onset of the LAP and the formation of the NBC, Raven and Iskin published "Through the Peephole: Lesbian Sensibility in Art" in *Chrysalis* (1977). Both Raven and Iskin had long been interested in the idea of defining a woman's or feminist sensibility (the distinction between the two was not entirely clear) in art-making practices. At the time that they published the article, feminist artists and art historians had been interested in looking at abstract art made by women artists to articulate an aesthetic that was uniquely female. One of the Woman's Building's founders—Judy Chicago—was a leading proponent of this idea. Chicago argued in her autobiography that women's abstract art was characterized by "central core" imagery, which she likened to female genitalia. Meanwhile, in an article written for the first issue of *Heresies,* Harmony Hammond attempted to articulate a feminist aesthetic for abstract painting.[23] For the lesbian issue of *Heresies* (1977), the editorial collective (which included Hammond) invited artists to answer the question "What Does Being a Lesbian Artist Mean to You?" Many of the artists, among them Jane Stedman, Monica Sjöö, and Debbie Jones, tried to find indications of a lesbian sensibility or sexuality in their artwork, whether it was functional (Stedman), figurative, or abstract (Jones). For Hammond, as for most of the artists who contributed to *Heresies*, lesbian sensibility was to be found in the aesthetic and tactile qualities of the object itself. Influenced by the writings of Monique Wittig, Hammond sought in her own art-making practice to "work on the edge between abstract form and political content."[24]

For Raven and Iskin, the lesbian aesthetic had less to do with the medium or appearance of the work than it did with the work's message. Tantamount to good lesbian art was that it somehow conveys a "positive woman-identified sensibility."[25] The work chosen by Raven and Iskin to illustrate "Through the Peephole" included work by Dara Robinson and Jerri Allyn that depicted lesbian relationships, Nancy Fried's bread sculptures of naked lesbians hanging out at home, and Candace Compton and Nancy Angelo's video *Nun and Deviant* (1976). When Raven and Iskin wrote "Through the Peephole," the ability to live and work as a lesbian was scarcely imaginable. The artwork that they advocated celebrated lesbian sameness rather than difference—lesbians suffered from unrequited love, misunderstandings, and longed for the stable home life imagined in Fried's bread dough sculptures. Jenni Sorkin has characterized this work as "ethical lesbianism—women advocating for social change, creating activist works and championing social causes through the visual and performing arts."[26] This concept of ethical lesbianism informed the work of the LAP. Ethical interaction is based upon a moral relationship between at least two conscious beings; therefore, the term "ethical" implies the presence of more than one person. It is not surprising, then, that the idea of community was so central to the NBC and the LAP.

Margo Hobbs Thompson has demonstrated that the idea of a shared lesbian sensibility seemed self-evident in the seventies. However, as Thompson has argued, "Attempts to unpack the tautology by defining that essence were frustrated by vagueness, the result of trying to account for the diversity of individual lesbian experiences and perspectives, and by reluctance to allow lesbian experience to be reduced to sexual preferences and activities."[27] Many years later, Hammond, in writing about her experience organizing "A Lesbian Art Show" (1978), concluded that no single "lesbian sensibility" characterized art made by women identified as lesbians. What emerged instead was a sense of community.[28] Significantly, Raven and Iskin were concerned with creating "a new space of freedom of thought, fantasy, and scale which allows for the creation of a lesbian art dealing with lesbianism as everything that is possible."[29] The idea was that certain qualities—reciprocity, mutuality, and equality—would emerge in art by lesbians once they became part of a lesbian community, which they defined along the lines of Rich's lesbian continuum. According to Iskin, "The muse that inspires one's work is one's *milieu*, one's support community, and for women artists it is the community of women at its broadest, and specifically the community of feminist women in the arts and various work-oriented feminist groups."[30] As Raven suggested, "Work produced in a feminist/lesbian community has the possibility of acknowledging the radical transformation of self through revolutionary social practice."[31] For Iskin and Raven, the new lesbian sensibility was both specific to the lesbian community and able to serve as a metaphor for the human condition.[32]

III. Constructing the LAP Community

At the time that they penned their article, Iskin and Raven lacked the community that they desired, hence Raven's attempt to create this community within the already sheltering walls of the Woman's Building. The idea of community—based on a collective and shared identity—was and is a powerful fantasy for many, particularly those who are disenfranchised. "From the earliest days of contemporary lesbian-feminism," Bonnie Zimmerman has written, "the notion of a unique lesbian space—sometimes actual, sometimes mythic or spiritual—has guided our visions and politics."[33] From the get-go, lesbian-identified women had been involved in the feminist art movement in Southern California. Lesbians were enrolled in the Feminist Art Program at Cal State Fresno and CalArts; lesbian students and teachers participated in the FSW at the Woman's Building; and established lesbian artists showed their work at the Woman's Building galleries. In Los Angeles, the idea of creating a lesbian community that was separate from the gay male community had been around since the early seventies, when the Westside Women's Center was founded in Venice.[34] A few years later, in 1976, the Woman's Building hosted its first lesbian conference; it was called la la la, which inspired the title of a song by Phranc. Very little documentation remains of this event, other than some video footage that is currently housed in the Getty archives.[35] The narrative of the video includes an explanation of the conference title, which turns out to be a double acronym that no one can remember: Los Angeles Leads the Advancement of Lesbians in the Arts, or Lesbians Are Living and Loving Amazons. From the ten minutes of footage, it is difficult to glean much of anything that happened at the first lesbian art conference. Iskin apparently gave a slide lecture presentation, and la la la t-shirts were made. The video documents some sort of workshop. In the first five minutes, Sheila Ruth, wearing a la la la t-shirt, asks two women to talk about the photography exhibition. During the second part of the video, Shirl Buss asks two unidentified women how they came out to their parents, ex-boyfriend, and best friend. What is apparent is that these women, one of whom mentions that she is not from Los Angeles, are at the conference in search of some kind of communal experience. The *la la la workshop* video is a documentation of this community building. As Alexandra Juhasz writes in this volume, "At once entirely about and for its own moment and community, feminist method and theory are at play in the consideration and construction of the multiplicity of time, space, and self that extends this one tape beyond video's cherished function as a playback machine that easily records and represents process."[36]

la la la provided a fleeting community that lasted for five days—the length of the conference. The women who signed on to the LAP were in search of a more permanent community, one in which they could interact day in and day out. For these women, community promised (but did not always deliver) a base for political mobilization, a model for behavior, insulation from homophobia and rejection, and a focus on art production and education that was specifically lesbian. In the late seventies, the categories of artist and lesbian feminist seemed mutually exclusive. The lack of community was mentioned repeatedly by the artists (almost all of whom were based on the East Coast) who contributed to a special issue of *Heresies* devoted to lesbian art and artists. Lesbian artists based in Los Angeles suffered from the same longing for community as the

Heresies collective artists, until Raven decided to challenge the masculinist and hetero-sexist bias of art history. All at once, a community existed. As Immergluck put it, "Suddenly, I had the opportunity to help create the State of Israel for lesbians. There wasn't any need to hide anymore: not *in* the culture or *outside* of the culture as a sub-culture."[37]

Communities based on a common identity such as lesbianism—even those such as the LAP/NBC that had members who had more or less similar backgrounds and interests—are difficult to maintain. The premise of a lesbian art community was prob-lematic because it assumed that all of its constituents were fundamentally the same, thus making it difficult for members of the community to have multiple identities and different allegiances. Almost from its inception, the NBC began to unravel, in part because the members were already linked together through a network of social and erotic alliances that shifted in the nine short months that the collective was in exis-tence, challenging the shared values and goals that were supposedly embraced by the community. Raven ended her relationship with Iskin at the same time that Wolverton ended her relationship with Cheryl Swannack, Raven's former lover. Raven resumed her earlier relationship with Swannack, creating a great deal of tension between Raven and Wolverton. Sterling and Fried, who were lovers at the beginning of 1977, ended their relationship as well. The desire for sameness and commonality also hampered the ability of the members of the NBC to listen to each other. Wolverton noted, "Our under-standing of 'collectivity' meant that we should all be the same, or equal; this assump-tion did not acknowledge our unequal experience, resources, ability and motivation."[38]

Nikki Sullivan has argued that community cannot actually exist except insofar as it actually does the opposite of what it sets out to do: "destabilizes the logic of identity in and through the invocation of multiplicity, heterogeneity, or *différance*."[39] The NBC sought to stabilize difference. The LAP, responding to the mistakes made with the NBC, began to destabilize difference. By the nineties, militant lesbian feminists who advo-cated separatism, community, vanilla sex or no sex, and feminist politics had become something of joke—caricatured as rigid and dogmatic in lesbian-themed movies such as *Go Fish* (1994, directed by Rose Troche) or *Better than Chocolate* (1999, directed by Anne Wheeler). The women involved with the NBC attempted to create a community based on their similarities. The community dissolved not so much due to their differ-ences—they really were not all that different—as it did due to their different desires. Sexual politics, even in a like-minded lesbian feminist art community, were messy and problematic. The bonds between these women ran the gamut of acquaintances to friends, sisters, and lovers. This bonding seemed to happen in spite of—or even because of—the restrictions placed on lesbian behavior by the members of the commu-nity. What came out of all of this was that the politics of desire often acted in contradic-tion to the politics of lesbian feminism. In trying to consciously perform the latter, the NBC demonstrated how the performance of gender and difference often works to undermine prescribed modes of behavior and identity formation. The collective performed lesbianism, but not in the way that they had foreseen.

Undaunted by the demise of the NBC, Wolverton and Raven remained committed to the LAP and to their notion of a Lesbian Art Community, flawed though it might be. This time around, they were careful to eschew the homogeneity that they felt had led to its failure. They also put in place a more prescriptive approach to interpersonal relationships, especially between one another, in an attempt to head off the problems that had plagued the NBC. They drew up and signed a contract, in which they agreed to meet once a week through May, use consciousness-raising to handle personal difficulties, and put in equal amounts of work on the projects sponsored by the LAP, including a projected publication during the third year of its existence. More importantly, Raven and Wolverton spent an inordinate amount of time analyzing their personal relationship as it pertained to a lesbian sensibility. One of the obstacles that confronted the two women was the difference in their respective backgrounds. Raven was a teacher at the FSW and had a PhD in art history; Wolverton, who was ten years younger, was still a student who had deliberately kept herself removed from the "patriarchal rat race." The two women redefined a traditional mentoring relationship into one that involved mentoring and "peership" on the part of both women, in spite of Raven's greater experience and education.[40] "A lesbian relationship," according to Wolverton, "must involve a process of mutual mentoring, the experience of learning from one another, and an acknowledgment of those things we exchange."[41] They agreed to acknowledge their attraction for one another while not acting on that attraction. This time, they sought a model of behavior that they believed was so universal and timeless that it could not fail—a model based upon the belief that there was a close relationship between women and nature, and that women could lead a more fulfilled life if only that relationship was acknowledged. The mutual attraction that they felt for one another was subsumed into a narrative about Goddess feminism in which present behavior was influenced by atavistic identities that had existed in prehistory. They developed a mentoring relationship that was part mother/daughter, part teacher/student, and part crone/maiden.

IV. Cultural Feminism and the LAP

At the time that Wolverton and Raven met to hash out a new version of the LAP, cultural feminism was in its ascendancy. Cultural feminism, which advocated that women build a separate culture that was uncontaminated by the patriarchy, was strongest on the West Coast, where not coincidentally the Woman's Building was located. The cultural feminist idea of building a separate educational and cultural facility for women was the premise of both the FSW and the Woman's Building. Probably the most attractive aspect of cultural feminism for Raven and Wolverton was the invocation of the Goddess and recourse to feminist spirituality. Goddess feminism, with its emphasis on the immanence of the Goddess in women's bodies and a holistic approach to nature, politics, and spirituality, was very appealing to West Coast feminists in the late seventies. It held particular appeal to lesbian feminists, who identified with the witch as a potent symbol of women's power. As Lillian Faderman has pointed out, "Lesbian-feminist spirituality was to resurrect the matriarchy, which would eliminate all of the destructive institutions of patriarchy—economic, political, sexual, educational—and return society to the maternal principle in which life is nurtured."[42] A matriarchy, by definition, needed a goddess rather than a god—hence, the interest in the Goddess and feminist spirituality.

Goddess feminism, as Kathryn Rountree has argued, has been a "thorny issue" for feminists within the academy, who are suspicious of supposedly essentialist ideas that "valorize fertility, nurturance and other 'maternal' qualities as 'natural,' universal and static feminine traits."[43] Although not unsympathetic to this project, Diana Fuss has argued, "What is missing in many of these treatises on lesbian identity is recognition of the precarious status of identity and a full awareness of the complicated processes of identity formation, both psychical and social."[44] Fuss's contention certainly has validity. However, what I am arguing here, vis-à-vis Butler, is that these treatises should not be read as *lacking* an awareness of the complicated process of identity formation. Rather, they should be viewed as attempts to construct identity through a complicated negotiation of what it meant to live and work as a lesbian artist in the seventies. In the case of the LAP, Goddess feminism was used to challenge and deconstruct traditional identities informed by patriarchal values. Wolverton and Raven hoped to provide an active model for lesbian relationships, a model in which the debased patriarchal form of the identities that characterized their relationship was transformed through recourse to the Goddess.

Laura Cottingham has observed, "Political and artistic feminist organizations were too often patterned on family structures even though, ironically, the home and the family were precisely what most seventies feminists sought to escape."[45] In retrospect, Wolverton and Raven realized that the "family" model used for the NBC had not worked. They sought a different model for their relationship, one not grounded in the patriarchy. They identified four aspects of their relationship that they felt could serve as templates for other lesbians: the Mentor/Peer, the Mother/Daughter, the Lovers, and the Triple Goddess (Nymph, Maiden, and Crone). The Mother/Daughter relationship was a blood bonding, a "psychic and biological union" that would ideally manifest in simultaneous menstrual cycles.[46] The Lovers relationship was similarly mythic, a fertile sexual relationship that resulted in the LAP, "the child of our union."[47] Goddesses were also seen as destroyers (Kali) and transformers (Demeter and Persephone). From destruction comes creation; the idea was much more appealing than that of nurturing. The aspect of the triple Goddess allowed them to see the connection of art and magic, both activities that involved "witches," which they viewed as the patriarchal term for lesbians.[48]

Coming to Lesbian Consciousness. 1979. Performance from *An Oral Herstory of Lesbianism*, directed by Terry Wolverton, part of the Lesbian Art Project. Woman's Building Image Archive. Otis College of Art and Design.

Probably the most innovative idea of the LAP was never fully implemented: the attempt to develop a pedagogical model for educating lesbian students. The LAP dubbed this approach "Sapphic" education, after the ancient Greek poetess Sappho, who had created an educational tradition for women 2400 years previously on the island of Mytilene (Lesbos) in Greece. Sapphic education was nonhierarchical, (w)holistic, and heavily indebted to "mythic and symbolic connections." It was not beholden to a traditional family model. The LAP identified "six roles or functions needed to fulfill the work of a lesbian educational community, ...a system in which all functions are interchangeable."[49] Three of the functions—the Lover, the Mother, and the Mentor—were derived from Raven's and Wolverton's exploration of lesbian identities. The other three—the Visionary, the Organizer, and the Artist—suggested the sort of exploration and creativity that the Sapphic model of education was conceived to encourage. The Sapphic model was also designed to sync with the "natural" rhythms of women's bodies, which was an idea that came from a Woman's Building artist in residence, Jere Van Syoc, who believed that women's bodies were connected to the cycles of the earth. Once that connection was acknowledged, it would be easier for women to learn. Each season had a particular theme and therefore different methods of learning. Autumn was "a time for gathering, self-discovery and exploration of [the lesbian] community." Autumn was therefore the time when most of the classes and workshops were held. Winter was "a time for study and contemplation," and involved making preparations for various projects that would appear in the spring, which was the time for blossoming and new growth. Summer was time off, a season for travel and making connections.[50]

One could argue that Wolverton and Raven oversimplified lesbian identities in their attempt to articulate a politics of identity that was not patriarchal and to construct a community based on shared goals, if not same desires. However, it would be inaccurate to suggest that they were attempting to erase differences and inconsistencies by turning to Goddess feminism as their model. It was precisely because they felt that the members of the earlier NBC were insensitive to each other's differences that they constructed a relationship that relied on feminist spirituality, rather than a familial model based on patriarchal principles, to enhance their sensitivity toward difference. They believed that their spirituality made it possible for them to acknowledge both their own individual identities and the individual identities of other lesbians. It also allowed them to acknowledge their sexuality—and sexual attraction for one another—without having to act on it. Feminist spirituality, with its emphasis on powerful women, elevated the status of the lesbian feminist—the ultimate woman-identified woman. At the same time, it reinforced the humanity—or humanness—of lesbians by emphasizing their commonality with other women of every race, ethnicity, class, and ability. Raven and Wolverton used feminist spirituality performatively rather than prescriptively; it was a way of being and thinking rather than an ideological system that precluded other possible identities.

V. Performing Lesbianism: *FEMINA: An IntraSpace Voyage* and *An Oral Herstory of Lesbianism*

The LAP sponsored two performance/theater pieces: *FEMINA: An IntraSpace Voyage* (1978) and *An Oral Herstory of Lesbianism* (1979). Created by Wolverton and Ann Shannon, *FEMINA* was based on an unpublished short story by Wolverton entitled "A Clear But Distant Memory." Conceived around the time that the first *Star Wars* was released, *FEMINA* was designed to be a low-tech, low-budget feminist antidote to the expensive, high-tech, and incredibly patriarchal science fiction narratives that were in theaters at the time. *FEMINA* told the story of a group of lesbians who fled a world corrupted by patriarchy in plastic pods, which they transported telepathically. The performance ended with them arriving on the planet Femina and telepathically birthing a female child for whom they had formed a nest. Unlike *Oral*, which was well documented, almost no photographs of *FEMINA* exist today. Judging from the script and the published reviews of the piece, however, it was fairly over the top in its presentation of lesbian science fiction. The women greeted each other with the word "OVO," which symbolized "of or from the ovaries" and came from a concept developed by Shannon that she termed "ovular thinking." The women also took on new names on the planet Femina such as Annchantment (Shannon), and D'Light (Wolverton). They were guided to the planet Femina by Dos Estrellas Sobre El Horizonte (Jade Satterthwaite), a messenger from the gynarchy who was "called by the sound of OVO."[51] "And so," Dos Estrellas intoned, "the daughters of the light riders are born into the Universe. Ovo! You can find them in your dreams."[52]

Wolverton viewed *FEMINA* as a metaphor for the LAP, which similarly transformed patriarchal institutions into their previous and prehistoric lesbian incarnations. When she and Shannon began work on the performance, Wolverton was anxious to put into practice some of the ideas that she and Raven had worked out about lesbian relationships. She therefore had the participants sign a contract (she signed a contract as well) agreeing to put in a certain amount of time and effort into the production, and commit to doing consciousness-raising and improvisational work. The eight women who collaborated on the performance—Wolverton, Shannon, Norma Fragoso, Chutney Lu Gunderson, Pam McDonald (Trucki Parts), Anna Hearn, Jade Satterthwaite, and Dyana Silberstein—did make some changes in *FEMINA* that deviated from the original story. More emphasis was placed on the departure, which had only been alluded to before. Although *FEMINA* was a science fiction piece, it was not "about hardware," according to Wolverton. "In all the recent futuristic art pieces—films like *2001, Star Wars, Close Encounters*—the vision has been to build an enormous piece of technological hardware and blast off. Working on *FEMINA*, we have learned that the Universe is not separate from ourselves [sic], our own bodies."[53]

FEMINA's mixture of Goddess spirituality, Armageddon predictions, and futuristic technology could be viewed as an early example of lesbian feminist camp.

ORAL: OLD STORY

Nancy enters in darkness, carrying cot, which she places downstage center. A spot finds her lying on the cot, her arms folded under her body which is tense and jittery. This is a posture of paralysis.

(Turns head) I'm coming *(Faces audience)* I'm not going in there. I'm *not!* I refuse. We've been planning her visit for over a year now. She was always so eager to come to see me. We used to be inseparable. Now she's here and she's brought *him* with her. *(Turns head)* Just a minute! *(Faces audience)* Since she's been here, we've made three times to be together, just her and me. Just the two of us. The first time, we were going to go have coffee — but then she had to take Bill to the dentist. Then, we were going to the movies, but then she just had to give Bill a ride to the beach to see his friends. And the third time, we were going to have dinner, but Bill felt left out, so we had to sit around and talk about how fascinating it must be to live *his* life, and do *his* job. *(Turns head, shouts angrily)* Wait a minute! *(Faces audience)* I could give a fuck about teaching gifted children how to read. I HATE HIM! *(Buries head, shaking with rage. Her body tenses, holding, then goes limp. She turns head, slightly, with resignation.)* Coming.

WRITTEN BY NANCY ANGELO

"SEX IS THE ISSUE, YOU KNOW...." This photo graced the program handed out to audiences for An Oral Herstory of Lesbianism.

ORAL: JANE

My lesbianism has to do with pushing past limits in my life, and also with acknowledging women who I love and who have taught me a lot. One woman in particular I have learned from is my therapist. Her name is Jane, and this piece is dedicated to her.

It's her hair, I think. I always notice it. How it's two colors — the same intensity — but two distinctly different colors, all there together. One of the colors is gray.

Sometimes I am invisible, but she sees me. Her presence surrounds me. It is necessary that she be here. That is what I need from her. I need her to exist. Really, nothing more.

I learned to love myself in the presence of a woman. I looked in a mirror; she looked on. I learned to stop the endless monologue in my head. It had droned on, telling me I was bad. She taught me her secret. I get the credit. It's perfect.

She is my mother. Though she did not carry my body in hers, she has given my body to me like a gift. It contains surprises. She tells me I am perfect just the way I am. She believes it too. She is on my side. She tells me to do what I want. She encourages my rebirth. There is air. I am not smothered. I can be visible and still breathe. And when I forget, she is there again to remind me.

WRITTEN BY SUE MABERRY

22

ORAL: ICE QUEEN

(Brook enters) I'm a wife, a mother. The world smiles at my baby, my better home, and garden. I wear dresses, pantyhose, Max Factor, White Shoulders, good diamonds and a strand of real pearls. I shop a lot. My credit's good, so I open charge accounts. My existence is valid. I have a husband. My husband calls me The Ice Queen, and every time he touches me, I freeze. Each night I inch to the edge of our bed. I go to the living room, I read male poets. I write angry poetry. My husband yells at me.

Please, come back to bed!

I go. My husband tells me ....

You think more of your girlfriends than you do of me! You're married to poetry! You can't even cook!

He says ....

It turns me on to see other men look at you.

My husband buys books on "How To Be a Better Lover." In ten years they fill our bedroom closet. My husband calls me The Ice Queen, and every time he touches me I freeze. I talk to my best friend as she takes a bath. I watch droplets hang on her breasts like jewels. I tell her I want a divorce.

Why? He's good to you, a good father. He makes a good living. He doesn't drink, beat you, or run around with other women. Why? Why a divorce?

Afternoons I masturbate, thinking of her. Thinking of untouchable jewels. I hate myself, my bitterness, this nameless desire for women. I grow thirty-two gall stones. The surgeon tells me that I almost died. The scar is horrible. He tells me my tension is killing me; wherever it comes from, I had better change it, get rid of it. I get a divorce.

WRITTEN BY BROOK HALLOR

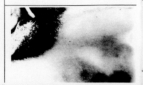

ORAL: FEMME

"Hey, look — I'm not kidding! Dykes on TV!" *Leslie turns a TV set around to face audience. On the set, there appears each woman in the cast, dressed up in extreme butch or femme drag. One by one they appear on the screen, while women watching comment on their "tough" or "sweet" appearances. Finally Chutney says, scornfully* "Look at that femme!" *Ali cast freezes except Chris, who moves downstage and says:*

Femme? *(Incredulous)* Femme? Oh no, here it comes again. That old "butch/femme" question that supposedly went out twenty years ago. But I bet you've decided which side I'm on, right? I'm wearing a skirt. And, I'm not an auto mechanic. Not only that, I don't fix my own plumbing, I don't chop wood, and I Hate Sports!

Now, I could have learned about these things, but I didn't want to. I like my long hair, my bright clothing, and music and art. But since this society has twisted these things into being symbols of submission to men — O.K. I know you've heard it all before ... but in fact, one of my femminist friends said to me, "You're a separatist? You don't look like one." And a lover, a lover, once told me, "When the revolution comes, you'll be only fit to entertain the troops."

At this point, lights change and the beat for the Butch/Femme Conga Line is heard. Chris freezes, while all cast begins to move to the beat, forming a conga line. One by one they move forward, to the beat, downstage to the audience.

WRITTEN BY TERRY WOLVERTON; DEVELOPED BY CHRISTINE WONG, BROOK HALLOR, ARLENE RAVEN AND CHERYL SWANNACK.

BROOK
I'm butch, cause I have short, clean finger nails.

CHUTNEY
I'm femme, because I drink diet sodas.

CATHERINE
I'm butch, cause I always make a score.

NANCY
I'm femme, because I can't make up my mind.

LOUISE
I'm butch, because I spit in public.

JERRI
I'm femme, because I made all the costumes.

ARLENE
I'm butch, because I have a bed in the back of my van.

CHERYL
I'm femme, because I'm good in the kitchen ... and in the bedroom.

CHERI
I'm butch, because I pick the restaurant, and even though I wear make-up, they always bring me the check.

SUE
I'm femme, because I blush.

LESLIE
I'm butch, because I know how to treat a lady.

The beat fades away, and all cast resume their freeze. Spot comes back up on Chris, who is flabbergasted by what she has just witnessed.

CHRIS
If the Women's Movement is supposed to be about honoring women, and the lesbian movement is supposed to be about loving women, why is it that the more "femme" you are, the more shit you get?

DEVELOPED BY CAST FROM AN IDEA BY CHERYL SWANNACK

23

ORAL: HAIR STORY

Cheri enters in darkness with a stool and faces the rear of the stage. Unseen, Nancy begins reading Cheri's words. Cheri sits on stool, lit in silhouette, her arms around herself. We see her hands caressing her back sensuously.

Travelling across country with my parents to see the Woman's Building, the summer before I was to attend the Feminist Studio Workshop. It was becoming apparent to me that I was a lesbian. I masturbated in the back of our camper van all the way to L.A. Making love to myself. Imagining making love to another woman. I had worn my hair in a crew cut for the last year, feeling more and more conspicuous and out of place in my school. *(Cheri slowly begins to turn to face the audience)* I walked into the Woman's Building: tan, braless, with short-cropped hair. *(Cheri covers her eyes with her fingers)* I knew they were lesbians. They were the first real lesbians I had ever seen. *(Cheri uncovers her eyes)* I looked exactly like them. I went back to Minneapolis to finish out my summer before moving to L.A. I moved in with a man for the first time in my life. I grew my hair. *(Cheri begins primping, applying make-up, fluffing her hair.)* I dyed it red. I had it curled. Still, I wasn't straight.

WRITTEN BY CHERI GAULKE

Tee A. Corinne, *Sex Is the Issue, You Know….*, 1979.
Pages 22–23, in *High Performance* 2. 4. (1979–80), about the performance *An Oral Herstory of Lesbianism* (directed by Terry Wolverton, 1979). University of Oregon, Tee A. Corinne Papers, Coll. 263. © *High Performance* Magazine, 1979.

145

Christine Wong, *Yellow Queer*, 1979. Performance from *An Oral Herstory of Lesbianism*, directed by Terry Wolverton, part of the Lesbian Art Project. © Bia Lowe.

Feminist camp, as Pamela Robertson has pointed out in her study of the genre, is often considered to be an oxymoron, as women are the objects—rather than the subjects—of traditional camp. Taking as her point of departure Mary Ann Doane's notion of the female masquerade, Robertson suggests that feminist camp is not recognized as such because it utilizes masquerade rather than drag. Arguing that feminist camp can be seen "as a kind of parodic play between subject and object in which the female spectator laughs at and plays with her own image," Robertson suggests that feminist camp has utopian aspects as a political tool for change.[54] The actresses who participated in *FEMINA* probably lacked the irony and distance necessary for a truly parodic performance—according to Wolverton, one woman tried to withdraw because she had enrolled in fall classes and wouldn't be able to go to the planet Femina after all.[55] Intentional or not, however, there was a bizarrely campy element to this play, with the actresses taking on the names of drag queens and the decidedly utopian projections about the possibility of reproduction without men (which was oddly prescient of a future in which lesbian women would be able to get pregnant without men). The lesbian actresses in *FEMINA* were not so much in drag as they were masquerading as natural women, women whose ultra-femininity was clearly a parody of stereotypical "feminine" qualities such as nurturing and empathy. In taking the connection between women, their bodies, and nature over the top, Shannon and Wolverton hinted at the constructed nature of *all* female identities and suggested that lesbians were neither more nor less "natural" than heterosexual women.

Raven and Wolverton had another opportunity to implement the Sapphic model of education while working on *An Oral Herstory of Lesbianism*, a theater project that premiered at the Woman's Building in the spring of 1979. The thirteen participants were Allyn, Angelo, Leslie Belt, Gaulke, Gunderson, Brook Hallock, Sue Maberry, Louise Moore, Raven, Catherine Stifter, Swannack, Wolverton, and Christine Wong. They prepared for *Oral* by meeting for a series of workshops, improvisational exercises, and theater events. During these carefully constructed events, they engaged in consciousness-raising, improvisational acting, guided fantasy meditations, and sound and movement games. The material for the performance was derived from these exercises. In keeping with the stated aims and goals of the Sapphic model of education, all of the participants had an equal voice, and the performance reflected the visions of many women. Wolverton stated, "We want to present *an* oral herstory, not *the* oral herstory of lesbians. We're not trying to say we can speak for everyone."[56] The performance thus reflected a winter of study, contemplation, and preparation. *Oral* was performed at the Woman's Building twelve times in May of 1979, for women-only audiences. As the audience arrived, they were directed to the second floor, where a ticket booth was set up and the "athletic girls"—a common trope in lesbian culture—performed in a roped-off area to the beat of disco music.[57] The audience was then directed to the third floor, where a "big pink tent, glowing from the inside" demarcated the stage upon which *Oral* was performed.[58]

Oral dealt primarily with the lived realities of being a lesbian in the seventies. It opened with a group of "athletic girls" cavorting about the space. Several scenes that followed dealt with butch/femme identity. For example, Wong lamented the fact that femmes were given such short shrift in the lesbian community. *Oral* incorporated many of the women's actual experiences of (be)coming out in a society that by and large viewed their identity as stigmatized and abject. Maberry described a high school crush. Gaulke talked about how her crew-cut hair signified her queerness before she even knew she was gay. Hallock related the story of her loveless marriage—and the desire that she had for her attractive neighbor. In *Jump Rope/Incest*, Belt talked about being molested by her grandfather. *Oral* also took on political correctness. In a mock birth scene, a fledging lesbian (Belt) emerged in the lesbian feminist world determined not to give up her best male friend, red meat, and cigarettes, in spite of warnings to the contrary. While the performers in *Oral* were willing to poke fun at lesbian feminist stereotypes, such as lesbian bed death or butch/femme stereotypes, they were less willing to take on the thorny issue of sexuality. In fact, *Oral* took a relatively chaste attitude towards sexuality (one performance was called *Stalking the Wild Orgasm*).[59] At the same time, a cover of *High Performance* magazine generated concern in the lesbian feminist community because the picture of two women kissing was tilted so that one appeared to be more dominant than the other, and thus replicated heterosexual modes of dominance.

VI. Difference

Oral concluded on a positive note with Raven reciting an abbreviated version of a longer poem that she had written:

> Our bonding
> creates light and heat
> (sparking, Mary Daly names, the fires of female friendship)
> And comfort. and nourishment.
> And danger. that the body/spirit of woman
> touching woman
> is a danger to death and killing
> endangering us in the death grip
> of the male bond.
> THE FUTURE IS FEMALE.[60]

Raven implied with this poem that lesbian bonding was a means by which socioeconomic, ethnic, and racial differences could be transcended. The female future that Raven predicted was one that included ALL women, even lesbians. Indeed, Raven and Wolverton wanted desperately to reach out to those lesbians who did not share their background—women of color, older women, working class women. They had little success, as is evidenced by the cast of *Oral*, which included only one non-Caucasian woman—Wong. Forced to represent *all* lesbians of color, Wong gamely performed "Yellow Queer" in *Oral*, running through the litany of problems that she faced when she wasn't quite white enough or straight enough. In an attempt to address the racial inequity of *Oral*, Wolverton chose Wong, and not Raven, as her co-author when asked to write an article about the LAP and *Oral* for the feminist publication *Frontiers*.[61] From its inception, *Frontiers* had devoted articles and issues to the cultural production of various groups of disenfranchised women, including Latinas, Native Americans, and African Americans. Wolverton would have run the risk of appearing exclusionary had she selected one of the other women who participated in *Oral*. In spite of the intentions of Wolverton and all of the women who worked on the project, *Oral* remained a product of white, middle-class, lesbian identity, rather than the truly diverse expression for which Wolverton had hoped. The LAP's inability to deal with race and class in any meaningful way was not a unique event in the history of lesbian feminism. As Faderman has demonstrated in *Odd Girls and Twilight Lovers*, racial and ethnic minority lesbians were justifiably suspicious of the white lesbian sisterhood, which seemed incapable of acknowledging the very different conditions experienced by lesbians who were working class and racial minorities.[62]

Ironically, given that Raven and Wolverton had tried so hard to provide a performance blueprint for lesbian relationships within the LAP community, it was unforeseen relationship politics that resulted in the end of the LAP. Wolverton's relationship with Swannack, which was never very good, deteriorated during the course of rehearsals for *Oral*. This in turn caused a rift between Wolverton and Raven. The following year, instead of working together on a book about the LAP as they had planned to do originally, Raven curated an exhibition of lesbian art for one gallery in the Woman's Building while Wolverton worked on the Great American Lesbian Art Show (GALAS) for another gallery in the Woman's Building. In spite of its success, *Oral* was the grand finale of the LAP, which more or less dissolved upon the conclusion of the performance.

VII. Changing the World

In an interview conducted with Wolverton, Raven recalled, "We truly thought we were changing the world in 1970, and I think that I have learned a great deal about what it takes to change the world and what kind of power you have to have, at what level you have to be."[63] With same sex marriage legalized (at least briefly) in California; openly gay sports stars, politicians, and actors; and an Oscar winning movie about gay cowboys, it is hard to remember just how marginalized the women involved with the LAP actually were. In the seventies, mainstream society—particularly in the Midwest and South—was only beginning to acknowledge that gay men and women existed and were deserving of civil rights. Openly gay women—even those whose educational and class privilege gave them a huge advantage otherwise—risked discrimination and outright persecution. One member of the NBC, emboldened by her newfound community, bravely wrote a coming-out letter to her family, only to be rejected by them. Swannack and Marguerite Elliot were harassed and beaten by the LAPD one night when closing the Woman's Building, most likely because they looked like "dykes": that is, wore unisex clothes, didn't shave their legs or armpits, and had very short hair. When Wolverton and Bia Lowe stapled a poster to a telephone pole advertising the "Family of Women" dance, they quickly photographed it and then pulled it down, afraid of the persecution and harassment they would experience were they to leave it up in a public place.[64] They contented themselves instead with making a poster of the photograph of the poster. This poster within a poster was displayed only within the safe confines of the Woman's Building, as an imaginary construction of utopia rather than a sign of the real. In the late seventies, proclaiming one's lesbianism in public took courage.

It is little wonder that the history of lesbian art at the Woman's Building is not a heroic history, but rather one that is full of ghosts. It is a history that does not appear in glossy catalogs or books (other than *Insurgent Muse*). It haunts contemporary exhibitions as an absence rather than a presence. For example, a flickering, slightly puce colored slide show of *Oral*, assembled by Jenni Sorkin, was part of *High Performance: The First 5 Years* (LACE, 2003, curated by Jenni Sorkin) and *WACK!* (Museum of Contemporary Art, Los Angeles, 2007, curated by Connie Butler). It is a history—or herstory—pieced together from anecdotes, various personal archives, half-forgotten recollections, and a lot of gossip. It is not a dramatic history—no one died of a drug overdose (although Wolverton did go through rehab), a dramatic suicide, or a sexually contracted disease. It is a history of relationships made and unmade, of wounded feelings, and unmet expectations. It is a history still skewed towards the narratives of its two most prolific chroniclers: Raven and Wolverton. This history leaves out quite a few events and art works: the la la la conference; a ritual performance that Swannack and Elliot performed in response to their harassment by the police, entitled *From Victim to Victory* (1975); the public service announcements made at the Los Angeles Woman's Video Center that tried to educate the public into being more accepting of gay people, particularly lesbians; the lesbian art show that Raven curated at the same time that Wolverton was working on GALAS; and some genuinely proto-queer work, such as Nancy Angelo's *On Joining the Order* (1977), an astonishingly erotic black and white video in which a young nun relates the story of her incestuous coupling with her father. There were also other artists: neon sculptor Lili Lakich, Kate Millet, Cynthia X, and Linda Montano working collaboratively with Pauline Oliveros in *Three Day Blindfold*, another proto-queer work. It was a history that tried to envision the future, but ultimately portrayed a present that had been, however slightly, ameliorated. In spite of being right there in front of us, it is a history that has yet to be acknowledged.

It seems appropriate, therefore, to conclude this essay with a return to the late seventies via a video made by three women, two of whom are no longer alive. In 1979, Kate Horsfield and the late Lyn Blumenthal filmed an oral history with Raven (who passed away in 2006), when Raven was still immersed in changing the world to make room for women who identified as lesbians. "Some of our greatest creators are lesbians. They would probably sue me if they heard me speaking about them in public... My work is a metaphor for transcending that. I'm proceeding from the point of the lesbian creator."[65] In 2002, Wolverton launched her book *Insurgent Muse* at the Woman's Building, which was by then no longer the Woman's Building but rather a collection of artist's studios.[66] Kaucyila Brooke wrote an article about the Woman's Building and *Insurgent Muse* for *X-TRA*, an art magazine based in Los Angeles. Brooke recalled that at the end of the launch party, Wolverton was approached by a former Woman's Building participant. The woman told Wolverton that she was glad that she had written her book, because she was beginning to believe that none of it had ever actually happened. Brooke states, "It is chilling to realize that feminist history had become so erased and dismissed that these women who lived it had begun to think it imaginary."[67]

This herstory did happen and has not disappeared. As Brooke notes, "Fortunately, this history is not lost but has been documented and will continue to be revisited in exhibitions, catalogues, art historical books and essays."[68] In fact, Brooke's work, which draws upon lesbian feminist ideas *and* queer theory, is a testament to Raven's vision of a lesbian creator. Perhaps the future was female after all.

Notes

1. Terry Castle, *The Apparitional Lesbian* (New York: Columbia University Press, 1993), 4–5.

2. Laura Meyer, "The Los Angeles Woman's Building and the Feminist Art Community, 1973–1991," *The Sons and Daughters of Los: Culture and Community in L.A.*, David E. James, ed. (Philadelphia: Temple University Press, 2003), 50–51.

3. Harmony Hammond, *Lesbian Art in America: A Contemporary History* (New York: Rizzoli, 2000), 53.

4. Terry Wolverton, "Even Closer Encounters," The Woman's Building Press Release, March 30, 1978, Personal Archives of Terry Wolverton, Los Angeles, CA; Terry Wolverton, "Feminist Theater, Entertaining Visions," *Spinning Off* 1.5 (1978): 2–3; Terry Wolverton and Christine Wong, "An Oral Herstory of Lesbianism," *Frontiers: A Journal of Women Studies: Lesbian History* 4.3 (1979): 52–53; Terry Wolverton, "Lesbian Art Project," *Heresies* 7 2.3 (1979): 14–19; Lesbian Art Project, "An Oral Herstory of Lesbianism," *High Performance* 2.4 (1979–80): 17–25; LAP, "Advertisement for Oral," *Lesbian Tide* 8.6 (1978): 6.

5. Judith Butler, *Bodies That Matter: On the Discursive Limits of "Sex"* (New York and London: Routledge, 1993), 95.

6. Judith Butler, *Undoing Gender* (New York and London: Routledge, 2004), 35.

7. Ibid., 3.

8. *Spinning Off* 1.1 (1978) advertised a lesbian worksharing day, a Valentine's Day Dance entitled "Dyke of Your Dreams," an astrology class conducted by Terry Wolverton, and a talk by Charlotte Bunch, the lesbian feminist editor of *Quest*. Number 2 (1978) included an announcement for a benefit for *FEMINA*. Number 3 (1978) announced a workshop by Barbara Hammer entitled "Sappho at the Woman's Building." Number 4 (1978) announced the premier of *FEMINA: An IntraSpace Voyage*. Number 10 (1978) announced lectures on Sapphic education and the lesbian body by Arlene Raven and Terry Wolverton. Number 11 (December 1978/January 1979) announced the forthcoming lectures of Adrienne Rich and Mary Daly, two influential writers who also identified as lesbians.

9. Castle, 28.

10. Hammond, 112–113.

11. Sue Maberry, email correspondence with the author, February 3, 2010.

12. Terry Wolverton, "Generations of Lesbian Art," *High Performance* 14 (1991): 10–11.

13. Terry Wolverton, *Insurgent Muse* (San Francisco: City Lights, 2002), 94.

14. Annamarie Jagose, *Queer Theory: An Introduction* (New York: New York University Press, 1996), 56.

15. Linda Garber, *Identity Poetics* (New York: Columbia University Press, 2001), 17.

16. Deirdre Heddon, *Autobiography and Performance* (London: Palgrave, 2008), 31.

17. For a history of queer theory, see Jagose, *Queer Theory*; Nikki Sullivan, *A Critical Introduction to Queer Theory* (New York: New York University Press, 2003); and Riki Anne Wilchins, *Queer Theory, Gender Theory: An Instant Primer* (Los Angeles: Alyson Books, 2004).

18. Alice Echols, *Daring to Be Bad: Radical Feminism in America, 1967–1975* (Minneapolis: University of Minnesota Press, 1989).

19. Adrienne Rich, "Compulsory Heterosexuality and Lesbian Existence," *Signs* 5.4 (1980): 631–660.

20. For most of the time that the worksharing events took place, Raven shared her home with Cheryl Swannack, who was her lover at the time. Raven lived in a beautiful old Victorian house, which became an important backdrop to the emerging lesbian consciousness of the members of the Natalie Barney Collective and the LAP.

21. Lesbian Art Project, "Progress of the First Two Months of Operation of the Lesbian Art Project," Handout, 1977. Personal Archives of T. Wolverton.

22. Pam Meecham and Julie Sheldon, *Modern Art: A Critical Introduction*, 2nd ed. (London and New York: Routledge, 2005), 242.

23. Harmony Hammond, "Feminist Abstract Art—A Political Viewpoint," *Heresies* 1.1 (1977): 66–70.

24. Hammond, *Lesbian Art in America*, 96.

25. Arlene Raven and Ruth Iskin, "Through the Peephole: Lesbian Sensibility in Art," *Chrysalis: A Magazine of Women's Culture* 4 (1977): 22.

26. Jenni Sorkin, "Arlene Raven: Homecoming," *Critical Matrix* 17 (2008): 82–89.

27. Margo Hobbs Thompson, "'Lesbians Are Not Women': Feminine and Lesbian Sensibilities in Harmony Hammond's Late-1970s Sculpture," *Journal of Lesbian Studies* 12.4 (2008): 435–54.

28. Hammond, 44–45.

29. Raven and Iskin, "Through the Peephole," 21.

30. Iskin, "Through the Peephole," 23. In "Through the Peephole," Raven and Iskin took turns authoring paragraphs. The author of the alternating paragraphs was identified.

31. Raven, "Through the Peephole," 21.

32. Ibid., 20.

33. Bonnie Zimmerman, *The Safe Sea of Women* (Boston: Beacon Press, 1990), 120.

34. Lillian Faderman and Stuart Timmons, *Gay L.A.: A History of Sexual Outlaws, Power Politics, and Lipstick Lesbians* (Berkeley and Los Angeles: University of California Press, 2006, 2009), 170. Prior to the Westside Women's Center, Del Whan had founded the Gay Women's Services Center in 1971.

35. *la la la workshop*, The Woman's Building, 1976. Video documentation of the second day of the la la la workshop held at the Woman's Building, June 5–6, 1976, 10 mins. Long Beach Museum of Art Video Archive, Getty Research Institute. Transferred by the Long Beach Museum of Art Foundation and the City of Long Beach, 2005.

36. Alexandra Juhasz, "A Process Archive: The Grand Circularity of Woman's Building Video," *Doin' It in Public: Feminism and Art at the Woman's Building* (Los Angeles: Otis College of Art and Design, 2011), 109.

37. Sharon Immergluck, "Natalie Barney Collective: An Afterthought," Manuscript, n.d. Personal Archives of T. Wolverton.

38. Terry Wolverton, "The Joy of Lesbian Work—A Story of the Lesbian Art Project," Manuscript, 1979, 12. Personal Archives of T. Wolverton.

39. Nikki Sullivan, *A Critical Introduction to Queer Theory* (New York: New York University Press, 2003), 148.

40. Wolverton, *Insurgent Muse*, 70–71.

41. Wolverton, "The Joy of Lesbian Work," 14.

42. Lillian Faderman, *Odd Girls and Twilight Lovers: A History of Lesbian Life in Twentieth Century America* New York: Penguin Books, 1991), 227.

43. Kathryn Rountree, "The Politics of the Goddess: Feminist Spirituality and the Essentialism Debate," *Social Analysis* 43.2 (1999), 138.

44. Diana Fuss, *Essentially Speaking* (New York: Routledge, 1989), 100.

45. Laura Cottingham, *Seeing Through the Seventies: Essays on Feminism and Art* (Amsterdam, The Netherlands: G+B Arts, 2000), 141.

46. Wolverton, "Joy of Lesbian Work," 18.

47. Ibid.

48. Ibid., 20.

49. Wolverton, "True Confessions: Lesbian Art Project Talks about the Sapphic Model of Education," TMs, n.d. [1978/1979], 8. Personal Archives of T. Wolverton.

50. Lesbian Art Project, "Program of Sapphic Education," TMs, 1978/1979. Personal Archives of T. Wolverton.

51. Ann Shannon and Terry Wolverton, "FEMINA: An IntraSpace Voyage," Performance script, 1978, 4. Personal Archives of T. Wolverton.

52. Ibid., 8.

53. Wolverton, quoted in "Even Closer Encounters," Woman's Building press release, March 30, 1978, 1. Personal Archives of T. Wolverton.

54. Pamela Robertson, *Guilty Pleasures: Feminist Camp from Mae West to Madonna* (Durham: Duke University Press, 1996), 17.

55. Wolverton, *Insurgent Muse*, 104.

56. Terry Wolverton, "Creating *An Oral Herstory of Lesbianism*: An Interview of Terry Wolverton by Terry Wolverton," TMs, 1979. Personal Archives of T. Wolverton.

57. Wolverton et al., *An Oral Herstory of Lesbianism*, performance script, 1979, 1. Personal Archives of T. Wolverton.

58. Ibid., 5.

59. Lesbian Art Project, "An Oral Herstory of Lesbianism," *High Performance* 2.4 (1979–1980): 17–25; Jenni Sorkin, "Envisioning High Performance," *Art Journal* 62.2 (2003): 36–51. *High Performance* engendered some controversy with Tee A. Corinne's solarized photograph of lesbian oral sex, which the first printer refused to publish.

60. Arlene Raven, "Visual Body of Vision: A Poem for/with Lesbian Visual Art," in Wolverton et al., *An Oral Herstory of Lesbianism*, performance script, not paginated .

61. Terry Wolverton and Christine Wong, "An Oral Herstory of Lesbianism," *Frontiers: A Journal of Women Studies: Lesbian History* 4.3 (1979): 52–53.

62. Faderman, *Odd Girls*, 240–241.

63. Terry Wolverton, "Looking Through a New Lens: An Interview with Arlene Raven," in *From Site to Vision: the Woman's Building in Contemporary Culture*, Sondra Hale and Terry Wolverton, eds. (Los Angeles: Woman's Building and Otis College of Art and Design, 2011), 134.

64. Wolverton, "Lesbian Art: A Partial Inventory," in *From Site to Vision*.

65. *Arlene Raven: Oral History*, videotape by Kate Horsfield and Lyn Blumenthal, 1979. Long Beach Museum of Art Video Archives, Getty Research Institute.

66. It was subsequently sold and the artists evicted.

67. Kaucyila Brooke, "She Does Not See What She Does Not Know," *X-TRA* 6.3 (2004), available online at http://www.x-traonline.org/past_articles.php?articleID=152 (accessed January 2, 2010).

68. Ibid.

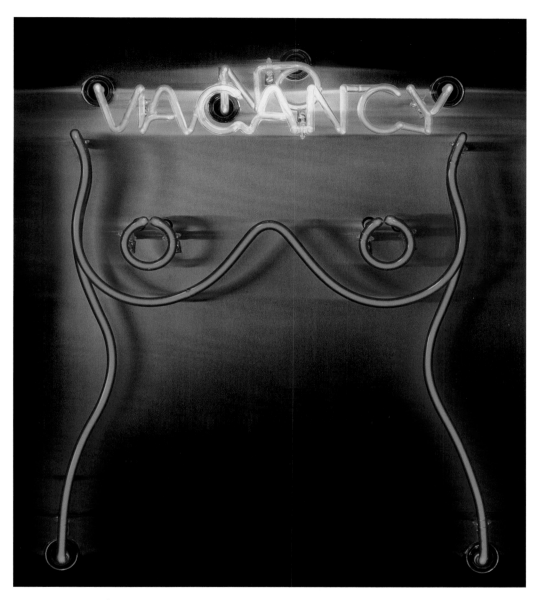

Lili Lakich, *Vacancy/No Vacancy*, 1972. Stainless steel, plexiglass, glass tubing with neon and argon, and electronic animator; 30" x 26" x 7". Collection of Marion Rothman, Del Mar, CA. © Lili Lakich.

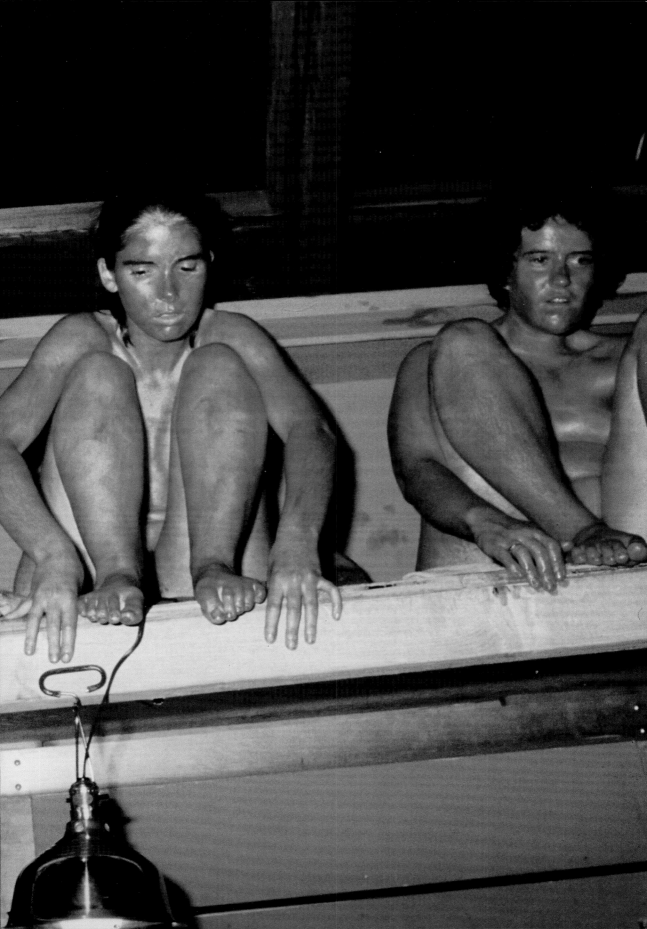

ENDING THE SILENCE

Vivien Green Fryd

Starting with its inception in 1973, the Woman's Building (WB) provided many women an open, supportive, and safe environment to explore the subject of sexual violence against the female body. Some of these artists were centered in the WB while others were associated with it; the boundaries that existed in the Los Angeles feminist art world during 1970s and early 1980s thus were amorphous. The WB fostered a strong sense of community throughout Southern California, and many of the artists collaborated in creating artworks imbued with a feminist consciousness that critiqued the media, deconstructed images of the patriarchal order, broke down barriers between public and private realms, and strove to end the silence about sexual violence against the female body. Through performances, paintings, videos, installations, posters, and exhibitions, these feminist artists contributed to the rape and incest crises discourses. They wielded their strategic agency through their art to empower women, reconstruct gender norms, and challenge cultural norms, attitudes, assumptions, and laws.

More specifically, the artists under the aegis of the WB studied within this essay participated in the processes of "bearing witness and giving testimony" that is central to traumatic events. "Testimony is coming to voice, an insistence on speaking and not being silenced or spoken for," and "giving shape to what once seemed overwhelming, incomprehensible, and formless."[1] As Nancy K. Miller and Jason Tougaw explain, "Testimony records a movement from individual experience to the collective archives, from personal trauma to public memory."[2] The feminist artists connected with the WB not only fought to end the silence about sexual violence in American culture and challenged patriarchal images of women that encouraged such violence, but they also made the trauma knowable and visible. As Cathy Caruth explains about traumas: "The striking juxtaposition of the unknowing, injurious repetition and the witness of the crying voice" demand a listener or viewer "for the belated repetition of trauma" that can only be known after the traumatic event.[3] In hindsight, the frequent repetition of the subject during the 1970s and early 1980s resulted in art that functioned as a ritualized site for witnessing, disrupting conventional patriarchy, empowering women, and urging social action.

The Rape Crisis Movement

In addressing these subjects in their art, artists in the WB joined the newly emerging rape crisis movement. A brief outline of the history of the movement follows, because it is relevant to a consideration of their artwork. Feminists in Berkeley, California, founded the first rape crisis center in early 1972. Similar centers were formed the following year in Washington, D.C., Ann Arbor, Boston, Philadelphia, and Minneapolis.[4] Anti-rape squads held rallies in Seattle and Los Angeles (1972), and Women Organized Against Rape (WOAR) took shape in 1973, when a small group of women challenged Philadelphia's police, hospitals, and courts "to treat survivors of sexual assault with dignity and compassion—and to confront the culture of violence against women that underlies the crime of rape."[5] The New York Radical Feminist Speak-Out on Rape (1971), the New York Radical Feminist Conference on Rape (1971), the Rape Speak-Out in San Francisco (1972), and the joint New York Radical Feminist-National Black Feminist Organization Speak-Out on Rape and Sexual Abuse (1974) all addressed rape from a woman's perspective.[6] In May 1976, the International Tribunal of Crimes against Women was held in Brussels. Over two thousand women from forty countries shared experiences "of sexual slavery, weekend sex tours, sexual mutilation, rape, battery, enforced participation in pornography, and murder," in an effort to give victims a voice, raise public awareness, and suggest solutions.[7] The National Organization for Women (NOW) joined the anti-rape movement, focusing on such short-term goals as a national communications network and educational campaigns. When NOW turned its attention to the Equal Rights Amendment, the National Coalition against Sexual Assault formed in 1977 to fill the gap and create a national structure for rape crisis advocacy.[8] Simultaneous with the rise of this anti-rape movement was the larger proliferation of images and representations of sexual violence in the mass media. Such images existed in profusion in the post-World War II pornography industry, an increasingly realistic movie industry, on television, and in photojournalism, contributing to a broader dissemination of images of sexual violence. Some of the feminist artists associated with the WB responded directly to media representations of violence against women.

Speak-outs and meetings in New York City inspired the feminist author and historian Susan Brownmiller to write *Against Our Will: Men, Women and Rape* (1975). This "rape classic," published in sixteen foreign editions, argues, "all rape is an exercise in power" in which women "are trained to be...victims." "Rape is not a crime of irrational, impulsive, uncontrollable lust," Brownmiller asserts, "but is a deliberate, hostile, violent act of degradation and possession...designed to intimidate and inspire fear" by the "would-be conqueror."[9] As the historian Roy Porter summarized her thesis, Brownmiller exposed rape as "not the sickness of perverts, but the sickness of patriarchy," and as a political crime.[10]

Other texts written during the 1970s made violence against women visible in the public sphere, ending the era of silence.[11] They overturned myths of rape as rapture by exposing the act as a crime of power and control. These anti-rape treatises supported efforts for legislation, which indicates the political activity that was happening at the same time. As Susan Griffin concluded in 1971, in one of the first widely read anti-rape texts, "Rape, the perfect combination of sex and violence, is the penultimate act" for wielding patriarchal power; it is "the quintessential act of our civilization."[12] Three years later, Catherine Calvert supported Griffin's conclusion in an essay in *Mademoiselle*, reporting that most psychologists consider rape to be "more a working out of hostility and aggression than any flowering of a frustrated sexual urge." Calvert depicted sexual violence as an arena in which power and powerlessness are played out, and advocated that it must be realigned in order to reach "a détente in the sexual free-fire zone that is the country of rape."[13]

In her pioneering 1986 article in the *Yale Law Journal*, Susan Estrich explained the legal difficulties confronting a woman who wanted to prosecute a man for what she calls "simple rape"—rape by a friend or neighbor—as opposed to "stranger rape," which she claimed was prosecuted more frequently and successfully than many other violent crimes.[14] Estrich articulated in the courtroom and classroom the problems that these feminists a decade earlier had protested against.

The anti-rape movement was an outgrowth of second-wave feminist consciousness-raising (C-R) groups and "speak-outs," where women publicly discussed that which had been silenced. C-R became the primary educational and organizing program of the women's liberation movement. Intended to raise awareness and understanding of women's lives and concerns, C-R groups underlined the idea that "personal" injuries and frustrations were not unique but common among women—that is, the issues were political. As one of the earliest sourcebooks about rape explained, "Through the process of consciousness-raising, women moved on from the discovery that sexual assault was not just an individual and unique experience to the realization that rape, as an issue, was a means of analyzing the psychological and political structures of oppression in our society."[15] Ellen Bass and Laura Davis's *The Courage to Heal* (1988) later would advocate C-R as a means for survivors of rape and sexual abuse to begin their recovery process.[16]

Representations of Rape in the Woman's Building

Artists participated in C-R groups in Judy Chicago's Feminist Art Program at Fresno State College in 1970–71, in a similar program at California Institute of the Arts (CalArts) facilitated by Chicago and Miriam Schapiro in 1971, and subsequently in courses taken and works produced through the Feminist Studio Workshop (FSW) at the Woman's Building. They repeatedly discovered, as one of the earliest sourcebooks about rape predicted, that the theme of rape was omnipresent in their discussions. As a way of vocalizing their concerns about the issue, they first turned to performance art. While performance remained a primary medium to address the subject, by the mid-1970s and early 1980s other art forms had evolved, including installations, drawings, videos, posters, and painting.

While participating in one of Chicago's classes at CalArts in the spring of 1971, Suzanne Lacy, who had studied under Sheila de Bretteville in the Woman's Design Program at CalArts, proposed a performance in which an audience would enter a large theater with low lights and listen to audio recordings of women narrating their stories of sexual abuse. Lacy and Chicago located seven women willing to share the horrors that they had experienced, and recorded their previously untold stories. These testimonies formed the background for *Ablutions* (1972), which Lacy created in collaboration with Chicago and two of Chicago's other students—Sandra Orgel and Aviva Rahmani. *Ablutions* was performed in the spring of 1972 in Los Angeles, just before Chicago left CalArts to form the WB with Arlene Raven and Sheila Levrant de Bretteville. The performance employed visceral items—one thousand unbroken egg yolks, twenty gallons of beef blood, wet gray clay, broken egg shells, piles of rope and chain, and beef kidneys that covered the floor and walls—along with women's bodies submerged in tubs of egg yolks, clay, and blood. *Ablutions* combined bodies, objects, and voice recordings to expose the horror of sexual violence against the female body and embody themes of female bondage, fertility, cleansing, and recovery.[17]

It must be noted that no self-help book for rape victims had yet been published at this point; *Ablutions* predated by seventeen years texts that encouraged victims to speak out, such as Bass and Davis's *Courage to Heal*. Significantly, Lacy, Chicago, Orgel, and Rahmani made an artwork that constituted an early testimony of sexual trauma, providing a precursor to works that artists connected with the WB would create to address similar themes. *Ablutions* represented an early attempt by feminist artists to consider their increasing concern with rape in American culture.

While teaching in the FSW at the WB, Lacy elaborated on the themes of *Ablutions* in *One Woman Shows* (1975). A community of women, assembled anonymously by a chain-letter process, sat together in the WB, facing Lacy. Lacy named herself as a woman who had been raped, a woman who is a whore, and a woman who loves women. Dressed in paint-soaked clothing in her persona as the "woman-who-was-raped," she read police statistics gathered from that day's rape reports. She then threw herself

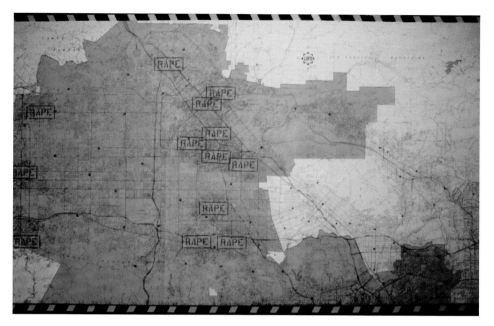

Suzanne Lacy, *Maps, Three Weeks in May*, 1977. Using daily police reports, two wall-sized maps of Los Angeles and a rubber stamp spelling "RAPE" were used to document where and when women were raped throughout the city. © Suzanne Lacy.

against a wall, leaving an imprint of black from her paint-soaked clothes.[18]

Ablutions and *One Woman Shows* were precursors for *Three Weeks in May*, which was sponsored by the Studio Watts Workshop (a community development corporation that worked with artists), the WB, and the City of Los Angeles. On Mother's Day in 1977, shortly after Los Angeles had been designated "Rape Capitol of the Nation," various events took place around the city that addressed the subject of sexual violence against women.[19] In its diversity, complexity, and range of activities and artworks, *Three Weeks in May* was extraordinary. The project included installations, speeches by politicians, interviews with hotline activists, self-defense demonstrations, speak-outs, media articles and programs, and performance art, all designed to grab media attention and generate awareness and discussion about rape in American culture. In addition to Lacy, a number of feminist artists were crucial to the deployment of *Three Weeks in May*. Other key participants included the general public (particularly the television-watching public and the live audiences who viewed the performances), police, politicians, self-defense instructors, anti-rape and anti-domestic violence activists, and the print and electronic media.[20]

Three Weeks in May centered on an installation, *Maps*, based on police statistics about the incidence of rape in the city. On the first map Lacy stenciled the word "RAPE"

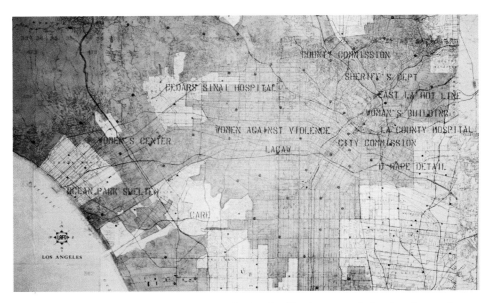

Suzanne Lacy, *Maps, Three Weeks in May*, 1977, Los Angeles. Map documents the location of women's organizations providing assistance and resistance. © Suzanne Lacy.

in four-inch, red letters over every location where a woman had been raped over a three-week's period. She updated the map daily, using data from the Los Angeles Police Department's central office. Around each red "RAPE" stamp, she inscribed fainter red markings that alluded to the estimate that there are nine unreported rapes for every one reported. A second map showed the locations of sites of assistance and resistance: rape prevention centers, rape hotlines, hospital emergency rooms, and crisis and counseling centers. This map was designed as a link to the "revelation of the problem" and to counteract any suggestion of "continuous victimization."[21]

In addition to literally mapping the confluence of rape and rape crisis centers in Los Angeles, Lacy coordinated thirty public and private activities during the three weeks "to 'activate' public awareness of the maps and to call attention to the reality of rape as a social phenomenon."[22] These included an opening press conference called at the recommendation of the city attorney and attended by him, the deputy mayor, Lacy, and Jim Woods of the Studio Watts Workshop; a Women's Coalition luncheon to explain the project to business and professional women; *Moment of Concern*, a moment of silence held on Mother's Day in various churches to commemorate victims of rape; *Breaking the Silence*, a private ritual attended by a select group of women and performed by Anne Gaulden and Melissa Hoffman; four performances by Leslie Labowitz; a guerrilla event in which Lacy, Judith Loischild, Phranc, and Hoffman chalked the red

Cheri Gaulke and Barbara Smith, *Liebestod*, 1977. Performance as part of *Three Weeks in May*. Pasadena, California. Photograph by Suzanne Lacy. Woman's Building Image Archive, Otis College of Art and Design.

outline of a woman's body on sidewalks throughout the city, adding the words, "a woman was raped near here," the date of the assault, and a flower; a performance entitled *Liebestod* by Cheri Gaulke and Barbara Smith for a group of women activists and law enforcement officials; a three-part performance entitled *She Who Would Fly* by Lacy and Labowitz; Laurel Klick's *Exorcism*, a ten-step private ritual to exorcise a sexual assault she experienced; and self-defense demonstrations at the Los Angeles Trade Technical School, the City Mall, and the ARCO Plaza. At a one-day rape speak-out at the WB, women revealed stories that had never been publicly acknowledged, while elected officials called press conferences and participated in rallies and activist events. The final event was a self-defense demonstration.[23]

Gaulke and Smith's *Liebestod* featured images of Chinese foot binding and other restrictions on women's freedom, reiterating some of the themes in *Ablutions*. The performance title, derived from Wagner's opera *Tristan und Isolde*, means "love-death," and also alludes to the suffering of Chinese women with bound feet. *Liebestod* was presented at a banquet attended by women from the American Civil Liberties Union; Women Against Violence Against Women, an activist organization devoted to

166

Suzanne Lacy, *She Who Would Fly*, 1977. View of installation and performance as part of *Three Weeks in May*, Los Angeles. © Suzanne Lacy.

stopping the use of images of physical and sexual violence against women in the mass media; the Ocean Park Battered Women's Shelter; and the Los Angeles Commission on Assaults Against Women. Some women shared their own experiences with rape during the event, providing testimonies of sexual trauma.

During the evening of May 21, 1977, Lacy and Labowitz opened up to the public *She Who Would Fly*, a personal, smaller scale performance and installation in the Studio Watts Workshop's Garage Gallery. Three to four visitors at a time were admitted into the gallery space, where they were confronted by a lamb cadaver with white-feathered wings suspended between floor and ceiling as if in flight. In Christian iconography, the lamb symbolizes Christ in the role of collective sacrifice and mute victim.[24] Women's testimonies of rape were pinned to their corresponding locations on maps that covered the walls. As the viewers read the stories, they eventually became aware that they were being watched by four nude women stained in red greasepaint, crouching "like vultures"[25] on a ledge above the door. Lacy describes these women as "avenging Valkeries" [sic], or "avenging angels, metaphors for a woman's consciousness that often splits from her body as it is raped," and also "bird-women [who] reminded visitors they were voyeurs to the pain of very real experiences."[26] The Valkyrie maidens of Odin, who choose the heroes to be slain in battle, are not objects of desire but women "who actively look rather than returning and confirming the gaze."[27] The masculine spectator's gaze, scopophilic and fetishizing, was thereby subverted. These predatory-looking, grotesque women watched over the female spectators to protect them from further violation, and over male spectators to create a "forced empathy, a moment of recognition which was the central aesthetic point: shock."[28] The installation created a viscerally difficult environment in which the viewer was forced into the role of witnessing trauma and performing what the artists considered "a ritual exorcism."[29]

Three Weeks in May succeeded in creating a vast community among feminist artists, lawmakers, police, media reporters, and the general public to bear witness to a variety of testimonies and performances of sexual trauma, not only ending the silence but also advocating changes in attitudes and the legal system, as well as encouraging women to learn self-defense.

Many of the activities connected with *Three Weeks in May* consisted of the repetitive nature of trauma—repeating activities like stamping the map or writing and reading testimonies. The phenomenological nature of trauma was also reenacted in *In Mourning and In Rage*, another collaboration between Lacy and Labowitz under the aegis of the WB. *In Mourning and In Rage*, which included participants from the Rape Hotline Alliance, the Los Angeles City Council, families of victims, and women from the community, was held in front of Los Angeles City Hall in 1977 to commemorate the victims of the serial rapist-murderer known as the Hillside Strangler. Seventy women gathered at the WB in Los Angeles and filled twenty-two cars. Led by a hearse and two motorcycle escorts, the motorcade traveled to City Hall, where news media and members

Suzanne Lacy and Leslie Labowitz, *In Mourning and In Rage*, 1977. Photograph documenting a performance conducted at City Hall protesting the media's portrayal of the Hillside Strangler's victims, Los Angeles.
© Suzanne Lacy.

of the City Council waited. Each car bore stickers: "Funeral" and "Stop Violence Against
Women." The funeral procession circled the building twice. Out of the hearse climbed
nine seven-foot-tall women robed in black with headdresses shaped like coffins and a
tall woman clothed in red with a scarlet headband. The women-in-black and woman-
in-scarlet formed a procession, two abreast, walking toward the steps in front of City
Hall. Simultaneously women from the motorcade positioned themselves on either side
of the steps, "forming a black-clothed chorus from a modern tragedy."[30] They unfurled
two banners, designed to fit a television screen, which read: "In Memory of Our
Sisters" and "Women Fight Back." The first mourner walked to the microphone and
proclaimed in an even yet impassioned tone, "I am here for the ten women who have
been raped and strangled between October 18th and November 29th." The chorus
chanted, "In memory of our sisters, we fight back," while the woman-in-scarlet
wrapped the first mourner in a red shawl. Each of the subsequent women read a statement that connected the "seemingly random incident of violence in Los Angeles with
the greater picture of nationwide violence toward women."[31] The second speaker, for
example, cited the three hundred and eighty-eight rapes in Los Angles during the

169

same six-week period that were not connected to the Hillside Strangler, while the third remembered the four thousand thirty-three women raped there during the previous year. Each speaker was covered with a red cloak and greeted by the chorus. The original woman-in-scarlet then approached a microphone and declared loudly and powerfully, "I am here for the rage of all women. I am here for women fighting back."

In fact, *In Mourning and In Rage* began "more in mourning and not in rage," but some of the participants at the WB who were rape survivors advocated a more activist stance that would show female empowerment. The women-in-black symbolized repressed anger and "the power of women who have historically banded together as mourners, and as givers of life and death in their culture," and as "powerful and defiant overseers of one's voyage into death." Bia Lowe suggested adding the woman-in-scarlet to the nine mourning figures in black in order to signify outward anger and self-defense, and to provide a powerful color against the prevailing black.[32]

Lacy and Labowitz's "performative method" blended "art and life, aesthetics and ethics to focus on the political significance of women's experience."[33] Their visceral presentation of *In Mourning and In Rage* resulted in some audience members weeping, as is evident in the video that documents the event (*In Mourning and In Rage*, by L.A. Women's Video Center).[34] They transformed a civic space into a site for grief, mourning, and remembrance. By speaking on behalf of murdered and violated women in Los Angeles and other places throughout the United States, the participants created a site of belated witnessing, memory, and testimony to that which had been silenced. The public bore witness via the event itself and its repetition in the media.[35] Like *Three Weeks in May*, *In Mourning and In Rage*'s repetitive format—repeating phrases and ritual actions, cloaking of speakers, and its chorus-like theatrical format—reenacted the phenomenological structure of trauma.

The videotape of the performance was shown at the WB on June 16, 1979. The video not only documented the event, but also served as "a vehicle for testimony, a screen of memory," and asked "that we bear witness to its act of witness."[36] The video, in other words, contributed to performing the act of bearing witness to unspeakable acts that had been formerly silenced, and participated in the process of repetition characteristic of trauma. Video was a new, experimental electronic medium at the time—black and white, produced on portable reel-to-reel equipment, and edited with a tape splicer. Through flickering light, discontinuous and grainy images, and scratchy sound (the results of over two hundred edits), the disjunctive narrative of *In Mourning and In Rage* evokes the disruption of lived experiences and psychic coherence that is associated with trauma.

Representations of Incest in the Woman's Building

Although rape had been a prominent theme during the early 1970s among second-wave feminists connected with the WB, the subject of incest was not addressed in

American culture until the end of the decade. In 1979, newspaper reporter Elaine Woo called incest "the last taboo."[37] Ellen Weber reported three years earlier in *Ms.* magazine: "One girl out of every four in the United States will be sexually abused in some way before she reaches the age of eighteen," and "the magnitude of the problem of incest is perhaps only matched by the degree of secrecy which surrounds it."[38] Louise Armstrong's "The Crime Nobody Talks About,"published in *Woman's Day* (March 1978), stated that more than one million cases of child abuse and neglect had been reported in 1975, with twelve percent involving sexual abuse. Florence Rush described incest in *The Best Kept Secret: Sexual Abuse of Children* (1980) as "a national epidemic."[39] Armstrong's *Kiss Daddy Goodnight* (1978), which included sixteen personal stories and a list of resources, was one of the first mass-market collections of first-person accounts of incest. Sandra Butler's *Conspiracy of Silence: The Trauma of Incest* (1978) similarly confronted this seemingly unspeakable subject before it attracted the interest of television, radio, newspapers, magazines, pediatricians, social workers, and therapists.[40] Later, Kathleen Brady's *Father's Days: A True Story of Incest* (1979); Rush's *The Best Kept Secret*; Judith Lewis Herman's *Father-Daughter Incest* (1981), which was preceded by an article published in 1977; and Ellen Bass and Laura Davis's *The Courage to Heal* addressed the topic.[41] As Armstrong observed, "Incest is a big secret— not because victims are hiding pleasure. There is no pleasure. Incest is a secret because it is a power situation where victims are punished and silenced by fear."[42]

As language was forming and research was becoming available to the general public, it is not surprising that a number of artists connected with the WB created visual and verbal testimonies about these sexual traumas that feminists and others identified as a major social problem. For example, the WB's Incest Awareness Project (1979–1981) was a series of events and activities designed to make incest a public issue, create positive images of women moving from victimhood to survivorship, and promote recovery. Author Rush spoke about child abuse at the WB through the Incest Awareness Project in July of 1980; Butler gave a lecture after Wolverton's performance of *In Silence Secrets Turn to Lies/Secrets Shared Become Sacred Truths* (October 1979) in conjunction with the exhibition "Bedtime Stories: Women Speak Out About Incest" (1979); and Susan Forward, author of *Betrayal of Innocence: Incest and Its Devastation* (1979), spoke at an Incest Awareness Project event.[43] Explaining her decision to participate in the Incest Awareness Project, Angelo remarked that although feminists, therapists, and social workers began to expose the horrors of incest and to treat survivors, "public ignorance and professional misunderstandings" still existed, especially in terms of "prevention, intervention and healing."[44]

As early as 1975, Linda Oldon led an extension class at the WB focusing on the subject of incest. Two artists connected to the WB—Paula Lumbard and Leslie Belt—also addressed incest. While in the Summer Art Program at the WB with Angelo, Lumbard performed *Incest I* (1976). She cut up a painting and handed out the pieces to her fellow

I HEARD A WOMAN SAY THAT THOSE OF US WHO EXPERIENCED
INCEST ARE FEROCIOUSLY INDEPENDENT.
SHE TALKED ABOUT THE STRENGTH IN US, ABOUT OUR
DETERMINATION AND DRIVE TO MAKE OUR OWN LIVES.
I SAW IN MYSELF REASONS FOR HOW SERIOUSLY I LIVE
MY LIFE AND CLAIM THAT AS POSITIVE AND POWERFUL.
I HEARD A WOMAN CALL HERSELF AN INCEST SURVIVOR.

a monthly newsletter of women's culture presented by Women's Community, Inc. 50¢

Spinning Off

October/November 1979

Art about Incest
(story on page 1)

**Four Full Pages of
Women's Art**
(see pages 4, 5, 8, 9)

Calendar of Events
(see page 6)

Once upon a time
she thought incest was
something she had to
carry around all by herself.

Above: **Paula Lumbard, *Self
Portrait/Liberation***, 1979.
Chalk pastel on brown paper,
40" x 50". © Paula Lumbard.

Left: **Cover of *Spinning Off*
newsletter announcing the
exhibition "Bedtime Stories:
Women Speak Out About
Incest."** October/November
1979. Woman's Building Image
Archive, Otis College of Art
and Design.

students as she told of her experiences. This performance marked the first time that Lumbard had spoken publicly about her childhood trauma.[45] In her monologue in *An Oral Herstory of Lesbianism* (1978), Belt jumped rope and recited a sing-song reminiscent of the familiar children's ditty, "Not Last Night but the Night Before." However, Belt's contained a jarring difference. The first stanza stated: "My grandfather was a child molester until the day he died; I was first molested by him at the age of five." She explained in sing-song manner while jumping rope that she remained silent around her father "cuz I was afraid of what he'd do," her grandfather "cuz he already knew," her mother "so she wouldn't be sad," and anyone else "cuz I thought I was bad."[46] Belt intended to take "the familiar and seemingly innocent meter of the childhood chant played against the hypnotic slapping of the rope" to create "a visceral experience of what it was like to be a child who was caught up in an adult's relentless desire."[47] The repetitive sound of jumping rope, combined with the rhyming structure of the song, iterated, enacted, and rewrote traumatic history in an attempt to gain mastery over tragic loss.

Angelo, who was a former student and later a faculty member in the FSW, addressed the subject of incest in a video called *Part 1, On Joining the Order: A Confession in which Angelica Furiosa Explains to Her Sisters How She Came to Be Among Them* (1977). This single-channel video was never intended to be an actual story of incest.[48] Performing as a nun—which Angelo had also done with Candace Compton in *Nun and Deviant* (1976)—Angelo created a fictional persona who confessed her incestuous relationship with her father and their mutual betrayal of her mother. The video created controversy. Los Angeles City Council member Ernani Bernardi blocked its inclusion in a federally funded art exhibition and the FBI questioned the artist to determine whether or not the work could be considered pornography.[49] Nevertheless, Angelo exhibited the work across the United States, in Europe, Australia, and New Zealand; while doing so, she discovered that many women in the audience felt compelled to share their own experiences.[50]

Discussion with Labowitz and audience responses to *On Joining the Order* led Angelo to elaborate further on the topic of incest. The resultant Incest Awareness Project, organized through the WB, was cosponsored by the Women's Resources Program of the Los Angeles Gay and Lesbian Community Services Center (LAGLCSC) and Ariadne: A Social Art Network. Ariadne was a loose umbrella and conceptual framework established by Lacy and Labowitz in 1978 for women artists, social activists, media specialists, and government officials to facilitate funding, organize art activities, and support artists' use of the media with the intention of addressing sexually explicit and violent imagery of women in American visual culture.[51] The many and varied activities of the Incest Awareness Project included "Bedtime Stories" (1978), an exhibition at the WB; art therapy workshops for children in the Los Angeles County's Sexual Abuse Program; community dialogues, counseling and referrals provided by the LAGLCSC; and a large-scale, multimedia project entitled *Equal Time in Equal Space*.[52]

"Bedtime Stories," curated by Lumbard and Belt, consisted of performances and static artworks by eighteen women and children who had experienced incest. "Rather than focusing on victimization," the exhibition "graphically" presented "a feminist perspective on the complex aspects of sexual abuse in the family," showing the journey from victim to recovery. To expose the "big secret" that involves the perpetrator's power over the victims, Belt wanted to allow women and children to speak out, feel empowered, and be able to recover.[53] They placed child-size furniture around the exhibition space, intending to convey the idea that, as Belt explained, "the teeny little bodies that fit comfortably in those chairs are being abused, pressed against, by adults twice their size."[54] The two-tone walls of the exhibition space moreover signified the child's experience of day and night as two different realities: yellow below for the daytime of normal activities, and black above for the looming nighttime, the "darkness of forced adult sexuality."[55] Lumbard and Belt, both incest survivors, intended to challenge the "secretive, or non-existent status" of incest and make its pervasiveness in American culture visible through video and performance.[56]

At the entrance of "Bedtime Stories" stood Lowe's life-size photomontage, *Once Upon a Time She Thought Incest Was Something She Had to Carry Around All by Herself*. A young girl in overalls holds aloft a globe on which a photograph of her smiling nuclear family appears in negative. Evoking the ancient Greek god Atlas, who was forced to carry the world on his shoulders, the girl has the strength to carry her own burden: the memories, guilt, shame, secrecy, and fear associated with incest. Lowe intended to show the girl "about to throw off the weight of keeping the family together," giving in-cest survivors "a sense of direction and community rather than the feelings of defeat and isolation that come from the family's conspiracy of silence."[57] *Once Upon a Time* also functioned as a logo for the Incest Awareness Project.[58]

The exhibition was divided into three sections to underscore the process a woman undergoes from incest victim to survivor. The first section addressed the secret of incest. Lumbard's charcoal drawing, *Incest #3*, shows the artist as a young girl on a bed in fetal position, which suggests her isolation and confusion about incest. A large bird behind her flies away, signifying recovery and her transformation from victim to survivor.[59] Diane Silberstein's *No Doll* consisted of five hundred color, Xeroxed paper dolls with open mouths. Lined up along the gallery walls, these likenesses of the artist bore a variety of expressions, which proceeded from grief to anger and finally to relief. Tyaga's *Telling*, a large, mixed-media drawing, also represented dolls. These life-size babies sat in disarray, seemingly abandoned, and expressing ferocious outrage. Powerlessness and disembodiment were also conveyed in Lyricon Jazzwomin McCaleb's installation *Silent Screams*, in which a stuffed military uniform sat in a chair surrounded by empty alcohol bottles with a little girl's dress on its lap. One white glove of the absent-yet-present military man held the child's dress while the other clutched a leather belt, which trailed on the floor "like a whip."[60]

The second section of the exhibition dealt with one of the consequences of incest: when a child becomes a liar to maintain the secret. On opening night, Terry Wolverton performed *In Silence Secrets Turn to Lies / Secrets Shared Become Sacred Truths*, which was inspired by memories of her molestation by her stepfather between the ages of five and eleven. Of the performance Wolverton said:

> I constructed a physical environment in which I could move through layers of experience; revealing first those secrets I had thought were too terrible to share, exposing the lies I told about myself to seem more acceptable, and finally moving into honesty and self-awareness.[61]

From a dark red canopy, Wolverton hung streamers upon which she wrote: "Do not say no; don't ask your stepfather to not get drunk; don't say that you do not want to touch your father's penis." In another section, she wrote on black streamers lies she had told herself: that she was ugly, unlovable, and not angry. In the performance, Wolverton ripped these words apart; over the discarded paper she poured a circle of salt for purification. She then entered the center of the room, sat on a chair, and read a letter informing her mother of her childhood sexual abuse. At the close of the performance, Wolverton invited the audience to write their own stories in a notebook; some added their own memories of similar childhood experiences.[62]

The third section of "Bedtime Stories" focused "on the strength women have found in themselves as survivors of incestuous assault." Here an installation entitled *Letters Home* (1979) contained letters by five women to men who had engaged them in sexual relations when they were children. Quimetta Perle's *Adolescent Journal* consisted of hand-embroidered excerpts from the journal she kept during the time of her incest experience.[63]

The Incest Awareness Project also sponsored the innovative, ten-day video installation *Equal Time in Equal Space (ETES)*, directed by Angelo and co-produced by the Women's Video Center with a media campaign led by Ariadne. In preparation for this complex project, Angelo facilitated meetings among seventeen women, who were of differing ages and came from a variety of backgrounds.[64] The women participated in journal writing, body work, and eleven C-R sessions over a period of ten weeks on a variety of topics: mothers, sexuality, anger and authority, class, race, religion, and feelings about speaking out about individual incest experiences. As the title indicates, the intention was "to give equal time and equal space to each woman's recollections and analyses of incest."[65] Divided into roles of performer, camerawoman, and organizer, the participants worked under the guidance of Angelo, who conceived of and facilitated the entire project.

This large-scale, multichannel video installation was designed for a small audience. Six video monitors were set up facing each other in a large circle, with audience members distributed evenly around them. Each monitor carried the image and voice of a different woman from the C-R groups: Anita Green, Lowe, Lumbard, McCaleb, Christine Wong, and Wolverton.[66] The viewers thus witnessed a C-R session on incest as the "monitors 'talked and listened' to each other, responding in such an appropriate and coordinated fashion that the audience soon forgot the technology and found themselves included in an intense and painfully honest group discussion."[67]

As medium, video "asks that we bear witness to its act of witness."[68] In this case, each video monitor "testifies to the act of having seen."[69] Angelo created a space for a series of witnessing. The video bears witness to each woman's testimony of sexual trauma. The audience members seated between each video constituted what Shoshana Felman calls "*second-degree witnesses* (witness of witnesses, witnesses of the testimonies)."[70] The result gave "shape to what once seemed overwhelming, incomprehensible, and formless" and created a public memory.[71] *ETES* expressed "outrage" for the "experiences of pain, betrayal, and loss of childhood," but also rejoiced in the fact that "these are women bearing witness together."[72] As the therapist Butler observed:

> I celebrate the coming together of the women who are in front of and behind this pain, the strength, the clarity, and the vision that emerges from our coming together to continue the acts of creation that are our lives and the lives of those who will follow us.[73]

In its use of the new technology of video as a vehicle for social change, *ETES* was experimental and visionary. The installation challenged the positioning of women as victims in the media, instead empowering women to speak out, end the silence, and move from victimhood to survivorship. Significantly, the artists adopted and publicized the term "incest survivor," as opposed to "victim."

ETES, in conjunction with Wolverton's *In Silence Secrets Turn to Lies*, Lowe's *Once Upon a Time*, and the works in the exhibition "Bedtime Stories," joined the growing body of literature being published contemporaneously about incest. Together, they shaped a discourse on the links between patriarchy, incest, and women's social subjugation.

Conclusion

During the 1970s and early 1980s, artists used performances, exhibitions, videos, posters, installations, and other media to create works that addressed sexual violence against the female body. Their works functioned as a ritualized site for witnessing, disrupting conventional histories, ending the silence by making the unknown known, and reenacting or performing the phenomenological structure of trauma. They created repetitive traumatic sites that surround, involve, and challenge the viewer to witness, acknowledge, remember, and end the silence about sexual trauma experienced by women.

Nancy Angelo, director and producer, *Equal Time in Equal Space*, 1980. Collaborative video installation as part of the Incest Awareness Project. Photograph by Bia Lowe. Woman's Building Image Archive, Otis College of Art and Design.

Looking back at the activism of the 1970s, feminist art historian Moira Roth asserted, in 1983, that the feminist movement had become "beleaguered" after "an amazing decade of achievement." She argued that feminists were "exhausted by, and sometimes disillusioned with, the struggles of the last decade" and were now confronted by a dominant "right-wing" ideology—manifested by the election of Ronald Reagan as president—that led artists to rethink their strategies.[74] Lacy concurred, writing that rape "dropped from view" during the 1980s, due to a "political and cultural backlash against feminism."[75] The anti-rape movement waned during this decade in part because NOW was focused upon the Equal Rights Amendment. As a result, no national effort with specific, short-term goals was directed against sexual violence.[76]

Examinations of rape and incest, which had existed as a kind of paradigmatic practice for feminist artists connected with the WB, thus dissipated by the mid-1980s. Many artists instead focused on issues related to ecology, nuclear threats, class, race (including African American, Asian American, Latino, and Hmong artists), and identity politics.[77] During this decade, the WB underwent profound changes in response to the social, political, and economic climates of the United States, including attempting to redefine and broaden its constituency to include more women outside of the white middle class by which it had previously been dominated. In 1991, the WB closed its doors. Three years later, Congress finally passed the first comprehensive federal legislation "to stop domestic violence, sexual assault, and stalking": The Violence Against Women Act (VAWA), which was reauthorized in 2000, again in 2005, and signed into law by President George W. Bush in 2006.[78]

Unfortunately, sexual violence against women still exists. Today, Eve Ensler is one example of a feminist carrying on the important task of creating works that testify against sexual violence against women. Ensler's *The Vagina Monologues* is an Obie-Award-winning play performed on college campuses throughout the United States and in over one hundred and nineteen theaters throughout the world. Ensler, who was born in 1953, originally performed the play in 1997 and published it in 1998. The play has since been translated into forty-five languages. Ensler originally intended her project to celebrate female sexuality and the female body,[79] but her interest shifted to preventing violence against women. In 1998, Ensler founded V-Day. Her website proclaims, "Today, V-Day is a global activist movement that supports anti-violence organizations throughout the world, helping them to continue and expand their core work on the ground, while drawing public attention to the larger fight to stop worldwide violence (including rape, battery, incest, female genital mutilation [FGM], sexual slavery) against women and girls."[80]

Ensler has visited over fifty countries, including Afghanistan, the Dominican Republic, Mexico, Zambia, the Republic of Congo, Pakistan, Egypt, and Iraq, speaking the unspeakable and providing a forum for silent victims. For example, Ensler worked with Filipina "comfort wives," who were kept as sexual slaves by Japanese troops during

WWII. In 2005, the sixtieth anniversary of the end of the war, Ensler launched the Global V-Day Campaign for Justice to "Comfort Women." Despite ostracism by family members because of the "shame" of their past, Filipinas spoke out for the first time about their horrific experiences. In 2008, more than three thousand five hundred V-Day events were scheduled in one thousand two hundred and fifty locations in the United States and around the world.

Feminist artists connected with the WB provided a model for Ensler and others who create art as a powerful vehicle for social change today. Although the artists connected with the WB largely ceased to create works about sexual violence after the Incest Awareness Project (and many of them, such as Angelo, did not pursue art making as a career), they provided a precedent by giving testimony and constructing and performing trauma for others to bear witness and give testimony, thereby ending the silence and contributing to cultural memory. The artists of the WB were part of the movement to politicize sexual violence against women, and they became powerful voices in the rape and incest crises discourses. Most significantly, they empowered women by ending the silence.

Notes

1. Hannah J. L. Feldman, "More Than Confessional: Testimony and the Subject of Rape," in *The Subject of Rape* (New York: Whitney Museum of American Art, 1993), 16–17; and Nancy K. Miller and Jason Tougaw, eds., *Extremities: Trauma, Testimony, and Community* (Urbana: University of Illinois Press, 2002), 7.

2. Miller and Tougaw, 13.

3. Cathy Caruth, *Unclaimed Experience: Trauma, Narrative, and History* (Baltimore: Johns Hopkins Press, 1996), 204.

4. Mary Ann Largen, "The Anti-Rape Movement Past and Present," in *Rape and Sexual Assault: A Research Handbook*, ed. Ann Wolbert Burgess (New York: Garland, 1985), 5. See also Susan Griffin, *Rape: The Politics of Consciousness* (New York: Harper & Row, 1986; reprint of 1979 original), 103–11. Griffin states that Washington, D.C., had the first rape crisis center.

5. Griffin, *Rape*, 111; Women Organized Against Rape website, http://www.woar.org/about-woar.html (accessed July 2, 2010).

6. Susan Brownmiller, *Against Our Will: Men, Women and Rape* (New York: Fawcett Columbine, 1975), 405. An account of the New York Feminists Rape Conference can be found in Noreen Connell and Cassandra Wilson, eds., *Rape: The First Sourcebook for Women* (New York: Plume Books, 1974), 59–112.

7. For information about this tribunal, see Diana E. H. Russell and Nicole Van de Ven, *Crimes Against Women: Proceedings of the International Tribunal* (Millbrae, CA: Las Femmes, 1976); and Suzanne Lacy, "Time, Bones, and Art: An Anatomy Lesson of Feminist Art and Sexual Violence," Suzanne Lacy Archives, Oakland, California, n.d., 9.

8. Largen, 11.

9. Brownmiller, *Against Our Will*, 153, 256, 309, 391. For the phrase "rape classic" and general information about Brownmiller and her book, see Brownmiller, "An Informal Bio," http://www.susanbrownmiller.com/susanbrownmiller/html/bio.html (accessed July 2, 2010). See also Brownmiller, "Against Our Will: Men, Women and Rape," http://www.susanbrownmiller.com/susanbrownmiller/html/against_our_will.html (accessed July 2, 2010).

10. Roy Porter, "Does Rape Have a Historical Meaning?" in *Rape*, Sylvana Tomaselli and Roy Porter, eds. (Oxford: Basil Blackwell, 1986), 218.

11. Nadya Burton, "Resistance to Prevention: Reconsidering Feminist Antiviolence Rhetoric," in *Violence Against Women: Philosophical Perspectives*, Stanley G. French, Wanda Teays, and Laura M. Purdy, eds. (Ithaca: Cornell University Press, 1998), 182–200.

12. Susan Griffin, "Rape: The All-American Crime," *Ramparts* 10 (1971): 29.

13. Catherine Calvert, "Is Rape What Women Really Want?" *Mademoiselle* 78 (March 1974), 134, 191.

14. Susan Estrich, "Rape," *Yale Law Journal* 95 (May 1986): 1097. She elaborated on these ideas in her book *Real Rape* (Cambridge, MA: Harvard University Press, 1987), 3–4.

15. Connell and Wilson, 3.

16. Ellen Bass and Laura Davis, *The Courage to Heal: A Guide for Women Survivors of Child Sexual Abuse* (New York: HarperCollins, 1994; 1st ed. 1988).

17. For information about *Ablutions*, see Judy Chicago, *Through the Flower: My Struggle as a Woman Artist* (New York: Penguin Books, 1975), 218–19; Sharon Irish, *Suzanne Lacy: Spaces Between* (Minneapolis: University of Minnesota Press, 2010), 15–18; Suzanne Lacy, "Time, Bones, and Art," 5–6; "Suzanne Lacy," interview by Moira Roth, March 16, 24, and September 27, 1990, Transcript, Smithsonian Archives of American Art Oral History Collection, Washington, D.C., http://www.aaa.si.edu/collections/oralhistories/transcripts/lacy90.htm (accessed July 2, 2010); and Stacy E. Schultz, "Naming in Order to Heal and Redeem: Violence Against Women in Performance," *n. paradoxa* 23 (2009): 38–39.

18. Suzanne Lacy, "Three Weeks in May," *Frontier: A Journal of Woman's Studies* 11 (1977): 9–10. See also Leslie Labowitz and Suzanne Lacy, "Evolution of a Feminist Art: Public Forms and Social Issues," *Heresies* 2 (1978): 80; and Irish, 46–49. After Lacy spoke, three women whom Lacy had invited moved to different parts of the space with the invited participants to perform simultaneously, creating "a patchwork quilt" in which a multitude of voices enacted "simultaneous rituals" ("Evolution of a Feminist Art").

19. Nancy Ward, Ad Hoc Committee on Rape, Department of Human Relations, Los Angeles County, 1976, as quoted in Lacy, "Three Weeks in May," 12. See also Meiling Cheng, *In Other Los Angeleses: Multicentric Performance Art* (Berkeley: University of California Press, 2002), 117. Cheng discusses *Three Weeks in May* as "a series of collaborative public actions" and as site-specific.

20. As Jennie Klein observes, "Three Weeks in May was not simply an activist event in which artists participated, but was instead a carefully designed performance designed to facilitate interaction between various groups and coalitions…[including] elected public officials, activists from the feminist community, media reporters, office workers, and feminist artists." See Klein, "The Ritual Body as Pedagogical Tool: The Performance Art of the Woman's Building," in *From Site to Vision: the Woman's Building in Contemporary Culture*, Sondra Hale and Terry Wolverton, eds. (Los Angeles: Woman's Building and Otis College of Art and Design, 2011), 210.

21. Lacy, "Time, Bones, and Art," 15; Lacy, "Three Weeks in May," 22.

22. Jeff Kelley, "The Body Politics of Suzanne Lacy," in *But Is It Art? The Spirit of Art as Activism*, ed. Nina Felshin (Seattle: Bay Press, 1995), 235.

23. Lacy, "Time, Bones, and Art," 16; and Kelley, 235–6. See also Vivien Green Fryd, "Suzanne Lacy's *Three Weeks in May*: Performance Art as 'Expanded Public Pedagogy,'" *National Women's Studies Association Journal* 19 (2007): 23–38.

24. Cheng addresses the iconography of the lamb within the context of Lacy's *Lamb Construction* (1973) performed at the WB. She later suggests that the lamb cadaver in *She Who Would Fly* signifies "women under attack." See Cheng, 112, 118.

25. Richard Newton, "She Who Would Fly: An Interview with Suzanne Lacy," in "The Art/Life Experiment," *High Performance* 1 (1978): 12.

26. Suzanne Lacy, "Artist Resource Site, Three Weeks in May: She Who Would Fly," September 27, 2003, http://www.suzannelacy.com/1970sviolence_3weeks_fly.htm (accessed July 2, 2010); Kelley, 238. See also Lacy, "Three Weeks in May," 54.

27. Griselda Pollock, "Modernity and the Spaces of Femininity," in *Vision and Difference: Femininity, Feminism and Histories of Art* (London: Routledge, 1988), 85.

28. Suzanne Lacy, letter to the author, January 10, 2004.

29. Suzanne Lacy and Leslie Labowitz, "Feminist Media Strategies for Political Performance," in *Cultures in Contention*, Douglas Kahn and Diane Neumaier, eds. (Seattle: Real Comet Press, 1985), 124.

30. Leslie Labowitz and Suzanne Lacy, "'In Mourning and In Rage,'" *Frontiers: A Journal of Women's Studies* 3 (1978): 52–55.

31. Suzanne Lacy, "In Mourning and In Rage (With Analysis Aforethought)," *Ikon* (1982): 6.

32. Labowitz and Lacy, "In Mourning and In Rage," 54; and Roth, "Conversation with Suzanne Lacy," 45.

33. Jennifer Fisher, "Interperformance: The Live Tableaux of Suzanne Lacy, Janine Antoni, and Marina Abramovic," *Art Journal* 56 (1997): 30.

34. *In Mourning and In Rage*, video created by Jerri Allyn, Nancy Angelo, Candace Compton, and Annette Hunt under the auspices of the Los Angeles Women's Video Center through the WB in consultation with Suzanne Lacy and Leslie Labowitz, 1977. Long Beach Museum of Art Video Archive, Getty Research Institute. Transferred by the Long Beach Museum of Art Foundation and the City of Long Beach, 2005.

35. I derive these terms and ideas about trauma from Lisa Saltzman's interpretation of Krzysztof Wodiczko's *Bunker Hill Monument* (1998) in "When Memory Speaks: A Monument Bears Witness," in *Trauma and Visuality in Modernity*, Lisa Saltzman and Eric Rosenberg, eds. (Hanover: Dartmouth College Press, 2006), 83–85.

36. For information about the techniques and equipment used in the WB, see Cecelia Dougherty, "Stories from a Generation: Video Art at the Woman's Building," in *From Site to Vision*, 308. For information about how video as a medium asks the viewer to bear witness, see Lisa Saltzman, *Making Memory Matter: Strategies of Remembrance in Contemporary Art* (Chicago: University of Chicago Press, 2006), 130.

37. Elaine Woo, "Bedtime Stories," *Los Angeles Herald Examiner*, October 23, 1979, B1.

38. Ellen Weber, "Sexual Abuse Begins at Home," *Ms.* magazine (April 1977), 64, 67.

39. Louise Armstrong, "The Crime Nobody Talks About," *Woman's Day* (March 1978), 52, 128; and Florence Rush, *The Best Kept Secret: Sexual Abuse of Children* (Englewood Cliffs: Prentice-Hall, 1980), 5.

40. Louise Armstrong, *Kiss Daddy Goodnight: A Speak-Out on Incest* (New York: Hawthorne Books, 1978); and Sandra Butler, *Conspiracy of Silence: The Trauma of Incest* (San Francisco: New Glide Publications, 1978).

41. Kathleen Brady, *Father's Days: A True Story of Incest* (New York: Seaview Books, 1979); Rush, *The Best Kept Secret*; Judith Herman and Lisa Hirschman, *Father-Daughter Incest* (Cambridge: Harvard University Press, 1981); Judith Herman and Lisa Hirschman, "Father-Daughter Incest," *Signs* 2 (1977): 735–56; and Bass and Davis, *The Courage to Heal*. For a discussion of these self-help books, see Rosaria Champagne, *The Politics of Survivorship: Incest, Women's Literature, and Feminist Theory* (New York: New York University Press, 1996), 14, 37–42. See also Diana E. H. Russell, *Secret Trauma: Incest in the Lives of Girls and Women* (New York: Basic Books, 1999), xviii, for information on the feminist books of the 1970s and 1980s. Florence Rush's book evolved from a presentation she gave on April 17, 1971, at a conference on rape sponsored by the New York Radical Feminists. See Rush, viii.

42. Armstrong, *Kiss Daddy Goodnight*, 215.

43. Susan Forward, *Betrayal of Innocence: Incest and Its Devastation* (Harmondsworth, England: Penguin Books, 1979).

44. Nancy Angelo, "Equal Time in Equal Space: Documentation of the Production and Exhibition of a Community Video Art Project on Women's Experiences of Incest," MA thesis, Goddard College 1982, 6. See also Michelle Moravec, "Feminism, the Public Sphere and the Incest Awareness Project at the Woman's Building," in *The Politics of Cultural Programming in Public Spaces*, Robert Gehl and Victoria Watts, eds. (Newcastle: Cambridge Scholars, 2010).

45. Paula Lumbard, email correspondence with the author, June 2, 2009.

46. Leslie Belt, manuscript for *Incest Piece*, from Catherine Stifter's archives.

47. Leslie Belt, email correspondence with the author, July 6 and 10, 2009.

48. Nancy Angelo, Part 1, *On Joining the Order: A Confession in which Angelica Furiosa Explains to Her Sisters How She Came to Be Among Them*, 1977. Videotape. Long Beach Museum of Art Video Archive, Getty Research Institute.

49. Moravec, 5.

50. Angelo, MA thesis, 9.

51. Irish, 74.

52. "'Incest': The Crime Nobody Talks About," press release by Ariadne and the Gay and Lesbian Community Services Center, n.d., *Ariadne Scrapbook*, n.p. See also Lacy and Labowitz, "Feminist Media Strategies for Political Performance," 132; and Terry Wolverton, *Insurgent Muse: Life and Art at the Woman's Building* (San Francisco:
City Lights, 2002), 127.

53. Annette Hunt and Nancy Angelo, "Bedtime Stories: Women Speak Out About Incest," *Spinning Off* (October/November 1979), 1. The exhibition went to Toronto in 1981 for an exhibition at the University College Playhouse at the University of Toronto.

54. Moravec, 11; and Diane Elvenstar, "Incest: A Second Reality for a Child," *Los Angeles Times*, October 22, 1979, 18.

55. Hunt and Angelo.

56. Paula Lumbard and Leslie Belt, "Statement by Curators of Bedtime Stories," in *Ariadne Scrapbook*, n.p.

57. Phyllis Rosser, "There's No Place Like Home," in *New Feminist Criticism: Art, Identity, and Action*, Joanna Frueh, Cassandra L. Langer, and Arlene Raven, eds. (New York: HarperCollins, 1994), 68. See also Moravec, 11.

58. Wolverton, *Insurgent Muse*, 128; and "Art Against Incest: Feminist Artists Challenge the Conspiracy of Silence," *FUSE* (July/August 1980): 280.

59. Moravec, 12.

60. Woo, B5.

61. Wolverton, *Insurgent Muse*, 130–31.

62. Ibid.

63. Woo, B5.

64. Angelo states that the ages ranged from late teens to mid-thirties, and their religious backgrounds were Lutheran, Catholic, Baptist, Jewish, Mormon, Presbyterian, and non-religious. Fifteen were Caucasian, one was an African American, another was Chinese American. Angelo, MA thesis, 32.

65. Moravec, 10.

66. Wolverton, "Art Against Incest," 281; *Insurgent Muse*, 134; and Angelo, MA thesis, 11.

67. Suzanne Lacy, interview with Moira Roth, March 16, 1990, transcript, Smithsonian Archives of American Art Oral History Collection, Washington, D.C., September 23, 2003, http://artarchives.si.edu.oralhist/lacy90.htm. See also Ruth Iskin, "Incest Survivors Go Public," *LA Weekly*, November 14–20, 1980, 4. In order for the tapes to play simultaneously, the decks were synchronized by pausing and playing each deck at the same time. For an

explanation of this technology, see Cecilia Dougherty, "Stories from a Generation: Video Art at the Woman's Building," in *From Site to Vision*, 312.

68. Saltzman, *Making Memory Matter*, 130.

69. Ibid.

70. Shoshana Felman, "The Return of the Voice: Claude Lanzmann's Shoah," in *Testimony: Crises of Witnessing in Literature, Psychology, and History*, Shoshana Felman and Dori Laub, eds. (New York: Routledge, 1992), 213.

71. Feldman, 16–17; and Miller and Tougaw, 7.

72. *Equal Time in Equal Space*, in *Ariadne Scrapbook*, n.p.; and Sandra Butler, "Cause for Outrage and Celebration," quoted in Angelo, M.A. thesis, appendix.

73. Butler, "Cause for Outrage and Celebration," from Angelo, M.A. thesis, appendix.

74. Moira Roth, ed., *The Amazing Decade: Women and Performance Art in America, 1970–1980* (Los Angeles: Astro Artz, 1983), 33.

75. Lacy, "Time Bones, and Art," 24.

76. Largen, 11.

77. For how race, identity politics, and class became issues among members of the Woman's Building, see Michelle Moravec and Sondra Hale, "'At Home at the Woman's Building (But Who Gets a Room of Her Own?): Women of Color and Community," in *From Site to Vision*.

78. Diane Stuart, "About the Violence Against Women Office," December 27, 2001, and reauthorized in 2010: http://www.ojp.usdoj.gov/.

79. Eve Ensler, *The Vagina Monologues* (New York: Villard, 1998).

80. V-Day website, http://www.vday.org/about/more-about/eveensler (accessed July 20, 2010).

Suzanne Lacy, *Three Weeks in May*, 1977. Los Angeles.
Documentation of guerrilla performance. © Suzanne Lacy.

Vivien Green Fryd, Professor and Chair of the History of Art Department at Vanderbilt University, is the author of *Art and Empire: The Politics of Ethnicity in the U.S. Capitol, 1815–1860* and *Art and the Crisis of Marriage: Georgia O'Keeffe and Edward Hopper*. She is currently working on a book manuscript titled *Against Our Will: Representing Sexual Trauma in Second-Wave Feminist American Art* and has published in various journals, including *Art Bulletin*, *American Art*, *Winterthur Portfolio*, and *American Art Journal*. She was the Spence and Rebecca Webb Wilson Fellow at the Robert Penn Warren Center of the Humanities 2008–2009 for Trauma Studies. She currently is a juror for the Smithsonian's Eldredge Prize for Distinguished Scholarship in American Art.

Cheri Gaulke's art and life were profoundly changed in 1975, when she moved from the Midwest to Los Angeles to join the Feminist Studio Workshop at the Woman's Building. There she embraced the notion that feminist art could *raise consciousness, invite dialogue, and transform culture*. She worked primarily in performance art from 1974 to 1992, addressing themes such as the body, religion, sexual identity, and the environment. In addition to her solo work, she co-founded collaborative performance groups Feminist Art Workers (1976–81) and Sisters Of Survival (1981–85). Gaulke has a BFA from Minneapolis College of Art and Design and an MFA from Goddard College in feminist art/education. She has received grants from the National Endowment for the Arts, California Arts Council, California Community Foundation, and the City of Los Angeles. As part of the Getty initiative Pacific Standard Time: Art in L.A. 1945–80, Gaulke's collaborative work will be featured in *Doin' It in Public: Feminism and Art at the Woman's Building*, and her solo performance work will be featured in *Los Angeles Goes Live* at Los Angeles Contemporary Exhibitions.

Dr. Alexandra Juhasz is Professor of Media Studies at Pitzer College. She makes and studies committed media practices that contribute to political change and individual and community growth. She is the author of *AIDS TV* (Duke, 1995), *Women of Vision: Histories in Feminist Film and Video* (Minnesota, 2001), *F is for Phony: Fake Documentary and Truth's Undoing*, co-edited with Jesse Lerner (Minnesota, 2005), and *Media Praxis: A Radical Web-Site Integrating Theory, Practice and Politics* (www.mediapraxis.org). Dr. Juhasz recently completed the feature documentaries *SCALE: Measuring Might in the Media Age* (2008) and *Video Remains* (2005). She is the producer of the feature films *The Watermelon Woman* (Cheryl Dunye, 1997) and *The OWLS* (Dunye, 2010). Her current work is on and about YouTube. Her born-digital, online "video-book" about YouTube, *Learning from YouTube*, is available online from MIT Press (Winter 2011).

Jennie Klein is an associate professor at Ohio University where she teaches contemporary art history and feminist art theory. She has published in *n. paradoxa*, *PAJ*, *Art Papers*, *Genders*, *Feminist Studies*, *Journal of Lesbian Studies*, and the *New Art Examiner*. She is presently completing a co-edited book on performance art, and is the editor of *Letters from Linda M. Montano* (Routledge, 2005) and co-editor with Myrel Chernick of *The M Word: Real Mothers in Contemporary Art* (Demeter Press, 2011). She has presented her work nationally and internationally, most recently in Kuopio, Finland.

Meg Linton is Director of Galleries and Exhibitions at Otis College of Art and Design. She is a project director and cocurator of the exhibition *Doin' It in Public: Feminism and Art at the Woman's Building*. Over the last seventeen years, she has organized numerous solo and group exhibitions of contemporary art and published dozens of related monographs and catalogs. Recent projects include: *Splendid Entities: 25 Years of Objects by Phyllis Green* with guest curators Jo Lauria and Tim Christian; *In the Land of Retinal Delights: The Juxtapoz Factor*, Laguna Art Museum; *Mark Dean Veca: Revenge of Phantasmagoria*, Instituto Cultural Cabañas, Guadalajara, Mexico; *Don Suggs: One Man Group Show*, a 38-year survey with cocurator Doug Harvey; *Nancy Chunn: Media Madness*; *Joan Tanner: On Tender Hooks*; and *Dissonance to Detour: Shahzia Sikander*. Prior to her arrival at Otis in 2003, she was the executive director of the Santa Barbara Contemporary Arts Forum.

Sue Maberry is Director of the Library and Instructional Technology at Otis College of Art and Design. She is a project director and cocurator of the exhibition *Doin' It in Public: Feminism and Art at the Woman's Building*. She attended the Feminist Studio Workshop at the Woman's Building from 1976 to 1977. She then served on staff of the WB in many different positions until 1987. While there, she collaborated with many artists and groups and is a cofounder of Sisters Of Survival. After receiving a Master's Degree in Library and Information Science from San Jose State University, she joined Otis in 1992 as the Director of the Library. After the Woman's Building closed in 1991, Maberry brought the WB slide archive to Otis and acquired financial support to digitize the thousands of images and create an online image database at a time when the Internet was new.

Michelle Moravec is Associate Professor of History at Rosemont College. A historian with a focus on the intersections of feminism, culture, and activism, she received her PhD in Women's History from the University of California, Los Angeles. She is the recipient of fellowships from the Getty Research Institute, the Archives of American Art, the Sallie Bingham Center for Women's History and Culture, and the Southern California Historical Society. In addition to conducting over fifty oral history interviews with participants in the feminist art movement, she has authored numerous essays about artists associated with the Woman's Building. Her current project investigates the overlapping concepts of women's culture in both feminist activist and academic communities during the 1970s and 1980s.

Elizabeth Pulsinelli is an artist and arts editor in Los Angeles. She has been the executive editor of the contemporary art quarterly *X-TRA* since 2007 and has served on the editorial board since 1998. Recent editing projects include catalogs for the artists Steve Roden, Ginny Bishton, and M.A. Peers (Pomona College Museum of Art); and Elizabeth Saveri (Armory Center for the Arts, Pasadena); and the books *Words Without Pictures* (LACMA and Aperture); *Sympathetic Seeing: Esther McCoy and the Heart of American Modernist Architecture and Design*, *How Many Billboards? Art In Stead*, and *Urban Future Manifestos* (MAK Center); *It Happened at Pomona: Art at the Edge of Los Angeles 1969–1973* (Pomona College Museum of Art); *Superficiality and Superexcrescense*, and *From Site to Vision: The Woman's Building in Contemporary Culture* (Ben Maltz Gallery, Otis College of Art and Design).

Susan Silton is a multidisciplinary visual artist based in Los Angeles whose simultaneous design practice is reflected in catalogs for institutions including The Hammer Museum and Museum of Contemporary Art, Los Angeles. She has often been cited for the catalog design for the 1994 exhibition *Sexual Politics: Judy Chicago's Dinner Party in Feminist Art History*, curated by Amelia Jones. As a visual artist, Silton's work has been exhibited nationally and internationally at venues including LACMA; Museum of Contemporary Art, San Diego; SFMOMA; Hammer Museum; Feigen Contemporary, NY; Susanne Vielmetter Los Angeles Projects; and Australian Centre for Contemporary Art. She has been awarded grants from the California Community Foundation; Department of Cultural Affairs, Los Angeles; and Durfee Foundation. Most recently she received an Art Matters grant for an ongoing project about whistling, which debuted in 2010 at LA><ART in a performance of the women's whistling group she formed, the Crowing Hens.

Jenni Sorkin is Assistant Professor of Critical Theory, Media, and Design at the University of Houston. She is currently completing a book manuscript titled *Live Form: Craft as Participation*, which examines the confluence of gender, artistic labor, and craft pedagogy from 1950 to 1975. Her writing has appeared in the *New Art Examiner*, *Art Journal*, *Art Monthly*, *NU: The Nordic Art Review*, *Frieze*, *The Journal of Modern Craft*, *Modern Painters*, and *Third Text*. She has written numerous in-depth catalog essays on feminist art and material culture topics. In 2010 she co-organized *Blind Spots/Puntos Ciegos: Feminisms, Cinema, and Performance* for the eighth edition of SITAC, the International Symposium of Contemporary Art Theory, held in Mexico City. She holds a PhD in the History of Art from Yale University. From 2010 to 2011, she was a Post-Doctoral Fellow at the Getty Research Institute in Los Angeles. She is the recipient of the 2004 Art Journal Award, given by the College Art Association.

Pacific Standard Time

Doin' It in Public: Feminism and Art at the Woman's Building has been organized by Otis College of Art and Design as part of Pacific Standard Time: Art in L.A. 1945–1980. This unprecedented collaboration brings together more than sixty cultural institutions from across Southern California for six months beginning October 2011 to tell the story of the birth of the L.A. art scene. Pacific Standard Time is an initiative of the Getty. The presenting sponsor is Bank of America.

Doin' It in Public: Feminism and Art at the Woman's Building is made possible by a generous grant from the Getty Foundation with additional funding provided by the Andy Warhol Foundation for the Visual Arts, Henry Luce Foundation, Department of Cultural Affairs of the City of Los Angeles, the Barbara Lee Family Foundation, and Supporters of the Woman's Building.

Project Directors and Curators
Meg Linton
Sue Maberry*

Project Advisors and Consultants
Jerri Allyn*
Nancy Angelo*
Cheri Gaulke*
Vivien Green Fryd
Sondra Hale
Alexandra Juhasz
Jennie Klein
Michelle Moravec
Elizabeth Pulsinelli
Jenni Sorkin
Susan Silton
Terry Wolverton*

Project Research Assistants
Jenay Meraz
Joanne Mitchell
Kayleigh Perkov
Julia Paoli
Paige Tighe

* Videotaped interview available online at www.otis.edu

Thank you!

A project like this that includes an exhibition, two books, online resources (timeline, bibliography, checklist, video interviews), and a series of public events requires a small army of artists, scholars, researchers, interns, institutions, collectors, and more to see it to fruition. We want to thank all those who have helped along the way. If we've left anyone out, we apologize and will make amends on the website and in any future printings.

Archives of American Art,
  Smithsonian
Armory Center for the Arts
Debra Ballard
Bonnie Barrett
Leslie Belt*
Nancy Buchanan*
Linda Bunting
California Institute of the Arts
Carol Chen*
Judy Chicago
Judy Chicago Papers,
  Schlesinger Library,
  Radcliffe Institute,
  Harvard University
Judith Dancoff
Johanna Demetrakas*
Sheila Levrant de Bretteville*
Marlena Donahue
Mary Beth Edelson
Feminist Art Workers*
Bruria Finkel*
Flomenhaft Gallery
Anne Gauldin*
Getty Research Institute
Amy Gantman
Parme Giuntini
Grand Central Art Center,
  CSUF
Vanalyne Green*
Kirsten Grimstad*
Betty Gordon*
Gilah Yelin Hirsch*
Maria Karras
Susan E. King*

Eloise Klein Healy*
Laurel Klick*
Tom Knechtel
Michele Kort*
Joyce Kozloff*
Deborah Krall*
Christy Kruse*
Leslie Labowitz-Starus*
Suzanne Lacy*
Los Angeles County Museum
  of Art, Research Library
L.A. Free Press
L.A. Women's Video Center*
Lili Lakich
Kris Lewis
Long Beach Museum of Art
Bia Lowe*
Paula Lumbard*
Helene Ly*
Barbara Margolies
Cynthia Marsh*
Rose Anne McCants
Deena Metzger*
Laura Meyer
Helen Million*
Robin Mitchell
Susan Mogul*
Mother Art*
Linda Nishio*
ONE National Gay &
  Lesbian Archives
Gloria Orenstein*
Otis Facilities and
  Tech Services
Phranc*

Denise Yarfitz Pierre*
Alexandra Pollyea
Margi Reeve
Susan Rennie*
Rachel Rosenthal*
Deborah Roundtree
Christine Rush
Laura Silagi*
Suzanne Siegel*
Sisters Of Survival*
Barbara T. Smith*
Cheryl Swannack*
Anne Swartz
Anne Swett
Joan Takayama-Ogawa
Through the Flower
  Archives
Jane Thurmond
Charles E. Young Research
  Library, UCLA Special
  Collections
University of Oregon
  Libraries
Linda Vallejo*
Video Data Bank
The Waitresses*
E.K. Waller
June Wayne*
Lilla Weinberger
Ruth Weisberg*
Faith Wilding*
Jeanne Willette
Nancy Youdelman

* Videotaped interview available online at www.otis.edu

THE PERSONAL IS POLITICAL